CLARENDON PLATO SERIES

Laws 10

CLARENDON PLATO SERIES

Volumes published:

Gorgias
Terence Irwin

Phaedo
David Gallop

Philebus
J. C. B. Gosling

Protagoras
C. C. W. Taylor

Theaetetus
John McDowell

Plato

Laws 10

Translated with a commentary
by
ROBERT MAYHEW

CLARENDON PRESS • OXFORD

OXFORD

UNIVERSITY PRESS

Great Clarendon Street, Oxford OX2 6DP

Oxford University Press is a department of the University of Oxford.
It furthers the University's objective of excellence in research, scholarship,
and education by publishing worldwide in

Oxford New York

Auckland Cape Town Dar es Salaam Hong Kong Karachi
Kuala Lumpur Madrid Melbourne Mexico City Nairobi
New Delhi Shanghai Taipei Toronto

With offices in

Argentina Austria Brazil Chile Czech Republic France Greece
Guatemala Hungary Italy Japan Poland Portugal Singapore
South Korea Switzerland Thailand Turkey Ukraine Vietnam

Oxford is a registered trade mark of Oxford University Press
in the UK and in certain other countries

Published in the United States
by Oxford University Press Inc., New York

British Library Cataloguing in Publication Data
Data available

Library of Congress Cataloging in Publication Data
Data available

Typeset by Laserwords Private Limited, Chennai, India
Printed in Great Britain
on acid-free paper by
Biddles Ltd, King's Lynn, Norfolk

ISBN 978–0–19–922596–5

1 3 5 7 9 10 8 6 4 2

Preface

In keeping with the aims of the Clarendon Plato Series, I have written the present work to serve the needs of philosophers and students of philosophy interested in Plato. My commentary is focused primarily on philosophical issues (broadly understood to include religion and politics), and deals with philological matters only when doing so serves to better explain those issues. Knowledge of Greek is not assumed, and the Greek that does appear has been transliterated (except in the Textual Notes).

My translation is based on the text of August Diès (1956). (The Stephanus line numbers printed in the margins of the translation and referred to in the commentary are based on the Diès edition.) I list and discuss my departures from Diès in the Textual Notes, and such departures are marked by asterisks in the translation. I have aimed to produce a translation as close to the Greek as possible without straying (too far) from acceptable English. As such, of the existing English translations of the *Laws*, mine is closest in spirit to Thomas Pangle's (1980), and perhaps farthest from Trevor Saunders's (1970)—though my *interpretation* of the *Laws* is much closer to Saunders's. I have tried as much as possible to render key terms consistently throughout (departing from this policy only when common sense seemed to dictate it). Noteworthy here is the word *nous*, which has traditionally been rendered 'intellect' or 'mind'. I have been convinced by Stephen Menn (1995) that 'reason' is a better translation, and have translated *nous* accordingly throughout.

Diogenes Laertius reports that 'some say that Philip of Opus transcribed the *Laws*, which was in wax' (3.37), perhaps suggesting that the dialogue was unfinished or in a less than polished state when Plato died. In Lucian's *Icaromenippus* Zeus jokes that the decline in visits to his temples has made his altars 'more frigid than the *Laws* of Plato' (24). The text of the *Laws* does often seem unpolished and 'frigid'—especially when compared to the *Symposium* or *Republic*, for example—and I have done little (above the level of punctuation) to attempt to improve upon the original. Nevertheless, it would be best not to attribute all the defects of my translation to Plato's Greek.

I wish to thank Seton Hall University for its continued support of my work: a University Research Council Summer Stipend in 2002 allowed me to concentrate my time on *Laws* 10 in the early stages of this project, and a sabbatical leave during the academic year 2006–7 enabled me (among other things) to put the finishing touches on this book. An Ayn Rand Institute Research Grant, for which I am very grateful, helped make this year-long sabbatical leave possible.

It has been a pleasure working with the personnel at Oxford University Press. I wish to thank Peter Momtchiloff for his encouragement and support, and Nadiah Al-Ammar and Jane Wheare for the superb job they did transforming my flawed typescript into a finished book.

The translation and commentary would not be what they are if not for the many helpful comments and criticisms of Christopher Bobonich and an anonymous advisor for Oxford University Press. Any remaining errors are my own.

Contents

Introduction

'God or some human—strangers, who is given credit for laying down your laws?' (1.624a1–2). This is the opening line of Plato's last and longest work, the *Laws*, translated somewhat awkwardly to capture the fact that the first word of the dialogue is *theos* ('god' or 'a god'). As the question indicates, the *Laws* is concerned with both politics and theology. The philosophical foundation of these two intersecting topics is most fully explored in Book 10.

The question that opens the *Laws* was asked by the Athenian Stranger. Here are the replies of the two other speakers in this dialogue, Kleinias and Megillus:

> *K.* A god, stranger, a god, to say what is most just. For us [i.e. the Cretans] it is Zeus, while for the Lakedaimonians, where this man is from, I think they claim it is Apollo. Is that so?
>
> *M.* Yes. (624a3–6)

Throughout the dialogue—and perhaps most of all in Book 10—the Athenian Stranger (hereafter 'the Athenian') is shown to be the sole interlocutor with a high degree of philosophical acumen. Aristotle treats him (by implication) precisely as if he were the Socrates of the *Republic* (see *Politics* 2.6); Leo Strauss (1975: 2) speculates that the *Crito* might suggest that the Athenian represents Socrates, had he escaped from Athens and gone to a faraway city, like one in Crete (53b4–d4); I take the Athenian to be pretty much a 'mouthpiece' for Plato.[1] Though no philosopher, the Cretan

---

[1] This seems to be the way Aristotle understood the Athenian (see *Politics* 2.10. 1271b1). On this way of taking the main speaker in a Platonic dialogue generally see the sensible comments of Kraut (1992; 25–30) and Sedley (2004; 6–8).

Kleinias is more astute—and more talkative—than the taciturn Megillus from Sparta. It is made clear at the outset that all three of these men are old (1.625b1–5).[2]

The Athenian asks about the Homeric story according to which Minos meets with Zeus every nine years to receive help in establishing laws for Crete (624a7–b3; cf. *Odyssey* 19.178–9). The *Minos* makes explicit what is left to implication here; namely, that these meetings took place at the cave of Zeus (319e2–3).[3] The Athenian says that it would be pleasant to discuss 'political systems and laws' (*politeias . . . kai nomôn* (*Laws* 1.625a6–7)), and suggests that the three of them do so while walking the long distance from Knossos (where the *Laws* begins) 'to the cave and temple of Zeus' (625b2). Kleinias and Megillus agree.

In the first two books of the *Laws* the three men, under the guidance of the Athenian, critically analyze Cretan and Spartan views on virtue, education, and law. In Book 3 they lay out the history of cities and their laws. A sudden and crucial turning point in the dialogue occurs at the end of Book 3 (702a2–e2), when the discussion moves from past history to a possible future (see Laks (2000; 262)). The Athenian states the ultimate reason for which they have been having their conversation: 'All these things have been said for the sake of seeing how a city might best be established [or 'governed', *oikoiê*], and how in private someone might best lead his own life' (702a7–b1). Then Plato has the Athenian ask this loaded question: 'as to whether we have made something useful, what test might we come up with for speaking among ourselves, Megillus and Kleinias?' (702b1–3). Kleinias reveals for the first time that he and nine of his fellow citizens have been delegated to establish laws for a new colony in Crete (702b4–c8), and he suggests that he and his two companions now build on their discussion and create a 'city in speech' to aid him with his assignment (702c8–d5; cf. *Republic*

---

[2] For some early indications of the differences between the three see *Laws* 1.641e2–4, 643a24, 644d4–6. For the little prosopographical information that exists on Kleinias and Megillus see Nails (2002; 101–2, 197–8).

[3] The *Minos* is a dialogue attributed to Plato, but of dubious authenticity.

2.369a6). Megillus and the Athenian agree. Their 'city in speech' is later referred to as 'the city of the Magnesians' (8.848d3; 9.860e7; 11.919d5; 12.946b6, 969a6–7). For simplicity's sake I sometimes call it 'Magnesia' (as do most scholars of the *Laws*).[4]

Crucial for understanding the *Laws*—including Book 10—is the fact that Plato considers the 'city in speech' presented therein to be a *second*-best city. In *Laws* 5 he writes: 'That city (*polis*) and that political system (*politeia*) are first, and those laws are best, where this old saying holds as much as possible throughout the entire city: it is said that the things of friends really are common' (739b8–c3). He briefly describes the communism of women, children, and property presented in the *Republic* (without mentioning that dialogue), says that such a city would be 'inhabited by gods or children of gods' (739d6–7), and calls this a model (*paradeigma*) political system (739e1–2). If the city they are creating 'in speech' ever actually came into being, he says, it would be closest to this model, and second best.

A city inhabited by gods (or ruled by philosopher-kings) does not need laws; the second-best city does. Plato makes precisely this point in *Laws* 9 (874e3–875d5). Humans, he says, must establish laws or else live like beasts. This is because there is no one among them who both knows what is best for humans with respect to politics, and is willing and able to do what is best based on this knowledge. For it is difficult to know that true politics aims at what is common, not at what is private, and even if someone did know this, it would be difficult to put this knowledge into practice—to focus on the good of the whole political community—and not to succumb to private desires. If a person with such knowledge *and* virtue did appear, Plato tells us, 'he would not need laws ruling over him; for no law or order is stronger than knowledge, nor is it right for reason to be subject or a slave to anyone, but to be ruler over everything' (875c5–d1). But since such people do not exist, 'one must choose what comes

---

[4] It is beyond the scope of this introduction to summarize the remainder of the *Laws*. For a brief overview of the structure of the dialogue see Saunders (1970; 5–14) and Laks (2000: 260–7).

second: order and law' (875d3–4; see also *Statesman* 293a6–297e5). Whereas philosopher-kings are the best way to approximate the gods ruling in a city, the rule of law is second best (see 4.713c2–714b1).

But laws, we soon discover, are not enough. The Athenian asks (expecting and receiving a negative response):

So should the one who is to arrange our laws provide no such preface at the beginning of the laws, but straightaway declare what must be done and what not, hold out as a threat the penalty, and then turn to another law, without adding to the laws being framed a single bit of encouragement or persuasion? (4.719e7–720a2)

The three men decide that nearly every law should be preceded by a prelude (*prooimion*), the purpose of which is persuasion—so that the law will not simply command, but will also teach, thus making the one who hears the prelude have a more favorable view of the law. (See 4.722c6-723e8, 5.734e3–6.)[5]

In *Laws* 10 Plato reaffirms the need for preludes:

Is [the legislator] simply to stand up before the city and threaten all the people that . . . they [must] affirm that the gods exist, and think and believe that [the gods] are such as the law affirms . . .? [Is he simply to threaten] that whoever does not show himself obedient to the laws, in one case must die, in another be punished with a beating and imprisonment, in another with dishonors, and in other cases with poverty and exile? But what about Persuasion for the people—should he, at the same time that he establishes the laws for them, refrain from adding arguments to make them as gentle as possible? (890b5–c8)

Book 10 is, in essence, a lengthy prelude to the laws on impiety, followed by the laws themselves. This prelude is the most deeply philosophical part of the entire dialogue. Nearly all of it is devoted to refuting what Plato considers three impious beliefs (the following are my labels, not his): atheism, deism (the view that the gods exist, but take no thought for humans), and traditional theism (the view that

---

[5] On the role of the preludes in the *Laws* see Nightingale (1993), Laks (2000: 285–90), and Bobonich (2002: 97–119).

the gods exist, but are appeasable through prayers and sacrifices). The philosophy of religion presented in *Laws* 10 is the filter through which must pass traditional Greek religion—however committed to traditional religion Plato seems to be throughout the *Laws*.

For instance, at *Laws* 4.715e7–718a6 the Athenian presents an address to the (hypothetical) newly arrived colonists, which begins: 'the god, according to the ancient account, holding the beginning and the end and the middle of all beings, completes his straight course revolving according to nature; and following him always is Justice, avenger of those who abandon the divine law' (715e7–716a3). He then says that the prudent man should follow god; that is, seek to be like him, which amounts to or involves being moderate. The noble, good, and happy man 'always communes with the gods', through prayer, votive offerings, and so on (716d5–7). Magnesia's commitment to traditional religion is made evident, for the Athenian says that they will aim to honor and/or worship (in this order): the Olympian gods; the gods of the underworld; spirits (*daimons*); heroes; ancestral gods (i.e. the souls of dead ancestors); and living parents.

In *Laws* 5 this commitment to traditional religion is confirmed. The Athenian says the following is true, whether one is establishing a new city from scratch or refounding an old city:

Concerning gods and temples—what [temples] should be established in the city for each of them [i.e. gods], and which gods or spirits they should be named after—no one possessing reason will attempt to change what comes from Delphi or Dodona or from Ammon [the most famous Greek oracles], or what the ancient stories suggest (in whatever way they suggest it, whether coming from apparitions or from an inspiration said to be from gods) ... Owing to such stories, people sanctified oracles, statues, altars, and shrines, and marked off a sacred grove for each of these. A lawgiver should change none of all of this in the slightest. (738b5–d1, see also 8.828a1–5; cf. *Republic* 4.427b1–c4)

It becomes clear from *Laws* 10, however, that the injunction to 'change none of all of this in the slightest' applies most of all to the *names* of the gods and the temples, and to the nature of the *rituals*, that accompany religion. For there will certainly have to be modifications to traditional religion.[6] The philosophical conclusions of *Laws* 10 put demands or limitations on Magnesian civic religion.

Stability and social cohesion require that the founders of the city keep as much of traditional religion as possible. There is no need for arguments proving the existence of Apollo or rationally validating the efficacy of the Oracle at Delphi. Nevertheless, civic religion must to an important extent pass the test of philosophical theology. Most significantly, it must meet the following three requirements, which in *Laws* 10 Plato claims are philosophically demonstrable:

1. The gods exist, are not themselves physical (or do not arise from what is physical), but are prior (ontologically and temporally) to the physical.
2. The gods are good—they do not neglect humans, and cannot be appeased by humans (e.g. through sacrifice and prayer) to overlook injustice.
3. There should be no private shrines and no private religion.

Much of traditional religion can meet these requirements: the names of the gods, the belief in prophecy, and many of the rituals of religion—as long as they are public. What must change are any beliefs or stories which present the gods as too anthropomorphic and anything less than good (taking on human forms, changing their forms, and acting like morally imperfect humans).

This is the primary function of the arguments and ideas of Book 10 from the perspective of the dialogue as a whole. The prelude of *Laws* 10 will (Plato hopes) ensure that the founders of Magnesia (or any city with such aspirations) will get right the crucially important establishment of religion. The importance of the philosophical-theological doctrines of Book 10 is made clear toward the end of the dialogue, in the discussion of the Nocturnal Council.[7]

---

[6] On the slightly provisional nature of the laws generally see *Laws* 6.769a7–771a4, 772c6–d4.

[7] On the Nocturnal Council, see Morrow (1960; ch. 9).

The Nocturnal Council is discussed in greatest detail in *Laws* 12 (the final book of the *Laws*). But it first makes its appearance in Book 10, where we learn that one of its functions is to admonish the honest (as opposed to dissembling) heretics—that is, to visit these heretics regularly in their special prison (where each prisoner is serving a sentence of at least five years) and attempt to convince them that the gods exist and are good (909a2–5). The composition of this Council is described in detail in *Laws* 12 (951d4–e5, 961a1–b8). Morrow provides a good summary:

> The Council is to consist of (1) the ten eldest guardians of the laws; (2) the 'priests who have been awarded *aristeia*' [i.e. received awards for excellence] . . . (3) the educator and all his predecessors in the office; (4) certain citizens who have traveled abroad and who on their return have been examined by the Council and adjudged worthy of membership; and (5) perhaps other citizens who have received awards of merit.   (1960; 503–4)

The Council must 'meet every day from dawn until the sun has risen' (12.951d7–8; cf. 961b6). In these meetings its members will discuss 'laws and their own city', as well as any areas of learning that contribute to this primary inquiry (951e5–952a4). Their main function is to safeguard the city and its laws (960d1–4). The Nocturnal Council is called an anchor, cast for the city's protection (961c4–6), as well as the soul and head of the city—and most of all, the reason (*nous*) in the soul of the city (961d1–962d2). It preserves the city by always aiming for the city's goal—which the Council does through knowing what the goal is, and how to attain it. This goal, we find out later, is *virtue* (963a1–4).

There are four virtues—reason (or prudence or wisdom), courage, moderation, and justice—and reason is their leader (963a6–9). This aspect of virtue—that it is one thing, and yet there are four *forms* (*eidê*) of virtue—explains why the members of the Nocturnal Council must explore an issue which had interested Plato at least as far back as the *Protagoras*: the unity of virtue. In *Laws* 12 this is connected to another issue, which interested Plato in later dialogues: the relationship among the forms (963c7–965e4). Plato says that sorting out the unity of virtue is necessary for the salvation of the city; but it is difficult and may elude even the members of the Nocturnal Council (who are the closest thing to philosopher-kings in the city of the *Laws*). Plato suggests that the members of the Council may be helped in this task by pursuing another topic (insofar as it is humanly possible to know such things): the existence and nature of the gods. I take it that since god *is* reason (*nous*), or at the very least intimately related to reason, and since reason is the leader of the virtues, Plato believes that by studying the nature of the gods—as the Athenian and his interlocutors do in *Laws* 10—the Nocturnal Council will more likely succeed in knowing fully the nature of (the unity of) virtue.

Plato revisits the nature and existence of the gods at 12.966c1–968a4. He writes that one cannot be a member of the Nocturnal Council who has not 'labored to grasp every proof concerning the existence of the gods' (966c7–8; see also 968a1–4). He then summarizes two key points from *Laws* 10: that soul is prior to matter, and that reason exists in or directs celestial objects. At the end of the *Laws* Plato says that if such a 'divine council' ever came into being, educated as he has described (i.e. concerning virtue and the gods), this would be the perfect guardian of the city and its laws (969b1–c3).

Laws 10 is important not only because it contains Plato's fullest and final discussion of the existence and nature of the gods (and one of the earliest sets of arguments for the existence of gods), but because the existence and nature of the gods—and the citizens' belief in the proper conception of the gods—are of central importance to the project of the *Laws* generally.

The commentary accompanying my translation is the first on *Laws* 10 to appear in English since the 1870 commentary (with Greek text) of the American Reverend Tayler Lewis, *Plato Against the Atheists; Or, The Tenth Book of the Dialogue on Laws*. Lewis wrote: 'Our object has not been merely to make a classical text-book, but to *recommend Plato* to the student or reader by every means through which attention could be drawn to our favourite author' (p.ix). He soon makes clear the urgency of this recommendation:

We believe that in this age there is a peculiar call for a deeper knowledge of Plato. Some acquaintance with his doctrine of ideas seems needed as a corrective to the tendency, so widely prevalent, to resolve all knowledge into an experimental induction of facts, not only in physical, but also in ethical and political science. If the Good, to adopt our author's own style, is something more than pleasure and happiness either present or anticipated—if the True is something higher than past, present, or future *facts* [. . .]—if God is something more than gravitation [. . .]—if there is a real foundation for the *moral* and religious, as distinct from, and not embraced in, the *natural*, or, in other words, if penalty and retribution are terms of far more solemn importance than modern jargon about physical consequences—then surely is it high time that there should be some disturbance of this placid taking for granted of the opposing views. (pp.xi–xii)

Lewis adds that the 'young man who is an enthusiastic student of Plato can never be . . . an infidel in religion'. His 'main object', he says, 'is to recommend this noble philosopher to the present generation of educated young men, especially to our young theologians' (p.xiii).

All this might have pleased Plato. And it would have delighted Lewis that the situation has changed in America in the approximately 140 years since his commentary appeared. Religion—and especially religion in alliance with political power—may not have the exalted position in academia that Lewis hoped for, but it is certainly on the rise in American culture generally. (It is on the rise in Europe too, though in a different form.)

My 'main object' in writing a commentary on Plato's *Laws* 10 was to aid scholars and students of philosophy and its history in becoming better acquainted with the *Laws* and its fascinating views on philosophical theology and their connection to Platonic political philosophy. If I had another, more cultural, aim, however, it would be radically different from Lewis's. For I would hope that a careful reading of *Laws* 10 might serve to make clearer and underscore the drastic consequences of taking seriously the idea that politics and religion should be intimately connected, and that the former should completely control the latter (or vice versa).

Plato, *Laws* 10

AS: *The Athenian Stranger*

K: *Kleinias*

M: *Megillus*

84a   AS. After assaults, let one comprehensive legal principle such as the following be stated covering acts of violence: No one is to carry off or lead away anything belonging to others, or use anything of one's neighbor, if he has not persuaded the owner. For all the evils mentioned have been, are, and will be dependant on such things. Gravest of the remaining [evils] are the unrestrained and hubristic acts of the young, and these are gravest of all when they affect hallowed things, and especially grave when they affect what is public and sacred—or common according to parts [of the

85a   city], being shared by a tribe or some other such [group]. Second and second gravest is when they affect private sacred things and tombs, and third, when someone is hubristic toward his parents (apart from what was discussed earlier). A fourth kind of hubris is when someone, ignoring the rulers, leads away or carries off or uses something of theirs without persuading them, and a fifth would be being hubristic with respect to the political rights of individual citizens in a way calling for legal justice. A law should be applied to each of these in common. For temple robbery has been discussed in summary—what the punishment ought to be, whether done violently or by stealth—but what the punishment ought to be for someone who (either by speaking or by acting) is hubristic towards the gods in word and in deed must be specified, once the exhortation has been laid down. Let it be as follows:
'No one who believes that the gods exist, according to the laws, has *ever* willingly committed an impious deed or uttered an illegal word, unless he is suffering from one of three things:

either this, he does not believe what I just said [i.e. that the gods exist]; or second, he believes they exist but do not take thought for humans; or third, he believes they are easily won over when influenced by sacrifices and prayers.'

c   *K.* So what should we do or even say to them?

   AS. Good man, let us first listen to them—to what I divine they say in derision and contempt for us.

   K. What's that?

   AS. They would probably say this, in their banter:
'Athenian Stranger, and Lakedaimonian, and Knossian, what you say is true. For some of us in no way believe in the gods at all, while others believe they are as you say. So we expect, just

d as you expected concerning the laws, that before you threaten us harshly, you first try to persuade and teach us that the gods exist, presenting adequate proof, and that they are too good to be charmed by some gifts into being turned away from justice. For now, hearing these and other such things from those said to be the best of the poets, orators, prophets, priests, and myriad upon myriad of others, most of us are not inclined to avoid unjust acts,

e but to do them and then attempt to make amends. So from legislators who claim to be not savage but gentle we expect persuasion first be used on us. If you do not *speak* much better than the others about the existence of the gods, but are *in fact* better with respect to the truth, then perhaps we might be persuaded by you. But try, if we say something reasonable, to reply to what we propose.'

   K. Well, stranger, doesn't it seem easy to speak the truth and to say that the gods exist?

886a *AS.* How?

   K. First, there's the earth and the sun and the stars and the whole universe, and the beautiful, orderly procession of the seasons, divided into years and months; and then there's the fact that all Greeks and barbarians believe that the gods exist.

   AS. Blessed man, I am *afraid*—I would never say that I'm ashamed —lest the wicked will somehow look down upon us. For you$_p$[1] don't know about the cause of our disagreement with them,

---

[1] In 886a8–c1 a subscript $_p$ indicates that in the Greek there is a plural 'you' or 'your'.

rather you~p~ believe that it is solely through a lack of control of pleasures and desires that their souls are impelled to the impious life.

K. But what besides these would be the cause, stranger?

AS. One which you~p~, living completely outside [their influence], would hardly know, but which would escape your~p~ notice.

K. What are you talking about now?

AS. A certain very grievous ignorance that seems to be the greatest wisdom.

K. What do you mean?

AS. There are among us [i.e. the Athenians] accounts set out in writing, which do not exist among you~p~ (because of the virtue of your political system, I understand), that speak about the gods (some with meters, others without): the most ancient say that the first nature of the heavens and the rest came into being, and, proceeding a bit beyond the beginning, they [i.e. the most ancient accounts] go through the birth of the gods, and how having come into being they [i.e. the gods] associated with one another. As to whether these [writings] do anything else fine or not fine to those who hear them, it is not easy to evaluate, because they are ancient; however, as to services to and honors due parents, I at least would never recommend them as beneficial or as what is spoken completely truthfully. Now let us dismiss the ancient material and bid it farewell, and let us speak about it in whatever way is dear to the gods; but what comes from our modern wise men let us censure to the extent that it is responsible for vicious things. Now the arguments of such people accomplish the following: when you and I present proofs that the gods exist, bringing forth these very things—sun and moon and stars and earth—as gods and divine beings, those misled by these wise men would say that these things are earth and stone and are not able to think about human affairs, but have somehow been well wrapped up in plausible stories.

K. Difficult indeed, stranger, is the argument you have described, even if it were one alone; but as there are in fact very many arguments, it is even more difficult.

AS. So what now? What do we say? What should we do? Shall we defend ourselves, as though someone were accusing us before impious people, who say to the accused, with respect to legislation, that we are doing terrible things in passing laws that the gods exist? Or shall we allow them to bid farewell, and [ourselves] return to the laws, lest our prelude become longer than the laws? For the discussion would not be brief if it were prolonged to provide those who desire to be impious with adequate arguments about the things they demanded we address, and cause them to fear and make them feel uneasy, and only then lay down the relevant laws.

K. But stranger, often (at least in our brief time together) we have said this very thing, that in the present case it is not necessary to honor the short speech more than the long—for no one hastens to pursue us, as the saying goes—and clearly it is ridiculous and base to appear to choose the shorter over the best. And it makes no small difference that somehow our arguments—that the gods exist and are good, honoring justice more than humans do—have some persuasiveness. For this would be just about our finest and best prelude on behalf of all the laws. So without being disgusted or rushed, and without holding back whatever capacity for persuasion we have from such arguments, let's go through them as sufficiently as possible.

AS. It seems to me that the argument you have just mentioned calls for a prayer, since you urge us on so eagerly. We should delay no longer in speaking. Come, then, how should someone speak without anger about the existence of gods? For it is indeed necessary to be harsh to and to hate those who have been and are now responsible for these arguments coming to us, as they do not believe the stories which, from the time they were young children still being nourished on milk, they heard from their nurses and mothers, presented like an incantation, sometimes playfully and sometimes seriously. They heard them in prayers at sacrifices, and they saw them in spectacles which are most pleasant for the young man to see and hear when accompanying the performance of sacrifices, and they saw their own parents, with the utmost seriousness, on behalf of themselves and their children, engaged in dialogue (through prayers and supplications) with gods who

887a

b

c

d

e

certainly did exist. And at the rising and the setting of the sun and moon they heard and saw the prostrations and adorations of both the Greeks and all the barbarians, in all sorts of misfortune and in prosperity, not as if they [i.e. the gods] do not exist, but as if they certainly exist and in no way give rise to any suspicion that they are not gods. Those people have contempt for all of this, and without a single sufficient argument (as those who have even a little intelligence would affirm), and they now compel us to say what we are saying. How could someone, with mild arguments, admonish and at the same time teach these people first of all that the gods exist? Still, it must be dared. For [both sides] ought not to be maddened at the same time: the one by gluttony for pleasure, the other by anger at such men. So let an introductory speech run as follows, without anger, for those who are in this way corrupted in thought, and let us speak mildly, extinguishing our anger, as if in a dialogue with a single one of them:

'Boy, you are young, and time as it passes will make you change many of the opinions you now hold into their opposites. So wait till then before becoming a judge about the greatest things; and the greatest, which you now regard as nothing, is to think correctly about the gods in order to live nobly—or not. First, in revealing to you some one great thing about them, I would never utter a falsehood. It is this: Neither you alone nor your friends are the first and foremost to have held this opinion about the gods, rather people who have this disease—many or few—are always appearing. And I, who have come across many of them, can tell you this: no one ever embraced from youth this opinion about the gods—that they don't exist—and continued into old age, steadfast in this way of thinking. The two other afflictions concerning the gods, however, do remain (not with many, but they remain with some): that the gods exist, but think nothing of human beings; and the one after this, that they *do* think about them, but are easily won over by sacrifices and prayers. You will wait, if you're persuaded by me, until a position concerning these things becomes as clear as possible to you, examining whether things are thus [i.e. as you now believe] or otherwise, inquiring from others and especially from the legislator; and during this time you won't dare do anything impious concerning the gods.

88a

Let he who sets up the laws for you attempt, now and in the future, to teach how these very things stand.'

K. What's been said so far, stranger, is fine with us.

AS. Completely, Megillus and Kleinias. But without noticing it, we have been exposed to an amazing argument.

K. Which do you mean?

e   *AS.* The one thought by many to be the wisest of all arguments.

K. Explain this more clearly.

AS. Some people say that all things that come into being, have come into being, and will come into being do so by nature, by art, or through chance.

K. Isn't that right?

889a   *AS.* It's likely, at least, that the wise men speak correctly. At any rate, let's follow them and investigate whatever the men on that side really happen to think.

K. Absolutely.

AS. It's likely, they claim, that the greatest and finest things are produced by nature and chance, while the smaller are by art, which takes over from nature the source of the greatest and primary works, and forms and crafts all the smaller things which we call artificial.

K. What do you mean?

b   *AS.* I'll state it more clearly still, as follows. They claim that fire, water, earth, and air all exist by nature and by chance, but none of these exists by art; and the bodies that come after these—those making up the earth, sun, moon, and stars—in turn came into being through these completely soulless beings. Each [element] is moved by chance, by the power each has; as they fell together, harmonizing in suitable ways—hot with cold, or dry in relation
c   to wet, and soft in relation to hard, and all such things which, by mixing with their opposites according to chance, have from necessity been mixed together—in this way, and according to these means, the entire heavens and all that is in the heavens were born, as well as, next, all the animals and plants, when all the seasons had come to be out of these, not through reason, they say, nor through some god nor through art, but, as we were

saying, by nature and chance. Art is late, coming to be later from these [i.e. animals]. Itself mortal from mortals, it later gave birth to certain playthings, which do not much share in the truth, but are images akin to the arts themselves, such as painting produces and music and whatever arts are ancillary to these. But some of the arts do in fact produce something that is serious—the ones whose capacities cooperate with nature, such as medicine, farming, and gymnastics. And, in particular, they say that some small part of politics cooperates with nature, but most of it is by art; and so, too, all legislation—whose enactments are not true—exists not by nature but by art.

K. What do you mean?

AS. The first thing these people claim about the gods, blessed one, is that they exist by art—not by nature but by certain laws—and that these [gods] are different in different locations, according to whatever each group agreed among themselves in laying down the laws. And in particular they claim that there are beautiful things by nature, though these differ from what is [beautiful] by law, while the just things do not exist by nature at all, rather that people continue to disagree with one another and are always altering these things [i.e. what are considered just], and whatever they alter and when, each is authoritative at that time, having come into being by art and by laws but certainly not by some nature.

This, my friends, is all from wise men—according to young people—who are prose writers and poets, who assert that what is most just is whatever can triumph by force; from which come the impieties that afflict young people, who hold that the gods are not such as the law commands they should be understood to be; and civil conflict occurs because of this, owing to those who drag people towards the 'correct life according to nature', which is in truth to live dominating the rest and not being a slave to others according to law.

K. What an account you've gone through, stranger, and what ruin for young people, both in cities as public places and in private households!

AS. You speak the truth, Kleinias. So what do you think the legislator ought to do, given that these views have been current for a long time? Is he simply to stand up before the city and threaten all the people that unless they affirm that the gods exist, and think and believe that [the gods] are such as the law affirms (and

c   the same could be said about the beautiful and the just and about all great matters and whatever aims at virtue and vice, that it is necessary to act in this way [i.e. as the law affirms] while thinking in whatever way the legislator has instructed in writing)—that whoever does not show himself obedient to the laws, in one case must die, in another be punished with a beating and imprisonment, in another with dishonors, and in other cases with poverty and exile? But what about Persuasion for the people—should he, at the same time that he establishes the laws for them, refrain from adding arguments to make them as gentle as possible?

d   K. Not at all, stranger, but if there happens to be even some small persuasion concerning these matters, the legislator of even a little worth should in no way grow tired, but should 'let loose his whole voice', as the saying goes, and become an ally of the ancient law's argument*[2] that the gods exist and all that you just now went through; in particular, he should support law itself and art, as existing by nature or by something not inferior to nature, if they are offspring of reason, according to the correct account. That is what you seem to me to be saying, and I believe you now.

e   AS. Most eager Kleinias, what now? Isn't it difficult to follow arguments in this way, when they are presented to crowds; and, further, don't they possess an immense length?

K. What, stranger? We put up with ourselves speaking at such length about drunkenness and music, but we're not going to endure this when it's about gods and such things? Further, it [i.e. a lengthy argument] is presumably a big help for *prudent* legislation, since

891a   the commands of law set down in writing remain completely the same, and ready to submit to examination for all time. So if they are difficult to listen to at the beginning there's no need to fear, because the slow learner will be able to return often and

---

[2] An asterisk indicates that the text corresponding to this part of the translation is discussed in the Textual Notes.

examine them; and if they are lengthy but useful it is in no way reasonable or holy, it seems to me, for any man not to support these arguments as much as possible.

M. What Kleinias says, stranger, seems excellent to me.

AS. Certainly, Megillus, we should do as he says. Indeed, if such arguments were not sown among all of mankind, so to speak, none of the arguments in defense of the gods' existence would be needed; but now they are necessary. So with the greatest laws being destroyed by vicious humans, who better to come to their defense than the legislator?

M. No one.

AS. But tell me again, Kleinias, for you must share in the arguments: the one saying these things apparently believes that fire and water and earth and air are first among all things and names these very things 'nature', while soul comes out of these later. But it's likely that this isn't merely apparent, but that he explicitly asserts these things to us in his argument.

K. Certainly.

AS. Now then, by Zeus, have we discovered something like a source of the unreasonable opinions of all those humans who have ever undertaken investigations into nature? Consider and examine the entire argument. For it is no small matter if those who handle impious arguments and lead others to them appeared to employ these arguments not well but erroneously. In fact, this seems to me to be the case.

K. You're right. But try to explain in what way [they're erroneous].

AS. Well, it's likely that rather unfamiliar arguments must now be handled.

K. There is no need to hesitate, stranger. For I understand that you think we'll be going outside legislation if we handle such arguments. But if there is no other way than this to come to an agreement that what are now described as gods according to law are correctly so described, then, you amazing man, it's necessary to speak in this way.

AS. So it seems I must now present this fairly uncustomary account: the arguments that produce the soul of the impious have declared that this—what *is* the first cause of the generation and destruction of all things—is *not* first but has come into being later, while what *is* later is earlier. This is why they have erred concerning the real existence of the gods.

892a   *K.* I don't understand.

AS. It's *soul*, comrade, that nearly everyone seems to have misunderstood: what it is, the power it has, and particularly (apart from other things about it) its generation—that it is among the first things, coming into being before all bodies, and that it more than anything governs their changes and all of their transformations. If this is how it is, then wouldn't what is related

b   to soul necessarily come into being before what belongs to body, since soul itself is older than body?

K. It is necessary.

AS. So opinion and supervision and reason and art and law would be prior to hard things and soft things and heavy things and light things. Indeed, the great and first works and actions would be those of art, being among the first, while 'nature' and the things that are 'by nature', which they incorrectly name in this way, would be later and governed by art and reason.

c   *K.* In what sense 'incorrectly'?

AS. By 'nature' they mean the generation [or source] of the first things; but if soul turns out to be first, not fire or air, and soul is among the first things to have come into being, then it may well be most correct to say that *it* especially is by nature. This is how things are if someone can demonstrate that soul is older than body, but not otherwise.

K. That's perfectly true.

d   *AS.* So shouldn't we next get ready to do just this?

K. Of course.

AS. Let us guard against a completely deceitful argument, lest in some way we, who are old, are taken in by its novelty, and it eludes us and makes us look ridiculous, in seeming to take on great things but to fail at smaller ones. So consider: Suppose we three had to cross a rapidly flowing river, and I, who happened to be the youngest of us and experienced with many currents, said that I should try first by myself, leaving you in safety, and investigate whether it is fordable for you older men as well, or however it is, and if it appears to be such I'll call to you and help you with my experience to ford it, but if it's not fordable for you the risk would fall to me—I would seem to speak reasonably. Indeed, the argument now coming up is very rapid and probably not fordable given your strength. So lest [the argument], going by and asking [questions of] you who are unaccustomed to answering, makes you dazed and dizzy, putting you in an unpleasant, undignified, and unseemly position, it seems to me that I should now do the following: first I'll question myself, while you listen in safety, and after this I'll answer myself in return, and I'll go through the entire argument in this way, until it has completely covered what concerns the soul and demonstrates that the soul is prior to body.

K. You seem to us to have spoken excellently, stranger. Do what you say.

AS. Come, then, if ever we should summon a god for help, let this be done now—let us summon them in all seriousness, at the demonstration of their own existence—and, holding on as if to some security rope, let us enter into the present argument.

When I am questioned about such matters, and asked such things as the following, it seems safest to answer in this way. When someone says, 'Stranger, is everything stationary and nothing in motion? Or is it completely opposite to that? Or are some things in motion and some at rest?'—'Presumably some are in motion', I'll reply, 'and some are at rest.'—'Then surely there is some place in which the stationary things are stationary and the things in motion are in motion.'—'How could it be otherwise?'—'And some would presumably do this [i.e. move] in one spot while others would do this in many?'—'Do you mean those things that have the power of standing still in the middle', we'll say, 'and to move in one place, just as the circumferences of circles said to stand still revolve?'—'Yes.'—'And we understand that in the case of *this* rotation, the largest circle and the smallest go around at the same time, and such motion distributes itself to the small and the large proportionally, being less or more according to proportion. This is why it [i.e. circular motion] has

93a

become a source of all sorts of wonder: at the same time it imparts to large and small circles slowness and swiftness in harmony, an occurrence that one would expect to be impossible.'—'That's absolutely true.'—'"What moves in many locations" appears to me to mean whatever moves in a motion by which it always changes to another place, sometimes possessing a base of one point, sometimes more (by rolling). Each time they [i.e. moving objects] encounter each other, they are split apart by the ones standing still, whereas with the others that come and are borne from the opposite direction, they combine and become one thing intermediate between the two [in nature].'—'I say that this is the way it is, as you say.'—'Further, when they combine there is growth, but when they separate there is decay, for as long as the established state of each thing remains; but if it doesn't remain, there is destruction by means of both [i.e. combination and separation]. Now when anything comes into being, what is it that happens? It is clear that when the principle, receiving growth, proceeds to the second change, and from this to the next and proceeds as far as the third, it provides perception to perceivers. Everything comes to be by changing and transforming in this way; and it is really being, as long as it remains the same; but if it changes into another state it is completely destroyed.'

So, friends, haven't we stated and numbered all forms of motion, except two?

K. Which two?

AS. My good man, those two for the sake of which virtually our entire present investigation is undertaken.

K. Speak more clearly.

AS. Presumably, it was for the sake of soul?

K. Certainly.

AS. So let there be one motion that is always capable of moving others but incapable of moving itself, and another that is always capable of moving itself and others, by combinations and separations, growths and the opposite, and generations and destructions—another one among all the motions.

K. Let this be so.

AS. Therefore, the one that always moves another and is changed by another we will make the ninth, while the one that moves itself and others—in harmony with all actions and all experiences, and accurately called the change and motion of all beings—this we will say is pretty much the tenth.

K. By all means.

AS. Which of our approximately ten motions would we judge most correctly to be the most influential of all and especially effective?

K. Presumably, we should assert that the one capable of moving itself excels in myriad ways, while all the others are inferior.

AS. That's right. So, shouldn't one or even two of our incorrect statements just now be changed?

K. Which are you talking about?

AS. What was said about the tenth was pretty much stated incorrectly.

K. How?

AS. According to our argument, it is first in generation and in influence. And the one after this we hold is second to this, though oddly it was just now said to be ninth.

K. What do you mean?

AS. This: If we hold that one thing changes another, and this other yet another, forever, will one of these changes ever be first? And how will that which is moved by another ever be first among the things that are altered? For that's impossible. But when something having moved itself alters another, and this other another, and in this way thousands upon thousands of things being moved come into being, what will be a principle of all of their motions except the change from what has moved itself?

K. Excellently put; there should be agreement with this.

AS. Let us speak further, in the following way, and again answer ourselves. If somehow everything were to come together and stand still, just as most of those men venture to say, which motion of the ones we spoke of would necessarily be the first to come to be among them? Surely the one that moves itself. For it would never be changed by another that is prior, since there is among them no prior change. So, as the source of all motions, and the first to come to be among what was standing still and

95a

to exist among what moves, we shall assert that the one that moves itself is necessarily the oldest and most powerful change of all, while the one that is altered by another and moves others is second.

K. That's perfectly true.

c   AS. So, now that we are at this point in the account, let us answer the following.

K. What?

AS. If we should see that this [i.e. self-moving motion] had come to be in something made of earth or water or what has the form of fire—separated or even mixed together—whatever would we say is the condition of such a thing?

K. Are you asking me if we'll say something is living when it moves itself?

AS. Yes.

K. Living—how could it not be?

AS. Well then, when we see soul in certain things, is it anything but the same in such cases? Should we agree that it's living?

K. It's nothing else.

d   AS. Hold on, by Zeus. Wouldn't you be willing to recognize three points concerning each thing?

K. What do you mean?

AS. One is the being, one is the definition of the being, and one is the name. Further, there are two questions you could ask about every being.

K. Why two?

AS. Sometimes each of us puts forward the name by itself and demands the definition, other times he puts forward the definition by itself and asks for the name. So, do we intend to say the following now?*

K. What?

e   AS. Presumably, being divisible into two exists in other things and also in number. The name for this in the case of number is 'even', and the definition is: 'a number divisible into two equal parts'.

K. Yes.

AS. I'm talking about that sort of thing. Aren't we referring to the same thing in either case, whether when asked for the definition we give the name, or asked for the name we give the definition? By the name 'even' and by the definition 'number divisible into two', aren't we referring to the same being?

K. Absolutely.

AS. So what is the definition of the thing the name of which is 'soul'? Do we have another besides the one just now stated: 'motion capable of moving itself'?

K. Do you claim that the definition 'to move itself' holds for the same being which we all refer to by the name 'soul'?

AS. *I* claim this. And if this is so, do we still regret that we have not sufficiently demonstrated that soul is the same being as the first generation and motion of what exists, what has come to be, and what will be, and further of all of their opposites, since it has been shown to be the cause of all change and of motion in all things?

K. No, it has been demonstrated most sufficiently that soul, being the source of motion, is the oldest of all things.

AS. So isn't the motion that comes to be in one thing because of another, but that itself never causes anything to move by itself, second, or however many numbers farther down someone would wish to count it, really being a change of soulless body?

K. Correct.

AS. So we spoke correctly, authoritatively, most truly and perfectly saying that soul has come to be prior to body, while body is second and later, and that soul rules, while body is ruled, according to nature.

K. That is most true.

AS. Now remember what we agreed to earlier: if soul were shown to be older than body, then the things of the soul would be older than the things of the body.

K. Certainly.

AS. Habits, moral characteristics, wishes, calculations, true opinions, supervision, and memory would have come into being prior to length of bodies, width, depth, and strength, if soul is prior to body.

K. Necessarily.

AS. So, after this, isn't it necessary to agree that soul is the cause of good things and bad, beautiful and ugly, just and unjust, and of all the [sets of] opposites—if we are going to posit it as the cause of all things?

K. How could it not be?

e AS. Indeed, since soul manages and resides in all things that anywhere are in motion, isn't it necessary to assert that it also manages the heavens?

K. What else?

AS. One soul or more than one? More—I'll answer for both of you. At any rate, we should assume no fewer than two: one that does what is good, and one capable of doing the opposite.

K. What you said is definitely correct.

AS. Very well. So soul drives all things in the heavens and on earth and in the sea through its own motions, the names of which 897a are wishing, investigating, supervising, deliberating, believing correctly and falsely, rejoicing and feeling pain, being bold and feeling fear, hating and loving, and through all of the related or primary-work motions, taking over the secondary-work motions of bodies, they drive all things to growth and decay, separation and combination, and to what follows these: heat and cold, heaviness and lightness, hard and soft, white and black, bitter b and sweet. Soul uses all of these, and every time it joins with reason—'god' correctly for the gods*—it guides all things toward what is correct and happy, but when it associates with lack-of-reason it produces in all things the opposite of these. Shall we set these down as being this way, or do we still suspect that it might be otherwise?

K. Not at all.

AS. So then which kind of soul should we claim is in control of the heavens and earth and the whole cycle? The one prudent and c full of virtue, or that which possesses neither? Do you want us to answer these questions as follows?

K. How?

AS. We should say: If, my amazing man, the entire course and movement of the heavens and of all the beings therein has the same nature as the motion and revolution and calculations of reason, and proceeds in a related way, then it is clear that one ought to claim that the best soul supervises the whole cosmos and leads it along just such a course.

K. Correct.

AS. But if they proceed in a frantic and disorderly way, then it's the vicious soul.

K. This too is correct.

AS. So, then, what nature does the motion of reason have? This question, friends, is difficult to answer prudently, which is why taking me on now to help with your answer is just.

K. You speak well.

AS. Therefore, let us not come up with the answer head-on from the opposite direction, like looking into the sun and bringing on night in the middle of the day, as if with mortal eyes we could ever see reason and know it sufficiently. It is safer to see by looking at an *image* of what is being asked about.

K. What do you mean?

AS. Let us take as the image the motion (of those ten motions) which reason resembles. Recalling it with you, I'll come up with our common answer.

K. What you say is most fine.

AS. So do we still remember this from what was said earlier, that of all things some are in motion and some at rest?

K. Yes.

98a AS. And, of those in motion, some move in one place, some move in more than one.

K. That's right.

AS. Of these two motions, the one moving always in one place must necessarily move around some midpoint, being an imitation of wheels turned on a lathe, and in every way it has the greatest possible kinship and likeness to the orbit of reason.

    K. What do you mean?

   AS. Certainly, if we said that in both cases—reason and the motion moving in one place—moving was (1) in relation to the same things, (2) in the same way, (3) in the same place, (4) around the same things, (5) toward the same things, and (6) according to one formula and one order, and illustrated both by the motions of a sphere turned on a lathe, we would never appear to be poor craftsmen of beautiful images in speech.

    K. What you say is most correct.

   AS. But wouldn't the motion that never moves (1) in the same way, nor (2) according to what is the same, nor (3) in the same place, nor (4) around the same things, nor (5) toward the same things, nor (6) in one place, nor (7) in an arrangement or order or some formula, be akin to complete lack-of-reason?

    K. Most truly it would.

   AS. So now it is no longer difficult to say right out that since according to us soul is what leads everything around, it ought to be claimed that the orbit of the heavens is led around from necessity, being supervised and ordered either by the best soul or by the opposite kind.

    K. But, stranger, judging from what has now been said, it isn't pious to say anything other than that soul—one or more—having complete virtue leads things around.

   AS. Kleinias, you have listened to the arguments brilliantly. But further attend to this.

    K. To what?

   AS. If soul leads around all of these—sun and moon and the other stars—then doesn't it [lead around] each one?

    K. Of course.

   AS. Let us produce the arguments for one of these, which we find obviously applies to all of the stars.

    K. Which one?

   AS. The sun. Every human sees its body, but no one sees its soul—nor indeed the soul of the body of any other living beings, whether living or dying. But there is a good reason to expect that this kind of thing, which is completely imperceptible to all bodily senses, exists by nature all around us, but is intelligible through reason alone. Indeed, through this and understanding, let us grasp the following concerning soul.

K. What?

AS. If soul does lead the sun, we will not be far off if we say it does this in one of three ways.

K. Which ways?

AS. Either soul resides within this visible round body, and as such conveys it everywhere, just as our soul carries us around everywhere; or from somewhere outside it procures for itself a body of fire or some kind of air (as is the view of certain people), and by force pushes body with body; or third, being itself void of body, but having some other extremely amazing powers, it guides [the sun].

K. Yes, this is necessary: that soul does at least one of these to lead all things.

AS. Now hold it. All men ought to regard this soul as a god, whether it leads light to all of us by being in the chariot of the sun, or from the outside, or however or in whatever way. Or what?

K. Yes, anyone who hasn't reached the ultimate in lack-of-reason.

AS. Indeed, concerning all the stars and the moon, and concerning years and months and all the seasons, what other account will we present but this same one: that since soul or souls—good ones with respect to complete virtue—appear to be the causes of all of these, we will claim that they are gods, whether they order the entire heavens by existing in bodies, being living beings, or in whatever way and however they do it? Is there anyone who could agree with this and still not hold that all things are full of gods?

K. Stranger, there is no one so deranged.

AS. Now then, Megillus and Kleinias, to the one who hitherto did not believe in the gods let us state our terms and dismiss him.

K. What terms?

AS. Either to demonstrate to us that we aren't speaking correctly when we posit soul as the first genesis of all things (and everything else that we said followed from this), or, if unable to speak better than us, to be persuaded by us and to live believing in the gods

99a

d   for the rest of his life. So let us see whether what we said about
           the gods existing to those who don't believe in the gods is already
           sufficient, or whether it's inadequate.

    K. Stranger, it least of all is inadequate.

   AS. Then let this be the end of our arguments with these people;
           however, we must now exhort the one who believes that the gods
           exist, but that they don't think about human affairs. We'll state:

           'Best of men, that you believe in gods is likely some kinship
           with the divine that leads you to what is of the same nature
e   and to honor and believe in its existence. But the private
           and public fortunes of vicious and unjust humans lead you to
           impiety, when in truth they are not happy, though they are
           improperly thought to be extremely happy—among the Muses
           who incorrectly sing their praises and according to all kinds of
           accounts. Or perhaps you see humans nearing the end of old age,
900a   leaving behind grandchildren in high honors, and now you are
           disturbed observing in all these cases (either through hearsay or
           even by seeing it all with your own eyes) that there are some who
           have engaged in many terrible acts of impiety, and through these
           very acts have gone from humble beginnings to tyrannies and pre-
           eminence. The result of all of this is that although owing to your
           kinship you are clearly unwilling to blame the gods as the cause of
b   such things, you are led—by poor reasoning and an inability to
           condemn the gods—to this present condition of yours: it seems
           that they exist, but that they despise and neglect human affairs.
           Therefore, in order that the belief you now hold not worsen your
           impious condition, and if somehow we are able as it were to ward
           off this belief with arguments when it approaches, let us try to
           connect the next argument to the one we discussed thoroughly
           from the beginning against the person who did not believe in
           gods at all, and make use of this latter in the present case.'

c   But you, Kleinias and Megillus, on behalf of the young man,
           take his place in answering, just as you did in the previous case.
           If something difficult comes up in the arguments, I will take over
           from you two, as I did just now, and take [you] across the river.

    K. Well spoken. You do these things in this way, and we'll do what
           you say to the extent that that's possible.

AS. But perhaps it would not be difficult to prove this* at least, that the gods supervise small matters no less* than the especially big matters. For presumably he heard and was present at what was just said: that, being good with respect to every virtue, the supervision of all things is perfectly appropriate to them.

K. He certainly heard this.

AS. So, after this, let them examine with us in common what virtue of the gods we meant when we agreed that they [i.e. the gods] were good. Come, do we claim that being moderate and possessing reason are characteristic of virtue, while the opposites are characteristic of vice?

K. We claim that.

AS. What else? That courage is characteristic of virtue, and cowardice of vice?

K. Certainly.

AS. And will we claim that some of these are shameful, while others are noble?

K. Necessarily.

AS. And whichever of these are base befit us, if anyone, whereas we say that neither the great nor the small of such things dwell among the gods?

K. Everyone would agree that this, too, is the case.

AS. What else? Will we attribute neglect and laziness and luxury to virtue of the soul, or what do you say?

K. What indeed?

AS. But to the opposite?

K. Yes.

01a *AS.* And the opposites of these to the opposite?

K. The opposite.

AS. So what then? Would everyone who is luxurious and negligent and lazy be according to us the sort the poet says are most 'like stingless drones'?[3]

K. Spoken most correctly.

---

[3] Hesiod, *Works and Days*, 304.

AS. Then the god should not be said to have just the sort of character that he himself hates, and anyone who attempts to utter such a thing should not be allowed to.

K. No he shouldn't. How could he be?

b   *AS.* It belongs to someone to act and to have special supervision over something, and his reason supervises the great things but neglects the small ones: according to what argument would we praise such a man and not strike a completely false note? Let's consider this as follows: Doesn't the one who acts in such a way act according to either of two forms, whether he is a god or a man?

K. Which ones do we mean?

c   *AS.* Either (1) he thinks it makes no difference to the whole if he neglects the small things, or (2) he neglects them through indolence and luxury, though it makes a difference. Or does neglect come to be in some other way? For, presumably, if it's *impossible* to supervise all things, then it won't be neglect of either small or great things, whether a god or some base person is unable to supervise them, being inferior and thus unable to supervise.

K. How could it?

d   *AS.* Now let the two of them answer the three of us. (They both agree the gods exist, though the other says they're appeasable through prayer, while this one says they neglect small things.) 'First, do you both claim that the gods know and see and hear everything, and that nothing of which there are perceptions and knowledge can escape them?' Is this the way these things are said to be,* or how?

K. This way.

AS. What else? Can the gods do whatever is possible to mortals and immortals?

K. How could they not concede that this too is so?

e   *AS.* Further, we five have agreed that they [i.e. the gods] are good—in fact, best.

K. Very much so.

AS. So isn't it impossible to agree that they do anything at all through indolence or luxury, if they are such as we agree? For according to us, at least, laziness is an offspring of cowardice, and indolence an offspring of laziness and luxury.

K. What you say is most true.

AS. None of the gods, then, is negligent from laziness and indolence, for presumably none shares in cowardice.

K. What you say is most correct.

02a *AS.* So what is left, if they do neglect the very small things in the universe: either they do this knowing that it is absolutely necessary † to supervise none†* of these things, or—what is left, except the opposite of knowledge?

K. Nothing.

AS. So which is it, very best of men: Should we put you down as saying that the gods are ignorant and through ignorance neglect what ought to be supervised, or that they know what they ought to do, as the basest of humans are said to do: they know it is better to act otherwise than how they are acting, but don't do so, because they succumb to pleasures or pains?

K. How could that be?

AS. So don't human affairs share in the nature of the ensouled, and isn't the human himself the most god-revering of all animals?

K. That's likely.

AS. Indeed, we claim that all mortal animals are possessions of the gods, as are the entire heavens.

K. How could this not be?

AS. So, then, let someone claim that these are small or great to the gods; for in neither case would it befit the owners to neglect us, since they are the most solicitous and the best. For let us consider the following, in addition to these points.

K. What?

AS. Concerning perception and power: are they not by nature opposite one another, with respect to ease and difficulty?

K. What do you mean?

AS. Presumably, it's more difficult to see and to hear what's small than what's big, while it's easier for everyone to carry and control and supervise what's small and few than their opposites.

d   K. Much more.

AS. If a whole [patient] is assigned to a doctor to treat, and [the doctor] wants and is able to supervise what's big, but neglects the small parts, will the entire [patient] ever fare well for him?

K. Absolutely not.

AS. Nor for captains or generals or household managers, nor for
e   certain statesmen or any other such men, will the many and great fare well apart from the few and small; for the stonemasons claim that large stones do not lie well without small ones.

K. How could they?

AS. So let us never suppose that *the god* is inferior to mortal craftsmen who the better they are the more exactly and perfectly they execute with one art the small and the large aspects of the work that is proper to them; nor suppose that the god who is
903a   most wise and willing and able to supervise will not supervise any of the small things, which are easily supervised, but will supervise the large things, just like some lazy or cowardly person who is indolent in the face of toil.

K. Let us in no way accept such an opinion about the gods, stranger. For we would be thinking a thought that is in no way holy or true.

AS. We seem to me now to have had a completely reasonable* dialogue with the one who likes to accuse the gods of negligence...

K. Yes.

AS. ...by forcing him, with arguments, to agree that he was not
b   speaking correctly. Yet it seems to me that some mythic incantations are still needed.

K. Which ones, my good man?

AS. Let us persuade the young man, with arguments, that:
'The universe is put together with a view to the safety and virtue of the whole by the one who supervises the universe, and each part, to the extent that it can, does and has done to it what

is fitting. Rulers have been positioned over the experience and activity of each of these parts, for all time, to the smallest detail, and they [i.e. the rulers] have achieved their goal to the utmost fraction. Even your part is one of these, stubborn man, and it always strains to look toward the universe, even though it is altogether small. But you have forgotten about this very fact, that all generation comes to be for the sake of this: that a happy existence may belong to the life of the universe; and it does not come to be for the sake of you, but you for the sake of it. For every doctor and every skilled craftsman does all his work for the sake of all; he makes a part straining for what is best in common, for the sake of the whole, and not the whole for the sake of a part. But you are irritated, not knowing how what concerns you turns out best for the whole and for you as well, in virtue of the power of your common generation. Since soul is always put together with bodies—sometimes with one, sometimes with another—and undergoes all kinds of changes through itself or through another soul, no other function is left for the game-player except to transfer the character that is becoming better to a better place, and the one becoming worse to a worse place, according to what is appropriate to each of them, such that each is allotted its proper fate.'

K. In what way do you mean?

AS. The way in which the supervision of the universe by the gods would be easy—this is what I seem to be explaining. For if someone, failing always to look to the whole, were to mold all things by changing their shapes—for example, having ensouled [or 'cold'] water come from fire, and not many things from one or one from many—then once they [i.e. all things] have taken part in a first or second or third generation, there would be an unlimited number of transformations in the arrangement of the cosmos. But in fact it is marvelously easy for the one who supervises the universe.

K. Again, what do you mean?

AS. This: 'Our King saw that all actions involve soul, and there is much virtue in them, but also much vice, and that, having come to be, soul with body is indestructible but not eternal, like the gods that exist according to law—for there would never b   have been generation of living beings if either of these two had been destroyed—and he grasped that whatever in soul is good is always naturally beneficial, while the vicious is harmful. Seeing all this, he presumably designed the position of each of the parts so that virtue would be victorious in the universe, and vice defeated, in the easiest and best way. Indeed, he has designed, with a view to this universe, that when a certain sort [of person] comes into being, it must always take a certain place and reside

c   in certain locations. But he leaves the cause for the coming to be of each particular sort of person to the will of each of us. For as one desires, and as one is with respect to soul, so (pretty much in every case) is the sort of person each of us becomes, for the most part.'

K. That's likely.

AS. 'So all things that are sharing in soul change, possessing within themselves the cause of the change, and in changing they are moved according to the order and law of destiny. When the change in character is smaller and less significant, there is smaller horizontal movement in space; when a change is more significant

d   and more unjust, the movement is into the depths and the places said to be below, which people call "Hades" and related names, which terrify them both in dreams while they are alive, and when they have been sundered from their bodies. But whenever a soul gets a larger share of vice or virtue, owing to its own will and to an increased influence from others, then, by mingling with a divine virtue it becomes exceptionally such; and it undergoes

e   an exceptional change of place and is transported along a sacred road to a better place elsewhere; but when the opposite happens it moves its own life to the opposite place. "This is the judgment of the gods who hold Olympus",[4] O child or young man, who believes he is neglected by the gods: the one who becomes more vicious is conveyed to the vicious souls, while the one who becomes better is conveyed to the better souls, in life and in every

905a   death, to experience and to do what is appropriate for like to do to like. From this judgment of the gods* neither you nor anyone else who's become luckless will ever boast of having escaped.

---

[4] Homer, *Odyssey*, 19.43.

Those who ordered this ordered it to be above all judgments, and it should be regarded with absolute care. For you will never be neglected by this judgment—not if you were so small as to sink into the depths of the earth, or so high as to fly to the heavens—but you will pay them the appropriate penalty, either while you remain here, or after you've been brought through to Hades or been carried over to a place even more savage* than this. The same account, you know, would also apply to those you see going from smallness to greatness by doing unholy deeds or some such actions, whom you suppose go from wretchedness to happiness, and in whose actions, as in mirrors, you believe you have observed the neglect of all the gods, not knowing how their contribution helps the universe. But, bravest of all men, how can you think it's not necessary to know this? If someone does not know it he would never see an impression, nor be able to offer an account, of life with respect to both happiness and an unhappy fortune. So if Kleinias here and our whole Council of Elders persuade you about this—that concerning the gods you don't know what you're saying—the god himself would assist you nobly. But if you should still need some further argument, listen to us address the third opponent, if you possess any reason whatsoever.'

For that the gods exist and supervise humans I at least would claim has been demonstrated by us, not completely poorly. But that the gods can be appeased by the unjust, if they receive gifts, is not something one should agree with, and one should refute it in every way possible.

K. Well said; let's do as you say.

AS. Come, by the gods themselves, in what way would they come to be appeased by us, if they could be? And what, or what sort, would they be? Presumably, they will necessarily be rulers, since they are to manage the entire heavens perfectly.*

K. That is so.

AS. But which of the rulers do they resemble? Or rather which [rulers] resemble them, of those we can compare to them, lesser to greater? Would drivers of competing teams [of horses] be such [as to resemble them], or captains of ships? Perhaps they might be compared to rulers of armies. Or they might even be like doctors

906a   caring for bodies in the war on disease, or farmers awaiting in fear seasons that tend to be difficult with respect to the generation of crops, or even overseers of flocks. For since we have agreed among ourselves that the heavens are full of many good things, and also of the opposite, and that there is more of what is not good, this sort of battle, we claim, is immortal and requires amazing vigilance, and the gods and spirits are our allies, while
b   we are the property of the gods and spirits. Injustice and hubris without prudence destroy us, while justice and moderation with prudence save us, and these reside in the ensouled powers of the gods, though one can clearly see some small amount of these residing in us as well. Now there are some souls residing on earth who have acquired unjust gain and are clearly beastly. Throwing themselves down before the souls of the guardians (dogs or shepherds or absolutely supreme masters), they persuade them with flattering speeches and prayers of enchantment of what
c   the claims of the vicious men assert: it is possible for them to have too much among humans, and to suffer no hardship. But presumably we claim that the error just named—having too much—is called 'disease' in fleshy bodies, 'plague' in the seasons and years, while in cities and political systems this same thing, the name having been changed, is 'injustice'.

  K. Absolutely.

d   *AS.* The one who says that the gods are always forgiving unjust humans and those who act unjustly, if one distributes to them some of what's been gained unjustly, must necessarily present this account: it's just as if wolves were to distribute to dogs a small part of what they've seized, and the dogs, tamed by the gifts, were to allow the wolves to tear the flocks to pieces. Is this not the account of those who claim that the gods are appeasable?

  K. It is.

  AS. So to which of those aforementioned guardians could any human favorably compare the gods and not become ridicu-
e   lous? To captains who 'turn from their course by the libation of wine and the burnt offering',[5] and overturn ship and sailors?

---

[5] Homer, *Iliad*, 9.500.

K. Not at all.

AS. And surely not to charioteers lined up for a race, persuaded by a gift to give over the victory to the other teams.

K. You would present a terrible image in giving this account.

AS. And surely not to generals or doctors or farmers or herdsmen, nor to the dogs charmed by wolves.

K. Silence! How could they be?

AS. But, to us, aren't all the gods the greatest of all guardians and over the greatest things?

K. By far.

AS. Then are we going to claim that those who guard the finest affairs, and are themselves distinguished with respect to virtue in guarding, are worse than dogs and average humans, who would never give over what is just for the sake of gifts given in an unholy way by unjust men?

K. In no way. This is an intolerable account, and anyone holding this opinion is in danger of being judged—most justly—the most vicious and most impious of all the impious, who are involved in every impiety.

AS. The three propositions—that the gods exist, that they supervise us, and that they in no way can be appeased so as to act contrary to justice—shall we perhaps claim that they have been sufficiently demonstrated?

K. How could we not? We, at least, vote for these arguments.

AS. Still, they were perhaps presented rather vehemently, owing to our love of victory over vicious humans; and we felt this love of victory, dear Kleinias, for the sake of this: lest the vicious ones should ever believe that if they were more powerful in arguments they could act however they wished, in accordance with each and every belief they have about the gods. A zeal, because of these things, has made us speak with youthful vigor. But if we have made even some small contribution to persuading these men in some way to hate themselves, and somehow to like the opposite character traits, the prelude to the laws on impiety would have been well spoken by us.

K. There is hope; and if not, at least the kind of account will not discredit the legislator.

AS. Now then, after the prelude an account that is like an expounder of the laws would be right for us, forewarning all the impious to abandon their ways for pious ones. For those who do not comply, let the law concerning impiety be as follows:[6]

'If anyone is impious in words or in deeds, let the one who encounters this defend [the law] by informing the magistrates, and the first magistrates who learn of it are to bring [the accused] before the court created to judge these cases according to the law. If some magistrate hears of it and does not do this, let *him* be brought to trial for impiety by anyone wanting to avenge the laws. If someone should be convicted, let the court assess one separate penalty for each of those who are impious. Let imprisonment be imposed in every case.'

There are three prisons in the city: (1) a common one near the marketplace for most prisoners, for the safekeeping of a number of bodies; (2) one near the meeting place of the Nocturnal Council, named the Sound-mind Center; and (3) one in the middle of the countryside, in some empty place that is as savage as possible, having as its name some word for punishment.

Since the causes of impiety are three (which we have gone through), and there are two [kinds] for each of these causes, then concerning divine things there will be six kinds of offenders worth distinguishing, and these do not require equal or similar penalties. For a just character could come by nature to one who does not believe in the gods at all: they come to hate vicious people and from a loathing for injustice do not venture to perform such actions, and flee from unjust humans and like the just. But others, in addition to the opinion that all things are empty of gods, may be afflicted by a lack of self control concerning pleasures and pains, and also have strong memories and sharp minds. Not believing in the gods is an affliction common in both, but with respect to the ruin of other humans

e

908a

b

c

---

[6] In what follows I have distinguished (through the use of quotation marks) what I believe is part of the official law on impiety, and what are the Athenian's additional comments on the law as it is being presented. Keep in mind that these are my additions, and that there are no such indicators in the text.

the one would do less evil, the other more. For the former would be full of candor in speaking about the gods and about sacrifices and oaths, and by ridiculing others would perhaps make some of them such as he is, if he doesn't receive a penalty. But the latter, while holding the same opinions as the former, is called 'naturally gifted', and is full of cunning and treachery. From these are produced many diviners and men knowing all kinds of magic; and from this sort sometimes also come tyrants and demagogues and generals, and those who plot by means of private rites, and the machinations of those called 'sophists'. Many forms of these [atheists] would arise, but those for whom it is worth establishing laws are two: (1) the dissembler commits faults that are worthy neither of one nor two deaths; (2) the other requires admonishment together with imprisonment. Similarly, the belief that the gods are neglectful also produces two different kinds, and the belief that they can be appeased produces another two. These having been distinguished in this way, [let the law continue]:

'The ones who have come to be impious through lack-of-reason, without vicious anger or character, let the judge place, according to law, in the Sound-mind Center for not less than five years; and during this time let no other citizens meet with them except members of the Nocturnal Council, who are to associate with them for admonishment and for the preservation of the soul. When the time of their imprisonment has come to an end, if any one of them seems to be of sound mind, let him reside among those of sound mind; but if not, and he is again convicted on such a charge, let him be punished with death.'

But there are those who become like beasts, in addition to not believing in the gods or believing them to be neglectful or appeasable. Despising humans, they lead the souls of many of the living while claiming to lead the souls of the dead and promising to persuade the gods, by bewitching them with sacrifices and prayers and incantations, and so they attempt to destroy utterly individuals and whole households and cities, for the sake of money.

'If one of these seems to be convicted, let the court punish him with imprisonment, according to the law, in the prison in the middle of the country. No free man is ever to visit such men,

but they will get food from slaves, as arranged by the Guardians
of the Laws. When he dies, he is to be cast beyond the borders
unburied; and if a free man should help bury him, let this person
be brought to trial for impiety by anyone who wishes. If he [i.e.
the convict] should leave behind children fit for the city, let the
Supervisors of Orphans care for them as well, as if they were
orphans in no way inferior to the others, from the day their
father is convicted at trial.'

A law should be laid down for all of these people in common,
which would make many of them offend less against the gods by
deed and by word, and particularly become less unreasonable,
by not allowing them to deal in the divine contrary to the law.
Let the following law be laid down for all of them without
qualification:

'Let no one possess shrines in private households. When it
occurs to someone to make a sacrifice, let him go to the public
ones and sacrifice, and hand over his offerings to the priests
and priestesses who supervise their consecration. Let him join in
prayer along with anyone else he wants to join in prayer with
him.'

Let these things happen for the following reasons: To found
shrines and gods is not easy; to do this correctly requires some
deep thought. It is customary for all women especially, and for
those who are sick in any way or in danger or distressed (however
one might be distressed), or, conversely, when they gain some
prosperity, to sanctify whatever is in front of them at the time
and to swear to offer sacrifices and promise to found shrines to
gods and spirits and children of gods. And because of fears from
apparitions seen when awake and from dreams, and similarly
recalling many such visions, they make remedies against each
of them by filling every house and every village with altars and
shrines, founding them in clear places or wherever someone
happened to have such experiences. For all of these reasons one
should act according to the law just presented; and, in addition to
these, so that the impious won't act deceptively in these matters
by founding shrines and altars in private households, believing
they can in secret make the gods agreeable through sacrifices
and prayers, thus increasing injustice infinitely, and bringing the
reproach of the gods against both the impious themselves and

those who (though they are better than them) tolerate them, such that the entire city catches their impiety (in a way justly). The god will not blame the legislator, however, for let this law be laid down:

'There is to be no possession of shrines to the gods in private households; and for anyone shown to possess and worship at shrines other than the public ones, if the person possessing [a private shrine]—man or even woman—has committed none of the grave and impious acts of injustice, let the one who perceives this report it to the Guardians of the Laws, who are to order the private shrines be carried off to the public ones. Let those who disobey be punished until the shrines are carried off. But if someone is shown to have committed an impiety not of a childish sort, but an act of impiety characteristic of unholy men—either by founding a shrine in private or by sacrificing in public to any gods whatsoever—let him be punished by death for making a sacrifice while being impure. After the Guardians of the Laws judge whether it is childish or not, and bring the accused before the court accordingly, let them impose the penalty for impiety in these cases.'

Commentary

1. PRELIMINARIES (884A1–888D6)

884a1–6

Laws 9 could be entitled 'Crime and Punishment'. Besides a theory of punishment, it covers a number of crimes, such as theft (including temple robbery), treason, and acts of violence—this last including killing (homicide and suicide), wounding, and finally assault. *Laws* 10 begins: 'After assaults . . .'. The Athenian Stranger (hereafter 'the Athenian') says that having covered violent crime, they should thus formulate a general law, which in brief is: respect the property of others. This concern for property colors the entire opening section. (One should not conclude from this concern for property that Plato is a proto-Lockean. On the conception of property in the *Laws* generally see 5.739b8–745b2 and Morrow (1960; ch. 4).)

The Athenian regards violations of this general law as the source of 'all the evils (*kaka*) mentioned' (either all violent crimes or all the crimes mentioned in *Laws* 9). Elsewhere in the *Laws* Plato claims that the desire for wealth and property is the root of some evil (see e.g. 5.729a2–4) and that excessive friendship for oneself is the source of all evils (see 5.731d6–732b4). There is no contradiction here, as I assume Plato would say that the lack of respect for another's property is one common manifestation of excessive self-love. (I translate *kakos* and its cognates as 'evil', or as 'vicious' and related terms, depending on the context.)

This opening might seem to be more appropriate as an end to Book 9 (but then the division of the *Laws* into its twelve books was not the work of Plato), for it completes the discussion of that book. Nevertheless, it is not out of place where it is, as it provides a transition to a central subject of *Laws* 10: impiety. Plato is in effect saying: 'having finished speaking of one serious set of crimes, let us turn to another'. He then proceeds to a discussion of the causes of impious crimes; namely, the different erroneous beliefs people hold about the gods. But there is likely a tighter connection between the opening of *Laws* 10 and what follows, if the impious crimes that Plato goes on to discuss all involve hubris directed against public or private *property* (which I believe is the best way to interpret the text). If this is correct, then the general law demanding respect for the property of others is meant to apply not only to the crimes of *Laws* 9, but to the especially grave impious crimes of *Laws* 10. They too would then be connected to a lack of respect for the property of others. Nevertheless, it becomes clear below that Plato holds that the *fundamental* cause of hubristic acts is a certain set of impious beliefs.

884a6–885a6

Plato writes: 'Gravest of the remaining are the unrestrained and hubristic acts of the young' (884a6–7). I take 'the remaining' to refer to the remaining crimes or offenses or evils generally (i.e. those not yet discussed in the *Laws*) and not simply to the remaining violent crimes (e.g. as Saunders translates it (1970; 410)). For the offenses the Athenian is about to discuss do not (all) fall under the heading 'violent crime'.

Of the remaining offenses, one special class (the gravest) is worthy of serious treatment, and hence comes after even violent crimes: the hubristic acts of the young. Plato presents the five worst kinds, in descending order of seriousness. All seem to involve public or private property.

(1) Hubristic acts directed at sacred things held in common

Plato further divides this sort of offense into two kinds: (a) What is holy and public. These are 'especially grave', no doubt because they offend against the gods *and* against the city as a whole (with the exception of the virtues, the two greatest values in the *Laws*). (b) What is holy and the property of some subdivision of the city. (On this division and its subdivisions see Saunders (1972; 90).)

We can better understand what kinds of offenses Plato has in mind, and against what institutions or people, if we look at how the city is divided. Earlier in the *Laws* he tells us that there will be 5,040 citizens (that number chosen, among other reasons, for its divisibility by a variety of numbers; see 5.738a2–b1). These citizens will be divided into twelve tribes (of 420 each), and each tribe will be further divided into twelve 'demes' (of 35 each). At the center of the city the founders will set up a sanctuary to Hestia, Zeus, and Athena, and this will be called the acropolis and be surrounded by a wall. (On where the temples are placed see 6.778c4–d3.) The twelve parts of the city—the land on which the twelve tribes reside—will then radiate out from this city center. Each of these parts of the city is to be considered sacred. And each tribe will be named after, and have a special connection to, some god, child of a god, spirit (*daimon*), or hero. In this connection, Plato mentions altars, oracles, temples, statues, shrines, and sanctuaries. (See 5.738b3–e2, 745b3–e6; 6.771a5–e1.) Although Plato mentions children of the gods, spirits, and heroes, the traditional twelve Olympian gods are all recognized in the *Laws* as important, and he writes toward the opening of Book 8: 'the law will state that there are twelve festivals for the twelve gods, from whom each tribe will be given a name' (828b7–c2). On the centrality of the Olympian gods (especially Zeus) in the religion of the *Laws* see Morrow (1960; 434–57).

So I take it that (1a) above refers, at the very least, to hubristic offenses directed against the acropolis, its sanctuary, and any of the temples, altars, personnel, etc. connected to Hestia, Zeus, and

Athena. (No details are given, but we can speculate that Plato has in mind robbery, vandalism, and perhaps assault against personnel associated with sacred property.) And virtually as offensive will be (1b): hubristic acts directed against any of the twelve tribes or 'demes' (qua sacred entities) and the temples, altars, etc. associated with them.

This category of crime must also include a subclass of the theft of public property; namely, theft of public property connected to civic religion or sacred things. (Temple robbery, which is especially heinous, receives special treatment below, in the commentary on 885a7–b3.) This is indeed a serious crime, according to Plato, because theft of public property per se is treated as extremely grave. In *Laws* 12 he says that if a citizen—given his upbringing—is caught stealing public property, the penalty is death, because such a person must be regarded as practically incurable (941b2–942a4). (See Saunders (1991; 294–6).) Note that the cause of such crime is said to be 'an erotic passion' (941c6). But I think it will become clear that although such passion can be a cause of crime, a more fundamental cause is a set of impious ideas (see pp. 55–8 below).

(2) Hubristic acts directed against private sacred things and tombs

It is obvious in what sense tombs are private. Each tomb contains a single person or members of a single family. Defiling or robbing tombs is no doubt what Plato is here referring to. But it is not entirely clear what he means by private sacred things generally. In *Laws* 4 Plato condones the existence of 'private buildings (or shrines, *hidrumata*) of the ancestral gods', as long as people worship there 'according to law' (717b4–5). This would seem to be just the sort of thing Plato had in mind. But note that at the end of *Laws* 10 he strictly forbids privately held shrines and altars (909d3–910d4). For example: 'Let no one possess shrines in private households' (909d7–8). So it is not clear what would fall under this heading (but see England (1921; 2. 508)).

An ancient Athenian reader of the *Laws*, encountering this passage about hubristic acts directed against sacred things held individually, might think of the mutilation of the herms in 415 BC. Price (1999; 82) writes: 'One night shortly before the Athenian expedition to Sicily set out, a gang of men mutilated most of the herms in Athens. The herms were plain rectangular shafts with the head of the god Hermes on top and a set of male genitalia half way up . . . . Following customs that went back to the later sixth century BC these herms were dedicated throughout Athens in large numbers outside houses and shrines.' (See Thucydides 6.27.) But, as Morrow points out, Plato nowhere mentions herms in the *Laws* (1960; 440). Nor is there any indication of sacred boundary stones or lines separating private dwellings.

Plato describes members of a family as sharers of sacred things, and he seems to connect such sacred familial sharing with being parts of a hearth (9.868c6–e5). So perhaps a hubristic act against a family hearth falls under this heading (a hearth being held by an individual family). In Book 12, in a discussion of votive offerings, Plato writes that the household hearth is held sacred by all of the gods, and thus need not be sanctified a second time. He clearly wants to forbid any private religious ceremonies sanctifying the hearth; further, he suggests that there are no private votive offerings in the home (12.955e5–956b3). In Plato's discussion of improper sexual practices, a man having sex with a woman who is not his wife, in his own home, *might* count as hubris against what is sacred and held individually (the hearth or home), though again this is by no means clear (see 8.841d1–e4).

Olive victory crowns, awarded for excellence in battle, are hung in a temple of one of the gods of war (12.943c4–8). Although they are displayed in public, their theft or destruction may well count as hubristic acts against privately held sacred things. (See also 12.946e5–7 for crowns of laurel given as prizes for civic excellence.)

Plato says that the name and year of birth of every child should be 'written down in the ancestral temples', and that for every family there will be a wall upon which is written the name of every living member (6.785a3–b2). Elsewhere Plato mentions memorial markers (8.844a6–7). The desecration of any of these would seem to fall under this category of hubristic act.

(3) Hubristic acts directed against one's parents

Plato here seems to exclude those violent crimes against parents mentioned in *Laws* 9, hence the addition of 'apart (*chôris*) from what was discussed earlier' (885a2–3). Note the gravity of those crimes: killing a parent (869a3–c7); deliberately wounding a parent (877b6–7); wounding a parent in anger (878d6–879a2). The first warrants the death penalty, the second the death penalty or something roughly equivalent, and the third the death penalty or worse (whatever that might be). The language used in Book 9 makes clear that Plato regards these as violent acts of an impious nature (see 879b8–c5). So either (a) Plato has in mind these acts against one's parents, and any others not mentioned so far, in which case his formulation 'apart from what was discussed earlier' remains problematic (but see Saunders (1991; 271)), or (b) all five kinds of hubristic acts listed at 10.884a6–885a6 refer to crimes against property, in which case Plato intends only the theft or destruction or desecration of the property of one's parents. I find (b) more likely, though neither interpretation is entirely satisfying.

On the proper attitude to one's parents and older people generally see *Laws* 4.717b4–718a3, 9.879b5–880a9, 11.930e4–932d8; and cf. *Republic* 5.457c10–464d11.

(4) Stealing what belongs to the rulers

Plato is here most likely describing a special class of theft of *private* property. This is supported by the fact that the language he uses ('someone, ignoring the rulers, leads away or carries off (*agê$_i$ ê pherê$_i$*) or uses something of theirs [i.e. the rulers] without persuading them', 885a3–5) is similar to the language used at the opening of Book

10 to describe the need for citizens to respect each other's property ('No one is to carry off or lead away (*pherein mêde agein*) anything belonging to others, or use anything of one's neighbor, if he has not persuaded the owner', 884a2–4).

(5) Hubristic acts directed against the 'political rights' of individual citizens

'Political rights' is an imperfect rendering of *to politikon*; it is usually translated here by civic or civil or political right(s). I use 'political' to keep the translation close to the Greek, though 'civic' or 'civil' might be preferable. Plato seems to have in mind hubristic acts against an *individual* (as opposed to the city or to groups that are part of the city), and specifically against an individual's *civic* or *political* 'rights' or property or life (in contrast to his religious or sacred 'rights' or property or life, to the extent that these can be separated from the civic or political). But what does this mean?

England argues that since (4) concerns the property rights of rulers, (5) must refer to the property rights of individual citizens (1921; 2. 444). This is possible, and would fit the idea that all five kinds of hubristic act are directed against property. On this view, (5) would thus refer to non-sacred private things. If England is right, then Plato is in effect saying that *all* theft of private property (or at least that of citizens) constitutes an impious crime. But the theft of *private* property is not always treated this way in the *Laws*; however, we see at the outset of *Laws* 10 that Plato takes the need to respect the property of others very seriously. On the theft of private property generally see *Laws* 9.857a2–b3, 11.933e7–934c5, and Saunders (1991; 280–6, 292–4).

Plato adds: 'calling for legal justice' (*dikên epikaloumenon*, 885a6). I take him to be saying that any theft that (a) is of a citizen's property *and* (b) requires legal justice as a remedy is hubristic and impious. If this is the correct interpretation, then disputes that can be worked out without initiating formal hearings would not be considered as serious (see *Laws* 5.743c5–d). But much remains murky here.

There is no need to consider this list exhaustive. Plato is presenting the five gravest hubristic acts of the young, though there may be others. In fact, if we interpret this as a list of hubristic acts directed at property, then it cannot be exhaustive, for at 885b1 Plato refers to how people are hubristic in deed and in word; but on the 'property interpretation' all of these impieties would be cases of hubristic *actions* and not of hubristic speech.

Stalley (1983; 167) accurately identifies the connection of this preliminary discussion to *Laws* 10 as a whole:

The first few pages of Book X...serve as an introduction to the main arguments on the existence and nature of the gods. Their chief purpose is to establish that these matters really are of concern to the legislator. They do this by arguing that atheism or incorrect religious belief is a serious cause of vice.

885a7–b3

Plato writes that a law covering each of the hubristic acts in common must be drafted. But they will not present such a law until after 'the exhortation' (885b2). (More on this exhortation in the next section.) In fact, they won't get to a presentation of the actual law on impiety until much later (beginning at 907d9).

Plato interrupts the call for a law on impiety to mention temple robbery (*hierosulia*, which can also be translated 'sacrilege'). Why mention this here? Perhaps because it would likely have come up in any discussion of hubristic acts against the gods, as a paradigmatic act of impious hubris. (See Euthyphro's first attempt at a definition of piety, at *Euthyphro* 5d9.) Plato is reminding us that it has already been covered (at 9.853d5–854e1), and that such a summary-discussion of one act of impiety (however major) is not sufficient.

On Plato's discussion of temple robbery in the *Laws* see Saunders (1991; 286–90) and Cohen (1983; 93–100). Saunders writes: 'Like the Athenian orators, Plato does not define sacrilege [i.e. temple robbery], but it seems to me certain that he means at least broadly what they meant; if his understanding of it had been substantially different, he would have explained just how.' He agrees with Lipsius' definition of *hierosulia*—'theft of sacred objects from sacred places' (1905–15: 442–3)—and adds: 'By "sacred objects" I mean *valuable* sacred objects (statues, arms, money, implements, etc. of precious metals and other material)' (1991; 286).

It is worth looking briefly at the *Laws* 9 discussion of temple robbery, especially as it creates some problems for our understanding of *Laws* 10.

Plato begins by saying that it is not likely that a citizen—who would have had a proper upbringing—would catch this 'disease'; we would rather expect a slave or foreigner to commit such a heinous crime. He then proceeds to discuss the law for temple robbery and similar incurable and difficult-to-cure crimes, and perhaps all serious crimes against the gods (note that following the conclusion to the discussion of temple robbery he writes 'after the matters concerning the gods', 9.856b6).

The prelude to the law against temple robbery (9.854b1–c5) is meant to discourage the person from thinking about committing such crimes. Plato says that the evil that moves the temple robber is neither human nor divine, but 'a certain maddening insect goad (*oistros*) that grows within humans as a result of injustices ancient and unexpiated' (854b3). At first this sounds like an aspect of traditional theism which Plato would want to reject, an outlook common in tragedy (see for example the opening of Sophocles' *Oedipus Tyrannus*, 1–101). (For an interesting, though unusual, reading of this passage see Dodds (1957; 177 n. 133).) As the preludes are primarily for popular consumption, one may be tempted to conclude that this is evidence that 'noble lies', which were defended in the *Republic*, are to be used in Magnesia, the city of the *Laws*, as well.

This may be; but it is also possible that Plato does not have in mind here the traditional conception of unexpiated injustices. For he writes: 'When any of these opinions (*dogmatôn*) grab you, go and perform the rites of expiation' (854b6–7), which besides going to temples includes associating with good people. England claims that *dogma* here refers to 'thoughts' (1921; 2. 379)—as in the temple robber's hard-to-shake thoughts about robbing temples—and he is followed by Saunders and Taylor in their translations. But I think it likely that the more usual 'opinions' is preferable, and that what Plato is calling ancient and unexpiated injustices are precisely the impious ideas discussed in greater detail in Book 10. They are unexpiated as long as they still exist in a city and have not been properly refuted and combated. They are ancient in that whereas some of the ideas are only as old as the sophists, others (those of certain preSocratics) go back two hundred years, whereas still others (the ideas that make up what I shall call traditional theism) are older than Homer and Hesiod. These are the ideas—neither human nor divine—that can grow in humans and cause them to commit evil deeds. This reading of the passage is certainly more consistent with the Book 10 account of the cause of crime (and with what we find in the *Laws* generally).

After the prelude comes the law on temple robbery itself, which first describes penalties for slaves and foreigners who commit such crimes. Plato then turns to citizens:

> If a citizen is ever shown to have done such a thing—to have perpetrated one of the great and unspeakable injustices against gods or parents or city—let the judge consider this man to be already incurable, reckoning that even though he received an education and upbringing from childhood, he did not abstain from the greatest evils. The penalty for this man is death, the least of evils, and he'll become a model to help others, once he has disappeared without fame beyond the borders of the countryside.   (854e1–855a2; cf. the Athenian attitude toward dealing with temple robbery, described by Xenophon, *Hellenica* 1.7.22.)

This passage would seem to apply the death penalty to many, if not all, impious hubristic acts. But when we get to the law on impiety towards the end of Book 10 we find that this is not the case.

Note that when Plato mentions temple robbery in Book 10 he suggests that he had earlier made a distinction between 'whether done violently or by stealth', but he had not.

Temple robbery would seem to fall under hubristic act (1a) or (1b), depending on which type of temple was robbed.

There is a need to state the punishment for speaking or acting in a hubristic way towards the gods, 'once the exhortation has been laid down'. Plato seems to be using 'exhortation' (*paramuthion*) both narrowly and broadly. Narrowly, it can refer to the next six lines (i.e. 885b4–9), for he introduces these lines with 'Let it [i.e. the exhortation] be as follows.' But as Plato won't be discussing punishments for impiety until much later, at the end of *Laws* 10 (see 908e6–909d2), he must also be using 'exhortation' broadly to refer to the entire prelude to the law on impiety; and all that follows—from here to the discussion of the law of impiety—is in fact a prelude to that law. As England points out (1921: 2. 445), *paramuthion* is sometimes used as a synonym for or together with *prooimion* (Plato's standard term for 'prelude') (see 9.880a7–8 and 11.923c2).

885b4–9

The exhortation in the narrower sense contains an ambiguity: 'believes that the gods exist, according to the laws' (*theous hêgoumenos einai kata nomous*, 885b4) could be taken to refer to believing that the gods exist (their divine nature left unstated here), or to believing that the gods exist *in the way that the laws demand or proclaim*. The phrase that follows—'he does not believe what I just said [i.e. that the gods exist]' (885b6–7)—which describes one of three views about the gods that the laws forbid, suggests that Plato's main concern in the ambiguous line is that a person believe that the gods exist. Nevertheless, Plato eventually makes it clear that it is important that people not simply believe in the gods, but that they believe in the gods in the way that the laws demand—namely, that the gods exist *and* are concerned about humans but cannot be bribed by prayers and sacrifices.

We move from ambiguity to confusion. The exhortation seems to be saying: No one who believes in the gods ever willingly commits an impious act unless he does not believe in the gods or at least not in the way the law demands. The idea of 'no one who believes in the gods . . . unless he does not believe in the gods' is strange. One might wonder why Plato did not instead say: (1) no one ever willingly commits an impious act unless (a) he is suffering from atheism or (b) he believes in the gods but suffers from one of two erroneous sorts of belief about them (more on these shortly); or (2) no one who believes in the gods ever willingly commits an impious act unless he suffers from one of two erroneous sorts of belief about them. Despite the confusing formulation, Plato *seems* to be saying (1), because he is certainly concerned about atheism as well as what he considers impious forms of theism.

So Plato appears to be saying the following: People who hold proper beliefs about the gods might *inadvertently* or *mistakenly* say or do something hubristic; but only those with improper beliefs will *knowingly* or *willingly* do so (but see *Laws* 5.731c1–7). The view of *akrasia* implied here—that the cause of a wrong action is ignorance or an incorrect belief—might seem to have more in common with an early Socratic-Platonic conception of *akrasia*, according to which no one knowingly does what is wrong, than it does with the treatment of *akrasia* in the *Republic*, which is based on the tripartite view of the soul and allows for a person to know that x is wrong but to do x anyway because of a strong desire to do x. But in the *Laws* Plato recognizes the possibility of *akrasia*, though he does not seem to base it on a tripartite conception of the soul—though see *Laws* 3.689a5–c3. (For an excellent discussion of Plato's conception of *akrasia* in the *Laws* and its relation to his earlier views see Bobonich (2002: ch. 3).) For example, later in Book 10 he rejects as absurd the idea that the gods could 'know what they ought to do, as the basest of humans are said to do: they know it is better to act otherwise than how they are acting, but don't do so, because they succumb to pleasures or pains' (902a8–b2). Clearly, unlike the gods, humans (or the basest humans, at any rate) can act against their better judgment 'because they succumb to pleasures or pains'.

Then what do we make of the suggestion in the present passage that only impious beliefs make possible the willful commission of these hubristic actions? Let us turn to a passage from *Laws* 1 crucial to understanding the conception of *akrasia* in this work:

Let us suppose that each of us living beings is a puppet of the gods, either put together for their play or for something serious. We do not know which, but we do know that these passions are in us, like sinews or cords, drawing us along and pulling each other in opposite directions and toward opposite actions, where virtue and vice lie divided. For the argument (*logos*) claims that each person should always follow one of the pulling [cords] and in no way abandon it, pulling it against the other sinews: this is the golden and sacred pull of calculation (*tou logismou agôgên chrusên kai hieran*), called the common law of the city (*tês poleôs koinon nomon*). The others are hard and iron, while this one is soft because it is golden; and the others resemble many different forms. We should always assist the most noble pull of the law (*têi kallistêi agôgêi têi tou nomou*), for although calculation is noble, it is gentle and not forceful, and its pull needs helpers so that the golden kind in us may be victorious over the other kinds. (644d7–645b1)

Who is pulling the cord of calculation? Each of us is, at least in part (see Bobonich (2002; 266))—along with the pull of the law, with which we ought to cooperate. (The pull of calculation must include a proper education: Plato writes that those who are correctly educated *usually* become good, *Laws* 1.644a6–b4.) It is beyond the scope of this commentary to discuss this passage in detail; but applying it to 10.885b4–9 it seems we can say that Plato holds that *akrasia* is not possible (or at least not likely) for anyone who knows the truth (or has true opinions) about the gods—that they exist and what their nature is. And he holds this not because of a Socratic conviction that *akrasia* is impossible, but because the pull of calculation (which in this case requires knowledge or true opinion of the existence and nature of the gods) is stronger than any cords pulling in the opposite direction—or at least tends to be strong enough to resist the kind of pull that would lead a person to commit a grave hubristic act of impiety. (It becomes clear later in *Laws* 10, when Plato distinguishes honest from dissembling heretics, that he does not think that someone who holds a false view of the gods will necessarily engage in impious acts. See 908b4–e5.)

There are three beliefs that a person might 'suffer from' which could cause him *knowingly* or *willingly* to do what is hubristic—such a person failing, because of these false beliefs, to resist the pull of passions connected to pleasures and pains. (The following labels are not Plato's. For simplicity's sake, I sometimes follow Saunders in referring to these impious offenders generally as *heretics*.)

(1) *Atheism:* not believing that the gods exist. (I follow the scholarly tradition in calling this atheism, though it would also include agnostics like Protagoras—in fact, there would seem to be more agnostics than atheists among the intellectuals Plato is targeting.)

(2) *Deism:* believing that the gods exist, but that they 'do not take thought for humans'. (Plato probably has in mind many of the theistic presocratics; for example, the early Ionians like Xenophanes, whose brand of 'natural theology' does not leave much room for religion.)

(3) *Traditional theism:* believing that the gods exist, but that they can be swayed by sacrifices and prayers. (This refers to the vast majority of ancient Greeks; an excellent example from Plato's own corpus is Kephalus, at *Republic* 1.330d1–331d10.)

(At *Laws* 12.948c2–d1 Plato gives a brief summary of these three impious beliefs and says that the third is the worst.)

Note that Plato is being simultaneously radical and reactionary: reactionary, in that he is going to defend a fairly robust conception of the gods against the presocratics and sophists ((1) and (2) above); and radical, in that he is going to reject an important part of the traditional Greek conception of the gods and religion ((3) above).

885c1–e6

Kleinias' first thoughts are about what to *do* about people who hold impious ideas and do impious deeds, though he immediately makes it clear that he is also unsure what to *say* to such people. The Athenian, however, recommends that they first listen to them—despite the fact that such people would look down upon the Athenian and his companions. (In the end, however, he will have a lot to recommend about not only what to say to these impious people, but what to do with them as well.)

The Athenian, speaking for a hypothetical young atheist, says the following:

Athenian Stranger, and Lakedaimonian, and Knossian, what you say is true. For some of us in no way believe in the gods at all, while others believe they are as you say. So we expect, just as you expected concerning the laws, that before you threaten us harshly, you first try to persuade (*peithein*) and teach us that the gods exist, presenting adequate proof, and that they are too good to be charmed by some gifts into being turned away from justice.... So from legislators who claim to be not savage (*agriôn*) but gentle (*hêmerôn*) we expect persuasion (*peithoi*) first be used on us.   (885c5–e3; see also 899c2–d4)

The Greek word *hêmeros*, which I translate here and elsewhere as 'gentle', can also be rendered 'tame'—especially in contrast with *agrios* ('of the field', and so 'wild' or 'savage'). Although I have chosen 'gentle', one cannot escape the fact that behind any contrast between *hêmeros* and *agrios* is the idea of what is tame and what is wild. When applied to legislators, as in the present passage, the language suggests gentle and cultivated rulers, in contrast to rulers who are savage, brutal, uncivilized. When applied to citizens to be persuaded (see 890b5–c8), the language suggests *taming* the people through persuasion.

In this and other passages Plato emphasizes the importance of persuasion in addition to the force of the law. This has prompted some scholars to regard the Plato who wrote the *Laws* as less authoritarian than the one who wrote the *Republic*. (See Bobonich (2000, 2002; 97–119); for a different view see Mayhew (2007).) In any case, a careful study of the relevant passages shows that persuasion is closely connected in Plato's mind with the need for compulsion, and that persuasion is not for him limited to rational argumentation. (See for example *Laws* 2.659c9–664c2. Towards the end of this passage Plato refers to the tale of Cadmus—who sowed dragon's teeth, which grew into armed men—and says that this myth 'is a great example [*mega paradeigma*] for the legislator of how it is possible to persuade young souls of anything' (663e9–664a1).) Note too that the passage just quoted is part of a hypothetical exchange between an imaginary atheist and the Athenian; no such exchange would be legal among the citizens of Magnesia, outside the special prison called the Sound-mind Center (see Mayhew (2007; 104–10)).

Listening to the impious consists first in listening to a hypothetical reply from such people. The gist of this reply is a demand that before the Athenian et al. resort to threats of force (however embodied by laws), they should try to persuade and teach the impious that their views are indeed wrong, 'presenting adequate proof' (885d3: cf. *Apology* 26a1–7). This, we are told, has been the procedure so far with respect to describing the laws. The Athenian, speaking for the imaginary young atheist, is referring to earlier discussions which stressed the need for argument and persuasion (and thus preludes) in addition to the laws, over laws alone which simply tell people what they must do. (See for example 4.719e7–720e9, 4.722b4–c4, 9.858d6–859a6.) This request is consistent with civility (which the Athenian and his companions should respect, as they are 'legislators who claim to be not savage but gentle', 885e1–2). In effect, the request is that the Athenian present a proof that the gods exist and that they are good (i.e. concerned about humans, but unwilling to be influenced by prayers and sacrifices). Fulfilling this request will generate the lengthy prelude to the law on impiety.

The assumption seems to be—and this will be confirmed later—that the impious are atheists, deists, and traditional theists because they have not heard arguments which would lead them to think otherwise. It is interesting that the emphasis is on traditional theism: since we hear 'these and other such things from those said to be the best of the poets, orators, prophets, priests, and myriad upon myriad of others, most of us are not inclined to avoid unjust acts, but to do them and then attempt to make amends' (885d4–e1; cf. *Republic* 2.365d8–e5). The 'myriad upon myriad' may very well *include* philosophers and sophists who are atheists or deists, but these cannot be the majority of such numbers. Also, 'poets, orators, prophets, priests' no doubt refers primarily or exclusively to those who have presented the traditional stories about the gods. This underscores the fact that Plato's target is not simply 5th and 4th century BC enlightenment thought, but traditional religion as well.

Does this passage represent Plato speaking on behalf of the impious, and against the likes of Kleinias and Megillus? Is he saying, in effect, that men like Kleinias and Megillus would be tempted to deal with such people in drastic, unphilosophical ways, though they should not? Perhaps to some extent this was Plato's intention. But I do not think we can answer this question fully without considering how Plato in fact advocates treating such people—when the dust settles, towards the end of *Laws* 10—which is very harshly indeed. Further, we must not forget that Plato (through the Athenian) is introducing to Kleinias and Megillus a huge new class of people who they are to consider impious under the law (namely, the traditional theists). It could be argued that in this sense Plato is indulging the likes of Kleinias and Megillus, not calming them or making them more respectful.

885e7–886a5

Kleinias replies to the impious the way many modern religious people would: Isn't it easy to prove that the gods exist? (He leaves out the part about the gods being good, but perhaps that is meant to be implied.) Kleinias presents two brief arguments for the existence of the gods.

(1) The Teleological-Cosmological Argument

The first argument is either a version of the teleological argument or it is a combination or conflation of versions of the cosmological and teleological arguments: 'there's the earth and the sun and the stars and the whole universe, and the beautiful, orderly procession of the seasons, divided into years and months' (886a2–4). I'm inclined to think this actually combines two arguments:

(1a) The Cosmological Argument

The earth and the sun and the stars—and the whole universe—exist.
They must have a cause.
Only gods could have caused them to exist.
Therefore, gods exist.

(It is possible that Kleinias' argument is even more basic: atheists say there aren't any gods, but what about the earth and sun and stars, which are gods? Cf. the statement of the Athenian at 886d5–7.)

(1b) The Teleological Argument

The beautiful, orderly procession of celestial objects, and the division of the year into seasons and months, can be explained only by some kind of conscious, intelligent organizer(s) of the universe.
Only god(s) could fulfill this description.
Therefore, god(s) must exist.

However much Plato thinks this is insufficient to defend theism, he will nevertheless hold a view—albeit a more sophisticated one—that has a lot in common with what Kleinias presents here (see 899b2–8). (At *Laws* 3.683c4–5 Megillus takes for granted that the seasons change owing to the work of the gods.) An earlier version of the teleological argument, somewhat comparable to this one, can be found in Xenophon, *Memorabilia* 4.3. (There is another version, in *Memorabilia* 1.4, but it is more sophisticated than any of the appeals in *Laws* 10 to the orderliness of the universe.)

(2) *The Argument from Common Consent*

This is perhaps the weakest argument for the existence of god(s) in the history of philosophy (see Martin (1990; 210–12)), and it is fitting that the Athenian not offer it.

Everyone (i.e. every Greek and barbarian) believes that the gods exist.
Therefore, the gods exist.

Note that Xenophanes came to a rather different conclusion based on what the Greeks and the barbarians believed about the gods (see DK 21B14–16); namely, that anthropomorphic gods are the creation of humans, not the other way around. The weakness of the argument from common consent is likely part of the reason Plato feels the need to go beyond Kleinias' arguments and present a more worked-out defense of theism.

886a6–b5

The Athenian says he is afraid lest the wicked will look down upon them, though he is not ashamed (*aidoumai*). Why afraid? Why not ashamed? On the latter, England believes feeling shame would imply respect for the wicked (1921; 2. 447); but I think the point is rather that good people should not be ashamed by what the wicked think of them. (Cf. *Republic* 5.452a7–e1 on why men should not feel shame about exercising with women, but should be concerned solely about the truth and not about mockery.) But then why would the Athenian be afraid? Because this is serious, and if these impious youths look down upon them, they won't take seriously his arguments for what he considers the proper form of theism—and that's his aim here. He understands (as Kleinias and Megillus do not) that the impiety of these youths is (or is based on) fundamental philosophical beliefs—beliefs which the Athenian hopes to change.

Kleinias and Megillus (and people like them) believe the cause of impious ideas is a lack of self-control concerning pleasures. I take it Plato is saying that such people maintain the following etiology of impiety:

> Strong desires (e.g. for sex and wealth) → immoral actions → need for impious ideas that support such actions or are consistent with such actions → further impious actions.

According to Plato, however, the actual cause is certain ideas (and those who promulgate them): 'A certain very grievous ignorance that seems to be the greatest wisdom (*phronêsis*)' (886b7–8). But, as we have seen, Plato has not returned to his older conception of *akrasia*; so it is unlikely that he is here claiming that the impious youths do what is wrong because given their views of the existence and/or nature of the gods, they have no reason to believe that their actions are immoral. Instead, what he must be saying (if he is consistent) is that such youths are pulled in one direction by strong cords of desire that can be resisted only by the cord of calculation (in this context, the right ideas about the gods and the arguments that support them) pulled in part by the law. This 'very grievous ignorance' is a cause in the sense of being the weakening or absence of resistance to the pull of strong desires.

Impious ideas → rejection of a proper religious and ethical outlook → lower (or no) resistance to acting on strong desires (e.g. for sex and wealth) → impious actions.

Now Kleinias and Megillus (and people like them) are wrong on this count because of their own ignorance—they have never encountered the ideas at the root of these youths' impiety. This is what Plato means when he says that they have been 'living completely outside'—that is, outside the influence of these ideas. (More on this in the next section.)

Note that in this section—and in contrast to most of the rest of Book 10—the Athenian refers to a plural 'you' (as noted in the translation). This is meant to include both Kleinias and Megillus and in general people *like* Kleinias and Megillus. What kind of people are these? As we have seen, people who mistake the actual cause of impiety, and who have not encountered these impious philosophical ideas.

886b6–e3

The Athenian says that the 'very grievous ignorance' that seems to be 'the greatest wisdom' exists among the Athenians, but not among 'you' (plural)—i.e. among Sparta and Crete (and similar cities)—because of the virtue of their political systems. This raises two questions: (1) What is this political virtue? (2) Why does the

Athenian say these ideas do not exist among cities like Sparta and Crete?

As is clear from the first two books of the *Laws*, Plato does not regard the political systems of the Spartans and Cretans as fully virtuous, so he must have in mind here certain aspects of their political systems that are virtuous (or at least virtuous relative to Athens, say). And in fact I think the answer to the first question must be (a) the strict regulation of the stories that one may tell in such cities, along with (b) the political and/or cultural opposition to the new philosophy and science, now so closely associated with Athens. How accurate is this characterization of Sparta and Crete? That depends in part on how we answer the second question.

As we shall see, the ideas at issue are, as England puts it, the 'old mythology' and the 'new philosophy' (1921; 2. 477). But *some* versions of the 'old mythology' (but not the new philosophy) certainly existed in Sparta and Crete, as Plato was well aware. So perhaps Plato is praising the absence of any active re-evaluation or reinterpretation of these stories of the sort that one finds in Athens—especially among the playwrights (and above all Euripides) and philosophers like Socrates (see e.g. the *Euthyphro*). But if this is what Plato is praising, isn't he guilty of a contradiction or hypocrisy, given that—aside from the presocratics and sophists, who rejected the ancient religion—no one has undertaken such a radical re-evaluation of Greek religion as Plato? In *Republic* 2–3, and by implication in *Laws* 10, Plato advocates the radical re-evaluation of traditional theism and the mythology that underpins it. Is Plato guilty of praising Sparta and Crete for their political virtue in not allowing for such radicalism, while at the same time practicing it himself? Perhaps. But I believe he would reply to the charge of inconsistency as follows: What he is praising among these cities is not the *content* of their ideas, but the practice of not allowing or encouraging intellectual innovations concerning ideas about the gods. True, he *does* undertake to radically alter traditional Greek myths. But once that has been properly accomplished there will be very little re-evaluation or innovation, and only under strict regulations (see *Laws* 6.769a7–e2, 777a6–d4; 7.797a7–d5; and Bobonich (2002; 395–408)). In that sense, he is in line with the Spartan approach.

Let us now look in greater detail at the religious ideas that Plato says exist in Athens but not in Crete or Sparta. Plato places these into two categories: (1) those from the ancients, and (2) those from the modern wise men. He also says that some write with, and others without, meter. One might be tempted to see this as matching the ancients (who tended to write in verse) and the moderns (who tended not to), but that is not necessarily the case.

(1) The ancients

The ancients have written about 'the first nature of the heavens and the rest'—i.e. the sky, earth, ocean, night, etc. (By 'first nature', I take it he means the nature of the first things and what it is that makes them the first.) Homer and especially Hesiod come to mind (Plato even mentions the 'birth of the gods' (*theogonian*, 886c5), which is virtually identical to the title of one of Hesiod's works); but there is no reason to think Plato did not mean to include others here as well; for example, the 'mixed' theogony of Pherecydes (see Kirk, Raven, and Schofield (1983; 50–71)).

Plato writes that because they are ancient it is not easy to say, in general, whether their writings have a good or bad influence. The implication seems to be that what is ancient should be considered innocent until proven guilty—that something very old is likely (or should be taken) to be good unless one can prove otherwise. But Plato is willing to mention one area in which the ancient stories are *not* beneficial: concerning the treatment of parents. (See also *Republic* 2.378d3; and cf. *Euthyphro* 5e6–6a3, 8b1–4.) The Athenian says he would not recommend such stories as beneficial or truthful. But Plato is not going to discuss the ancients here, including any problems he might have with them.

Plato's primary concern in *Laws* 10 is to demonstrate that the gods exist (by showing that soul is prior to matter) and that the gods are good—i.e. they care about us and cannot be persuaded by sacrifices and prayer. With that established, it seems he will leave it to others to determine which traditional stories about the gods are (a) compatible with what he has demonstrated and (b) beneficial to the city; and which need to be revised or omitted because they fail to meet these criteria. (See *Republic* 2.376e2–3.398b9 for the sort of attitude Plato probably still has in the *Laws*.) In *Laws* 3 Plato claims that poets sometimes happen upon the truth (682a3–5).

In the *Republic* Socrates et al. are reluctant to legislate the details of the best city's religion, and so they leave such things to the Oracle of Apollo at Delphi (4.427b1–c4). This is consistent with what Plato says throughout the *Laws* (see 5.738b5–c3; 6.759c6–d1, d4–8; 8.828a1–5; 9.856d8–e2, 865b2–3; 11.914a1–5; 12.947d4–6). Tate is surprised at this 'curious deference to the Delphic oracle' (1936*b*; 143); but he shouldn't be, as Plato's conception of how the Delphic Oracle is to be 'used' is always limited (or vague): e.g. choosing certain officials from a select group, creating certain laws, helping to determine which sacrifices to make. (On prophecy and the Oracle of Delphi in the *Laws* see Morrow (1960; 404–11, 427–34).)

(2) The modern wise men

In this section all Plato tells us about these thinkers is that they deny that the earth and celestial bodies are gods or otherwise divine. Plato has no intention of holding back with these thinkers as he did with the ancients. And the implication is that answering them requires far more intellectual firepower than was found in Kleinias' arguments. Plato plans to censure these thinkers to the extent that they cause harm. But what harm do they cause? Their arguments lead people to conclude that what are normally considered gods—sun, moon, stars, earth—are mere matter, and moreover (and consequently) that there are no gods capable of thinking about human affairs and acting properly towards humans.

These modern wise men are confident about their views, though they are in the minority. Why do they think so many people can be wrong about the gods? Because these people have been fed a number of stories that make their religious beliefs plausible. The sun, for example, is said by these moderns actually to be a fiery stone; but it has been 'wrapped up' in stories that make it easy for people to believe it is a god.

Plato can here assume such arguments are harmful because it was agreed earlier that the hubristic impious acts of the young are caused by such impious ideas.

Interestingly, it is stated explicitly that the modern wise men—the philosophers and scientists—are responsible for arguments in support of atheism and deism. But it is left to implication that the ancients are responsible for the third wrong position, traditional theism. Plato said that they would bid such ideas farewell, but of course he won't—at least not fully. Traditional theism is a major target in *Laws* 10. What he won't do is attack this head-on or explicitly say that what he is doing is attacking the traditional beliefs that most Greeks hold—though attack them he will (though he might consider what he's doing correction, not rejection). Perhaps the Athenian needs to respect the likes of Kleinias and Megillus while radically reappraising traditional theism.

886e4–887c5

Kleinias says: 'Difficult indeed, stranger, is the argument you have described, even if it were one alone; but as there are in fact very many arguments, it is even more difficult' (886e4–6). The one argument or account (*logos*) that Kleinias refers to is the one according to which the earth and celestial objects are not gods but matter. It is important that Plato singled this argument out, as this issue—whether natural objects and forces are divine or purely material—is for Plato the fundamental one. Note that whereas Kleinias initially thought the atheists et al. were easy to answer, he now finds the task daunting.

Kleinias says that there are very many arguments in favor of incorrect views concerning the gods. This could mean that he is ignoring the Athenian's advice that they disregard the ancient accounts, or he might simply be exaggerating the Athenian's clear implication that there are some (more than one) modern arguments for impious views. (And in fact many such arguments existed, considering the number of presocratic philosophers and sophists there were.)

The Athenian says that the impious youths would no doubt claim that he and his two companions 'are doing terrible things in passing laws that the gods exist' (887a1–2). This is probably accurate. The philosophers and scientists at that time (though not youths) would likely have been opposed to laws against impiety and too much interference by the city in their activities. (On the status of freedom of thought in ancient Greece see Dover (1988).) How should the three interlocutors respond? Here is their basic choice: (1) Ignore the impious, i.e. do not respond to their arguments or to the claim that laws against them are unfair, and proceed to formulate the law against impiety. (2) Defend themselves, i.e. present arguments in defense of the idea that the gods exist and are good—arguments which in effect support the law against impiety.

It is important to note that those in power—in this case Kleinias and the other colonists who were set the task of founding the laws of Magnesia—can do this: they need not argue with those who hold dissenting views. Plato is well aware of this option. He makes it clear in this section that whichever the Athenian and the others choose, they will be attempting to get the impious to fear the laws; the difference is that in case (2) they will bring this fear about through arguments, they believe, and not merely through force. If Plato appears to be in favor of arguments over mere political force, why does he have the Athenian still speak in terms of fear? As Plato sees it, his arguments will demonstrate the truth of the proper form of theism, which will lead the impious who are persuaded by these arguments to realize that they are wrong, which will lead them to fear the consequences of these impious beliefs, which will lead them to change their views on these issues.

Does choice (1) have anything to commend it? Yes, the Athenian says, for not confronting the impious in argument would prevent the prelude to the law on impiety from becoming longer than the law itself. This implies that (a) the defense of the existence and nature of the gods that makes up the bulk of *Laws* 10 is a substantial part of the prelude to the law on impiety, and (b) any proper defense of the existence and nature of the gods must be lengthy (*pace* Kleinias).

Kleinias defends (2), thereby choosing it for them. He offers two related points in support of it: (a) they should not honor short speeches over longer ones, especially if they are not pressed for time (and they are not)—and he points out that this has been their policy so far (see for example 4.721e4–722b4, 9.858a7–c2); and (b) it is no small matter whether they make their case persuasively (i.e. with sufficient arguments), and, as was stated before, that will require lengthy arguments.

Kleinias says that 'no one hastens to pursue us, as the saying goes' (887b3–4). I have been unable to find any information about this saying, and England's brief comment (1921; 2. 449) is not helpful.

887c6–888a8

The Athenian does not himself offer up a prayer, though he suggests that such a call for help from the gods is implied in the urgency with which Kleinias supports the need for arguments against atheism. But later in *Laws* 10, right before he launches into his lengthy argument for the existence of the gods, the Athenian *will* evoke the aid of the gods (893b1; cf. *Timaeus* 27c6–7).

The Athenian brings up a somewhat surprising subject: how to speak to such people without anger. Moreover, in what follows the Athenian does nothing to allay any potential anger Kleinias and Megillus may come to feel. In fact, Kleinias has shown no signs of anger, only occasional enthusiasm and surprise (and Megillus has for the most part been mute, and never angry so far as a reader can tell). So broaching the subject would more likely stoke any potential anger in their souls. Those interested in esoteric readings of Plato could make a lot of this passage; but Plato's purpose might simply be to answer anyone in his audience (e.g. students in the Academy around the time he was composing the *Laws*) inclined to approach such impious youths in anger.

Plato next presents an argument for why it is reasonable to hate atheists. The gist of it is that young atheists must have done something terribly wrong, or there must be something terribly wrong with them, since they ignored or rejected or otherwise were not influenced by the following:

(a) stories they heard about the gods when they were very young;
(b) prayers they heard and spectacles they saw connected to religious rituals (and note that these spectacles tend to be pleasurable, especially to young boys, and that pleasure of this kind aids in a child developing the right ideas and character—see e.g. *Laws* 2.653a5–c9);
(c) the fact that their parents engaged in prayer to and supplication before the gods, who were definitely held to exist;
(d) in general, the fact that Greeks and barbarians (i.e. all people), in good fortune and in bad, treat the sun and moon as if they were definitely gods.

There is a somewhat unclear line in the text connected to this last point: 'not as if they do not exist, but as if they certainly exist and in no way give rise to any suspicion that they are not gods' (887e5–7). What does the 'they' refer to? It could refer to 'the sun and moon', in which case we are left with the odd implication that some people doubt that the sun and moon exist. So it more likely refers to 'the gods', in which case the Athenian is stressing that not only do people commonly believe that the gods exist, but there is no suspicion that they are not gods.

According to Plato it is understandable to hate the atheist not only because he defends false and dangerous views, but also (what is stressed here) because of the reasons just given (a–d). This attitude toward the atheist has implications for Plato's conception of persuasion. Plato clearly thinks that on the issue of the *existence* of the gods, at the very least, a person should believe what he has been raised to believe, and that there is something wrong with the person who does not—so much so that, in the case of atheism, he deserves the hatred of decent people.

Now one might raise the following objection: Isn't Plato presenting the same weak arguments that Kleinias used earlier, at 886a2–5 (namely, appealing to the existence and nature of the sun and moon and stars and to the fact that Greeks and barbarians believe that the gods exist)? He would likely respond that the point here is not how powerful these arguments are, but the fact that the young atheists were not influenced in their childhood by the theistic beliefs of their parents and virtually everyone else around them. On just this point, Tate comments: 'Yet we know from *Rep.* II 381e[1–6] that mothers are among the worst offenders who pervert the young by telling false tales about the gods' (1936*b*; 142). But Plato could reply that however distorted the stories of (non-Magnesian) mothers might have been, they did not go so far as to say that the gods do not exist. He might further respond that he is here talking about parents in Magnesia, who will tell the right tales. Or he could say that the damage done by such mothers is a different issue; what he is concerned with in this passage is the character of the child who would grow up unaffected by the tales told by his parents.

The Athenian finished his argument with a reminder that the impious 'have contempt for all of this' (887e7), i.e. the stories and beliefs and religious practices of their parents and fellow citizens and in fact of all peoples.

That these young atheists reject the traditional stories about the existence of the gods is bad enough. But what is worse is that they do so without adequate argumentation—as is obvious, Plato says, to anyone with reason (*nous*). Plato cannot of course be denying that they have arguments—he not long ago said that the problem was that they *did* have arguments, especially concerning the material nature of the earth and celestial objects. What he is claiming is that they do not have *sufficient* arguments. But at present this is simply an assertion; he will later have to try to prove this by arguing for the existence and goodness of the gods.

The implication in this passage is that we should hate anyone for whom such an upbringing did not 'take'. There must be something wrong, Plato seems to be saying, with anyone who was constantly exposed to such stories, which were accepted as true by virtually everyone, and yet came to reject them. What then are we to make of Plato, who challenged a number of sacredly held traditional beliefs (e.g. that Zeus castrated and overthrew his father)? I assume he would make a distinction between those who *correct* rather than *reject* the traditional stories and beliefs. The Platonic critique of traditional theism is radical, he might claim, but not morally destructive (on the contrary, he would argue), as are atheism and deism.

This passage is revealing in what it says about the Platonic conception of the efficacy and importance of upbringing and education. Aside from a few exceptions, Plato seems to hold, children will tend to take the form of the mold imposed on them. Hence the crucial importance of education in Plato's political thought, in the *Laws* as well as the *Republic*. (Much of the first two books of the *Laws* deals with the proper upbringing of children.)

So the problem of the Athenian and his interlocutors is this: They have every right to hate these impious young men, and thus to be angered by them. However, if they are going to attempt to reason with them—as Kleinias and the Athenian have already agreed is best—they must use gentle words and arguments. Only in this way can they successfully teach such men the truth about the gods. Plato is underscoring the difference between angry admonition (such as one might use with a child or slave) and rational argumentation.

Plato says this must be dared, because they do not want both sides 'maddened at the same time: the one by gluttony for pleasure, the other by anger at such men' (888a3–5). (Perhaps as an example of the need for mild language, Plato is using 'us' politely, to refer to all the parties together—the Athenian and his interlocutors, as well as the impious youths.) Kleinias, Megillus, and the Athenian are the potentially angry (for he believes they have every right to be), and the impious youths are the gluttons for pleasure. The Athenian said earlier that Kleinias was wrong to think that the desire for pleasure motivated such people (886a8–b1); however, as we have seen, what is likely meant is that their impious beliefs led them to lack self-control with respect to pleasures, in that such beliefs render them unable to resist pleasures.

888a8–d6

The Athenian's address discussed in this section will form part of the prelude to the law on impiety, though it is aimed at one part of the citizenry: the young people who hold any of the three impious ideas described earlier. (See England (1921; 2. 451) on the term *prorrêsis* (888a5), which I translate 'introductory speech'.) But why is it addressed solely to the young? In what comes later it certainly sounds as if at least some older people will hold atheistic and deistic ideas. And many older people, like Kephalus toward the beginning of the *Republic*, will hold the improper beliefs connected with traditional theism. It is likely that Plato regards impious older people as beyond hope, and/or as not responsive to what he is going to say to the young who hold these ideas. That is, the older ones will have to be treated or handled differently, as we discover later in Book 10.

Plato clearly hopes that the vast majority of young people in Magnesia will hold the views that they have been brought up to believe: that there are gods, and that the gods are good—i.e. concerned about humans, and incapable of being swayed by prayers and sacrifices. But some of the young will suffer from the 'disease' (*noson*, 888b8) of impiety. This is the special group addressed here. So this address is not to be regarded as what will primarily keep the young in line. That falls to their proper upbringing and education. Rather, it is aimed at those who fall through the cracks. (Four lines after Plato speaks of impiety as an illness, he refers to impious ideas as '*pathê* concerning the gods' (888c3). *Pathê* often means 'passions', but here I think it is best translated as 'afflictions' or 'conditions'.)

Note that Plato is not here interested in presenting an argument for the existence of good gods. That will come later. His aim instead is to argue for why one should remain open to the arguments for the existence of good gods.

The point Plato stresses is that the young who hold these improper views (unlike most of the young) ought not to hold them firmly. He says that they are likely to change their minds over time. Based on his experience with such people, this is what happens to most who hold such views. First (and most important), he claims that no one who is an atheist when young maintains this view until old age. He offers no evidence for this; and later in *Laws* 10 he suggests that some non-youths will be atheists (see e.g. 908a8–909d6). What should we make of this? Did these older atheists accept their atheism later in life? There is no indication of that. I think it probable that Plato condones the Athenian stretching the truth in the hopes of steering the young toward a more important truth. As for deists and traditional theists, however, we are told that some (though not many) maintain such views until their old age.

But whatever impious position one has accepted, he says, the important point is not to hold it as set in stone. (Clearly, Plato would not give the same advice to young people who have accepted the proper, sanctioned-by-law beliefs about the gods. For them, the object *is* to have their beliefs set in stone as firmly and as quickly as possible.) He tells them to proceed as if the jury is still out on the issue of the nature and existence of the gods: study the issue carefully, and listen to the arguments of others and especially of the legislators. That is, listen to the kinds of arguments that the Athenian is about to present about the gods. It is unclear whether Plato wants every young person to study 'theology' carefully and listen to arguments about it, or whether that is 'medicine' for the theologically or philosophically 'ill' alone. (On how much astronomy and mathematics connected to theology Plato in the *Laws* thinks the young should study see 7.809c1–e2, 817e5–818d8, 820e8–822d1; and cf. 12.967d4–968a4.) But the preludes to the laws—including to the laws on impiety—will be available to anyone with questions or doubts.

Perhaps the most important bit of advice contained in this address is: while considering these difficult issues, do not dare to do anything impious (cf. Descartes, *Discourse on Method,* pt. 3 (AT 22)). Plato's aim here is dual: to protect the city from the impious actions of the young; and, to protect the soul of the impious young person, which can only get worse with increased impious action.

Recall that Plato's main concern is the hubristic *acts* of the young. If all goes well, the young people of Magnesia will fall into two categories: (1) the majority—those who were properly molded by their upbringing, and thus hold proper beliefs about the gods and act accordingly; (2) the minority—those who do not hold proper views about the gods, but who refrain from improper actions while they consider these tough issues. Consequently, in Magnesia there *should* be no hubristic acts of the young. The majority will grow up to be properly behaving adults, and most of the minority will shed their impious beliefs and make the proper adjustments. The impious few who remain will be dealt with harshly, as described later in *Laws* 10.

II. ATHEISM (888d7–899d3)

888d7–889e2

The Athenian and his interlocutors must now confront the atheist account of the world—the one thought by many (but not *the* many) to be wisest.

I should mention at the outset that a lot of ink has been spilled over who precisely Plato is attacking in what follows. I think such scholarly endeavors are misplaced. As Vlastos puts it:

He [Plato] has in mind the most mature physical systems, including atomism; but he draws no fine distinctions and makes no honorable exemptions, for he is convinced that all those who sowed the materialist wind must be held responsible for the whirlwind, i.e., the conventional theory of justice . . . (1995*a*: 86 n. 177)

On the atheistic outlook, anything that has ever come into being has done so by nature, by chance, or by art; and the greatest and finest things come to be by nature and chance, while the smaller things (those we call 'artificial') come to be by art.

Plato writes that art 'takes over from nature the source (*genesin*) of the greatest and primary works, and forms and crafts all the smaller things which we call artificial' (889a6–8). The language is a bit odd—and most translators embellish their translations here—but I think the meaning is relatively clear. The 'greatest and primary works' are the formation of the earth and the celestial bodies—which according to the atheist occur by nature and chance. Humans take what is available from nature—the elements and compounds that exist by nature (more on these shortly) and that are in fact the source (*genesis*) or material constituents of the earth and celestial bodies—and use art to transform this matter into artifacts, which are of course smaller (not simply in size but in grandeur) than what exists by nature.

Kleinias and Megillus remain puzzled about the nature of atheism, so Plato has the Athenian clarify and elaborate on this outlook. Saunders aptly describes Plato's elaboration at 889b1–e2 of the atheistic cosmology as 'stuffed with vague words of uncertain reference' (1972; 91). In some cases I have in my translation placed in square brackets those words for which the reference is not given and not entirely clear.

According to the atheist, Plato tells us, here are the things that exist, and what accounts for their coming into being:

(1) The four elements

Fire, water, earth, and air all exist by nature and by chance, not by art. As we shall see, each seems to possess by nature a certain set of characteristics or the potential for them; e.g. hot or cold, hard or soft, wet or dry. By 'nature', Plato is referring to the powers or capacities each element (or combination of elements) has, given its identity. Water will do certain things and react to other elements in certain ways, because of what it is; the same is true of fire, earth, air, and all the combinations of these elements. Further, in saying the elements exist by nature the atheist is also claiming that they are the very first things (891c2–3), which is to say that nothing—and certainly no creator—preceded them. The atheist would contrast things that exist by nature with man-made things (that is, things that are the product of art). Plato tells us later in *Laws* 10 that the atheist uses 'by nature' incorrectly (892b8). For his own theistic view, by contrast, is that god or soul is pre-eminently by nature—that is, among the first things (to this extent he agrees with the atheist's usage)—and that something is by nature if it is the product of divine art and intelligence (890d6–7, 892b6–c5).

Why does Plato claim that according to the atheist the elements exist *by chance* as well? Chance or luck (*tuchê*) in the context of human life sometimes refers simply to one's fate or fortune; but what concerns us here is its use to refer to events that are unforeseen, unplanned-for, coincidental. For example, whether a couple has children or not is a matter of chance (Plato's assumption being that every married couple wants children and tries to have them); so is dying intestate or being chosen by lot to hold some office. (See *Laws* 3.686b2–7, 690c5–8, 702b4–c1; 4.709a1–d3, 710c7–d5; 9.877e1–878a4; 11.920d4 920d4 922b2–4, 924d1–2.) In this human context theists too recognize and must take into account such chance events (see especially 4.709a1–d3). But Plato is here discussing cosmology—the origin of the existence and nature of the universe—and in this context the idea of chance separates the atheist and the theist. What Plato is saying is that according to the atheist the elements exist by chance because they simply happen to exist and possess the natures they do—without any design or planning or intelligence behind them. (As in the context of human life, chance refers to what is unplanned-for.) But for the theist the existence and nature of the elements is a matter of art, design, intelligence—not chance.

Plato describes the elements, on this account, as 'completely soulless beings' (889b5). This must mean that by their nature they are neither capable of moving themselves (895e10–896a2) nor directed by a divine soul (898d8–899a6).

It is important to note that Plato does not seem to be saying that according to the atheistic conception of the universe earth, air, fire, and water must be the four *basic* elements that explain everything else in the universe (as was the view of Empedocles). Instead, he is saying that what are often held to be basic material elements of the world are, on this view, not the result of art. He is certainly not excluding 'atheists' who claim that earth, air, fire, and water are each the result of combinations of atoms (as e.g. Democritus and Leukippus would claim) or that air is primary to all of them (e.g. Anaximenes) or that fire is (e.g. Heraclitus) or that earth and water are (e.g. Xenophanes). The important point is that according to the atheist account of the universe, the elements—whether fundamental or explained by some material(s) even more basic—do not exist as a result of divine art. So, as I mentioned earlier, it is not necessary to attempt to determine who precisely Plato has in mind in this passage. As England writes: 'It is against any system which denies *psuchê* or *nous* to have had any share in creation that he [Plato] is fighting, and though the arguments put into the mouths of his opponents remind us now of one school, now of another, he probably had no particular school in mind' (1921; 2. 453). England is wrong, however, to conclude that 'Anaxagoras' *Nous* has no place in the philosophical system here combated' (1921; 2. 453). For, as is clear from the *Phaedo*, Anaxagoras' *nous* (or reason) is not at all what Plato intends when he says that reason and art are behind the four elements and the rest of the material world (see 97b8–98d6; and cf. *Apology* 26d1–e2). In sum, I do not think Plato has in mind particular presocratic philosophers, but simply the movement of 'atheistic' natural philosophy in general.

Finally, I think it is possible that Plato's model for atheism is in part the *Timaeus* conception of earth, air, fire and water, only without the demiurge. See the discussion in the *Timaeus* of the four elements and their combination (31b4–32c4 and 49a6–50a4).

(2) Combinations of the elements

The 'bodies that come after these' (889b3)—where 'these' refers to the four elements—are combinations of the elements. These, too, exist by nature and by chance, not by art. And Plato makes clear in this passage and at *Laws* 12.967c4 that these combinations of elements are, like the elements themselves, soulless beings.

Some commentators skip step (2), apparently thinking that Plato moves straight from the four elements to the heavenly bodies. But Saunders (1972: 92–3) quite rightly argues that the 'composite bodies' (as England calls them (1921; 453)) come after these (*meta tauta*, 889b3) four elements and produce or beget what comes next: the heavenly bodies. I think this better fits the claim, made earlier in *Laws* 10, that according to the atheist the sun and moon and stars and the earth are not gods but (composed of) stones and earth (886d5–e3; see also 12.967c2–5 and *Apology* 26d1–5).

(3) The heavenly bodies (the earth, sun, moon, and stars)

The formation of the heavenly bodies, on the atheistic view, is a result of elements and combinations of elements moved by nature and chance. 'Nature' not only refers to the capacities each element or combination of elements has; it could also be applied to certain forces or 'natural laws' (our language, not Plato's) according to which elements and combinations of elements interact: for instance, the one Plato mentions, whereby opposite characteristics attract. (And it is important to stress that this is simply an example; Plato will not be limiting his criticism to natural philosophers who describe and analyze the natural world in terms of the attraction of opposite qualities.)

Plato describes as follows the natural force by which opposite characteristics attract: the elements and their attributes 'fell together, harmonizing in suitable ways—hot with cold, or dry in relation to wet, and soft in relation to hard, and all such things which, by mixing with their opposites according to chance, have from necessity been mixed together' (889b6–c2). Plato seems to be saying that the atheist recognizes that natural processes do not simply involve the mechanistic actions and reactions of matter. There operate in nature harmonious forces, according to which opposites attract and combine to form the universe as we know it. As we shall see, what Plato finds impossible is the notion that this all happened by chance, i.e. without any intelligent guidance or design. (This might in part explain why Plato chose to attack this model of presocratic philosophy and science, rather than the atomistic model with its 'billiard-ball' mechanics.)

According to the atheistic outlook nature and chance are intimately connected and have cosmological priority over art (*technê*). As we have seen, 'chance' refers to the fact, as the atheist sees it, that each element just happens to exist and have the nature it does, though 'chance' must also refer to whatever materials *happen* to be around and *happen* to be moving in this particular direction and at this particular speed, etc. For example, this particular earth-water mixture happens to collide with that particular clump of air-water-earth mixture, traveling in this direction and at that speed, etc., and the result just happens, by chance, to contribute to the formation of this planet with these complex features, etc. The important point for Plato is that on this view the entire process takes place without reason, art, design.

Both processes—elements interacting to form compounds and compounds interacting to form heavenly bodies—involve necessity: what happens *must* happen, given the (chance) nature and (chance) motion of each of the four elements and of their various combinations. It is clear from the *Timaeus* that a theist like Plato has nothing against necessity per se (see 47e3–48b3). But again the significant point is that for the atheist necessity is merely material, we could say, and not directed by an intellect.

(4) *The seasons*

Similarly, the seasons come to be 'not through reason . . . nor through some god nor through art, but . . . by nature and chance' (889c5–6).

The regular change of seasons, and their natures, are—on the atheistic view—explained solely in terms of the nature and movements of the heavenly bodies, without any reference to intelligent design or guidance. That the existence and nature of the seasons is conducive to the production and maintenance of life, Plato would say, is purely a matter of chance on this view.

The referent of 'these' (*toutôn*) in 'the seasons had come to be out of these' (889c4–5) is unclear. Saunders writes that 'Translators commonly ignore or fudge this word . . . and commentators are silent as to its reference' (1972; 93). In my translation I have ignored the word, in a manner of speaking, since I am not clear about its referent. This 'these' could certainly refer to the four elements—and indeed, according to the atheist, the seasons do *ultimately* come to be by nature and chance out of the actions and interactions of the four elements. Saunders objects that it would be 'odd to speak of the seasons as arising from the elements *simpliciter*'; instead, he suggests that 'these' refers to 'the entire heavens and all that is in the heavens' (as I translate the Greek at 889c3–4) (1972: 93–4). Now just as it is true that the seasons come to be out of the four elements indirectly, in another sense (namely, directly) they come to be out of the heavens and all that is in them (including the movement of the heavenly bodies). But that does not mean Plato specifically had the heavens in mind in writing 'these' here. So I have left the ambiguity in my translation.

(5) Animals and plants

The coming to be of living beings is made possible by the seasons—and more fundamentally by the existence and nature of the elements and their chance actions and interactions—and is likewise not by art. For a succinct account of the theistic view of the creation of life, endorsed by Plato, see *Sophist* 265c1–e6. (For a less succinct account, probably endorsed by Plato, see *Timaeus* 69a5–77c5.)

(6) Art

On the atheist world-view the appearance of animals (and particularly or especially humans) is a precondition of the coming to be of art (*technê*). This is what Plato means in saying that on this view 'Art is late, coming to be later from these (*toutôn*)' (889c7). Here is another demonstrative pronoun the referent of which is unclear. I follow Saunders (1972; 94), who argues that it likely refers to the word 'animals' (*zô¡a*) at 889c4.

Art is itself mortal because it is the product of mortals: it comes into being and could go out of existence, depending on the prior existence of humans who have developed the arts. It is possible that Plato has in mind other animals, if for example one counts birds' nests and spiders' webs as the products of art. But he does not mention these explicitly.

The beginning of *Laws* 3 suggests that human art does not appear (or may not have appeared) simultaneously with the coming to be of humans. The Athenian and his interlocutors discuss the nature of human life following a devastating flood—the most recent of an endless cycle of cities coming into being and then being destroyed by floods and plagues and other disasters (676b9–c5, 677a4–6). The only people who escaped destruction were mountain herdsman, and they were inexperienced in the arts—and especially those arts associated with city dwelling (677b1–9). All tools were destroyed, as well as all serious and important arts, including politics (677c4–7). But some arts did survive: herding and hunting, if they can be considered arts (679a1–4), molding of clay (pottery and perhaps brick work), and weaving—and consequently the making of clothing, bedding, houses (presumably mud huts or houses made of brick), and equipment for cooking and other activities (679a4–b3). In their naive simplicity these primitive people believed that whatever they heard about the gods and humans was true (679c2–8). This implies some kind of storytelling, but not necessarily at the level of an art. What more can be said about the arts they lacked? Plato implies that any inventions (e.g. carpentry and the invention of many tools) associated with the legendary inventor Daedalus were discovered only recently (within the last one or two millennia), as were the alphabet (invented by Palemedes), and many inventions in the realm of music (Orpheus, Marsyas, Olympos, and Amphion are named) (677d1–6). Other arts which primitive humans lacked were: those connected to transportation over land and sea (678c6–8); metal work and wood work (678c9–e6); arts of war (678e2–4, 679d2–6); and arts connected with lawsuits and other activities involving disputes among citizens (679d6–e4). This scenario—in which cities and civilizations and the arts have been destroyed in the distant past and will no doubt be destroyed again—illustrates in what sense art is, according to the atheist, mortal. For Plato, of course, such destruction implies only that *human* art has temporarily gone out of existence, but not divine art and reason; so art itself for Plato is not mortal.

Plato speaks of two kinds of art: (a) art that produces something serious (*spoudaion*, 889d4) and (b) certain playthings or toys (*paidias tinas*, 889d1):

(a) Serious arts
Serious arts are those which cooperate with nature, e.g. medicine, farming, gymnastics, and (at least in part) politics. These cooperate with nature in that in making use of these arts reason assists what exists by nature and aims at achieving what is best by nature. For example, health and physical fitness are our natural states (ill health is unnatural or against our nature); by nature, we must eat and exercise (and combat disease) to survive; so, medicine, gymnastics, and agriculture—arts that aim at and contribute to health and physical fitness and the maintenance of life—are all serious. (On medicine being in accordance with, or helping, nature see *Laws* 4.720b2–e5, 9.857c6–e1, 12.961e8–962a3; but cf. 4.709a1–c6. On gymnastics see 2.673a7–10, 7.789b5–d7, 795b4–e7, and perhaps 1.625c6–d4.)

(b) Non-serious arts

The non-serious arts—the playthings or toys—are those 'which do not much share in the truth, but are images akin to the arts themselves, such as painting produces and music and whatever arts are ancillary to these' (889d2–4). (I agree with England (1921; 454) that 'arts…ancillary to these' refers to other mimetic arts, like drama and narrative.) Plato writes that art 'later gave birth to certain playthings' (889d1), which I take to mean that according to this account the non-serious arts appeared later than the serious ones.

In *Laws* 2 Plato tells us what he means when he calls something a plaything; which is to say, non-serious: 'whenever something does no harm or good worthy of serious discussion' (667e7–8). Does he believe that all mimetic arts are non-serious? The esthetic theory of the *Laws* has received little scholarly attention, but as I understand it, Plato believes that mimetic art can be serious (in the positive sense) when it imitates the truth—for instance, true beauty and virtue. Music that imitates what is truly beautiful or a tragedy that imitates action which is truly courageous is serious and important. (See *Laws* 2.665d1–666a1, 667a10–670e4; 4.719c1–e5; 7.795e1–7, 796b3–d1, 812b9–c7, 814d7–817d8.) The *Republic* provides us with excellent illustrations of Plato's conviction that mimetic art can be *dangerous* and thus worthy of serious concern (see 2.376e1–3.398b4).

However, according to Plato positive serious mimetic art implies the actual, non-subjective existence of something called 'beauty' or 'virtue', and, as we have seen, the best by nature. (For Plato, even in the *Laws*, these would ultimately be Forms. For example, see 12.965b7–e4.) But for the atheist and sophist, on Plato's view (and he treats them interchangeably here), beauty and virtue and every other moral concept is in the eye of the beholder, and thus mimetic art can be non-serious only. An atheist can make some connection between nature or what is true and the arts of medicine and gymnastics and even a portion of politics. But (Plato claims) there can be for the atheist no connection between the mimetic arts and anything real.

That is why Plato writes, in describing the atheist world-view, that the mimetic arts are non-serious. (To regard them as dangerous, and thus serious in the negative sense, the products of mimetic art that do not share in the truth would still require some kind of objective standard, which again Plato claims the sophists and atheists lack.)

The products of mimetic arts are 'images akin to the arts them-selves' (889d2–3). That is, like the arts themselves, they are mortal and from mortals (see England (1921; 454)), and, most of all, they too do not share in truth. Note that even at its best Plato believes mimetic art is still merely an *imitation* of the truth—and actually two steps removed from reality (i.e. from the Forms), according to the *Republic*. In fact, mimetic poetry is forbidden in the city in speech of the *Republic* (see 10.595a1–608b7). (On the similarities between Plato's conception of mimetic art, as discussed in *Republic* 10, and the view he attributes to the atheist in *Laws* 10 see Tate (1936*a*).)

But what most of all separates Plato and the atheist here is this: the atheist thinks that mimetic creation is one of the last steps in the history of the world (and, as we shall see, the human invention of gods is one of the last kinds of mimetic creation), whereas Plato thinks mimetic creation is the first. As we come to find in the rest of *Laws* 10 (e.g. 902e5–903e1), according to Plato god(s), through art, create(s) or rather order(s) the universe. (See also the *Timaeus*, e.g. 28b2–34b9.) Divine mimetic art is serious indeed; and the atheist not only ranks this too low, he leaves it out entirely.

The importance of the preceding is that according to the atheist art is the end not the beginning of the process, and therefore poli-tics—including laws and legislation, the subject of this dialogue—is the result of human art alone and is not necessarily consistent with nature (which for Plato means consistent with divine art and reason, and with the truth). The *Laws* opens with this question: 'God or some human—strangers, who is given credit for laying down your laws?' (1.624a1–2). Of course, the atheist's answer must be: a human.

Plato next elaborates on the atheistic conception of the *political* art. In doing so, he distinguishes between the small part of politics and the large:

(*a*) *The small part of politics: that which cooperates with nature*

Humans, by their nature, come together to form political communities. To the extent that human reason cooperates with and assists in the formation of a political community, and aims at some genuine human end (e.g. security), it exists by nature or at least cooperates with nature. According to the atheist this is the small part of politics—i.e. there is not much in politics which fits this description. I think the famous *Sisyphus* fragment attributed to Critias (and to Euripides) illustrates precisely what Plato is talking about (as well as the point, made earlier, that on this conception the gods are a product of human art):

> There was a time when the life of humans was without order and bestial and the servant of power, when there was no reward for the good nor again did punishment come to the evil. Next it seems to me that humans established laws for punishment, so that justice might be tyrant <over all equally> and hold hubris as a slave, and anyone who transgressed was penalized. Next, since the laws inhibited them from doing overt deeds by force, but they did them in secret, it seems to me that at this point some careful and wise man <for the first time> invented for mortals the fear of gods, so that there might be some fear among the evil, even if in secret they do or say or think <something>. Hence, then, he introduced divinity.   (DK 88B25.1–16; see also Prodicus DK 84B5)

The creation of cities and certain laws to protect people from harming each other falls under the small part of politics—it certainly involves human art, and aims at a genuine human end and thus is rooted in nature.

(*b*) *The large part of politics: that which exists by art*

For the atheist this part of politics is or includes the whole of legislation, whose 'enactments' (*theseis*), according to the atheist, 'are not true', i.e. are not 'by nature but by art' (889e1–2).

There is some controversy over how best to translate *theseis*. England claims that it 'is probably not used in its *legal* sense of *enactment*, but (as in *Rep.* 335a2) in the philosophical sense of *affirmation, definition, assumption*' (1921; 2. 455). But I do think 'enactment' is best, because the point Plato is making is that according to the atheist the laws and decrees (the enactments) of the legislators are not true, because they are not based in reality or nature (see e.g. Antiphon, P.Oxy. 1364 fr. 1, discussed in Pendrick (2002; 158–75)). Of course, Plato thinks the philosophical assumptions of the atheists are false, but that is not the point he's making here.

Human beings are capable of inventing all sorts of laws which have nothing to do with human nature, human well-being, the natural beginnings of political communities, etc. (for example: an oligarchic law that stipulates that a citizen must possess a specified amount of wealth in order to take part in the running of the city). And in fact many of the laws and decrees that humans have enacted run counter to all of these. The entire realm of legislation, on this view, is not by nature but by art, i.e. human invention. Such laws are not true for all humans—they are not absolutes—they are simply 'true' for whatever culture or city or group of people happen to believe they are true, or want to impose them on others irrespective of their truth.

Plato's target seems no longer to be the natural philosopher or scientist, but the sophist. Historically there was likely *some* connection between the atheistic or deistic views of the natural philosophers and the moral relativism of the sophists. (I take 'relativism' broadly here to refer to the view that there are no objective moral truths and/or no moral absolutes. Betts (1989) has argued that no sophist, with the possible exception of Protagoras, was a relativist; but he employs a rather narrow conception of relativism.) For Plato this connection was a necessary one: rejecting the (right kind of) gods is tantamount to accepting moral relativism; thus, he easily moves from the one to the other.

Of course, Plato is not denying that politics is an art. What he is claiming is that *all* of the political art, *properly understood*, cooperates with nature and as such is true; none of it is mere human invention.

(See *Laws* 1.650b6–9 and 9.875a2–d5. At 3.677c5 he makes it clear that he regards politics as a serious art.)

889e3–890a9

Kleinias asks for clarification of the atheist's claim that legislation is not by nature but by art; i.e. is man-made. This leads to a discussion of the connection, as Plato sees it, between atheism and moral relativism.

There is an ambiguity in the opening line of this section, when Plato writes 'these (*toutous*) are different in different locations, according to whatever each group agreed among themselves in laying down the laws' (889e5–6), for 'these' can refer to 'the gods' or 'the laws'. Plato is either saying (1) the *laws* differ from place to place according to what people agree to in establishing the laws, or (2) the *gods* differ from place to place according to what people agree to in establishing the laws. England supports (2), claiming that taking 'these' as 'the laws' turns 'the statement into an empty truism' (1921; 2. 455). Saunders argues for (1) (1972; 96), but I think England is right, and have written 'the gods' (in brackets) in my translation, though ultimately both readings make essentially the same point concerning the relativism of both laws and beliefs about the gods.

So the first point Plato makes is that according to the atheist the gods, like the laws, are human inventions; and consequently there are different gods in different places. The fragment from Critias quoted in the previous section provides a good example of this outlook, as do the passages from Xenophanes that attack the anthropomorphic conception of the gods (DK 21B14–16). Later in this section Plato writes that these atheists 'are prose writers and poets' (890a3), and Xenophanes and Critias provide an example of each one respectively.

Plato recognizes that atheists might concede that some things that fall under *ta kala* (which has a broad range of meanings: the beautiful, the fine, the noble) can exist by nature. England correctly identifies what Plato has in mind: '*physical* beauty is assumed to be *phusei* [by nature], but when *kalos* is used in a *moral* sense, it is a matter of *thesis* [enactment]' (1921; 2. 456). But Plato focuses the discussion on justice, where he believes there is no room for confusion. Atheists claim that justice does not exist by nature, which is why people disagree about what it is (more so than on other issues; see *Theaetetus* 172a1–b6).

But that justice is relative (on the conception of relativism described above), and different people have difference notions of what is just, does not mean that atheists lack their own conception of justice. They have one, which they see as coming from the fact that there is no justice by nature. Plato refers to the wise men ('according to young people') who assert that justice is 'whatever can triumph by force' (890a2–4). Plato is clearly thinking of certain sophists, for example Thrasymachus, who as a character in Plato's *Republic* says: 'justice is nothing other than the advantage of the stronger' (1.338c2–3) (see also Callicles in the *Gorgias* 483a8–d6). But I do not think the sophists are his only target. Twice in the *Laws* (3.690b4–c3; 4.715a1–2; cf. *Gorgias* 484b4–9) Plato refers to a poem of Pindar (fr. 169 Snell), which includes the line: 'Law is king of all [and] pushes through and makes just the greatest violence.' (See Pangle (1980; 522–3 n. 24).) Noteworthy too are the Athenian side of the Melian Dialogue, and the fate of Melos at the hands of Athens, described by Thucydides (5.84–116). At one point in the Melian Dialogue the Athenians say: 'the just, according to human reasoning, is an issue among those equal in power, while the possible is what the superior accomplish and the weak yield to' (1.89). This attitude is no doubt part of what Plato is reacting to in *Laws* 10, because he is concerned not only about impious ideas but about their application and consequences as well.

Clearly, Plato believes that atheism leads to moral relativism, which in turn leads to the sophistic conception of justice, which finally leads to 'the impieties that afflict young people' (890a4–5). So he is here expanding on what he said at the opening of *Laws* 10; namely, that impious ideas (in this case atheism) lead to the hubristic acts of the young:

Atheism → moral relativism → corrupt conception of justice → impious acts.

This set of impious acts appears to be broader than (though it includes) the hubristic acts of the young discussed at the outset of *Laws* 10. For he now says that the sophistic conception of justice leads young people to want to dominate others (in the way just described), rather than (what is presented as proper by Plato) 'being a slave to others according to law' (890a8–9).

The *Laws* is consistent with the *Republic* here. Consider this passage from *Republic* 9:

Why do you think vulgar and manual labor bring reproach? Or shall we say it is for any other reason than that when the best part is by nature so weak in someone, it cannot rule the beasts in him, but can only serve them, and can learn only the things that flatter them? . . . Therefore, in order that such a person be ruled by something similar to what rules the best person, we say that he ought to be the slave of that best person who has the divine rule within himself. It is not to harm the slave that we think he ought to be ruled, as Thrasymachus supposed about the ruled, but because it is better for all to be ruled by what is divine and prudent, especially when one has it as one's own within oneself, but if not, then imposed from outside, so that as far as possible all will be alike and friends, governed by the same thing . . . (590c1–d6)

In both the *Republic* and the *Laws* the choices seem to be (1) rule by brute force or be enslaved by brute force (Thrasymachus), or (2) rule according to what is 'divine and prudent' or be a 'slave' to what is 'divine and prudent' (Plato). So in either case the choice is rule or be a slave—but Plato wants us to be good rulers or good slaves (cf. *Laws* 2.669c3–d5; 3.694a3–b7, 701b5–e8; 4.720b2–e5; 9.857c4–e5; 11.930d1–e2).

This is not the only dichotomy in *Laws* 10 that many philosophers would regard as false, and behind it is another dichotomy: reject the proper belief in the gods and be vicious (or impious), or believe in the proper gods and be virtuous. Now this does not amount to the divine-command theory of ethics; however, in this and other sections of *Laws* 10 Plato *seems* to accept the view that without the gods there are or can be no ethical truths. This should come as a surprise, (1) given what Plato wrote earlier in his life in the *Euthyphro*, and (2) given that however little emphasis there is in the *Laws* on the Forms it is clear that they still play an important role in Plato's philosophy.

In the *Euthyphro* Socrates asks Euthyphro, who has just defined piety as what all the gods love: 'Is the pious loved by the gods because it is pious, or is it pious because it is loved by the gods?' (10a2–3). Plato thinks piety has a nature of its own—independent of what the gods think of pious people, actions, etc.—which he *hopes* we can discover (5d1–5, 10b7–e3). With the *Euthyphro* language in mind, we can ask the Plato of *Laws* 10 about justice (and virtue generally): 'Is the just created (or made possible) by the gods because it is just, or is it just because it is created (or made possible) by the gods?' The Plato who wrote the *Euthyphro* would have chosen the former. In the *Republic* as well Plato answers the sophistic conception of justice not with an appeal to the gods (or at least not primarily), but with an account anchored in the nature of the human soul and ultimately in the Form of Justice and the Form of the Good. But how the Plato of *Laws* 10 would answer is unclear.

Bobonich explains the relationship in the *Laws* between theology and ethics as follows:

The theology advanced in Book 10 is based on what Plato takes to be true claims about divinity. Moreover, Magnesia's theology gives Plato a way to articulate a standard of objectivity that does not require full metaphysical detail. The main targets of Plato's attack on atheism are those who deny the objectivity of value. And in an implicit rejection of Protagorean relativism, Magnesians are taught that god, not man, is the measure of all things (*Laws* 716c). This is not, however, to make Euthyphro's mistake, since although the Athenian does not go into details, he makes clear that ethical standards are not dependent on god. (2002; 208)

But Bobonich may be too easy on Plato. For even as stated, there is a tension between 'god is the measure of all things' and 'ethical standards are not dependent on god'.

It seems likely that in the *Laws* Plato maintains that justice (and virtue generally) is not simply what the gods decree it is (see his discussion in Book 12 of the Forms of the virtues). But it remains the case that Plato chose to put a strong emphasis on the need, ethically, for citizens to have proper beliefs about the gods. If argument and persuasion are in fact major values in the *Laws*, couldn't Plato have emphasized the case for virtue without such an emphasis on religious belief? Likewise, couldn't the rulers of Magnesia properly instill virtues in citizens without reference to the gods? Given the strong connection Plato sees between atheism and relativism, the answers to these questions are unclear.

One possible explanation for this discrepancy is that Plato changed his mind. In the *Laws* he genuinely *is* appealing to the gods as part of the foundation for law and morality. In some sense he gave up on a complete case for ethics that is neither the product of divine nor human decree, and to that extent, although he does not uphold the divine-command theory of ethics, he does maintain that there is a strong connection between an absolutist (i.e. non-relativistic) ethics and the existence of the gods. In the *Republic* he discussed the natural basis of ethics, but in the end relied on the absolutism of the Forms (and even the immortality of the soul and—perhaps with a nod in the direction of the *Laws*—the Myth of Er). In the *Laws*, however, he ultimately relies more heavily on the existence and goodness of the gods.

Another possibility is that Plato is not always presenting his own views on the matter; rather, he is describing what laws (and preludes) he thinks are necessary for non-philosophers like Kleinias and Megillus. This reading is like the other in that it sees Plato in the *Laws* as ultimately relying more heavily on the gods than he did in the *Republic*; it is different, however, in that on this interpretation there is no change in Plato's own metaphysics—i.e. in his view of what is the case with respect to the existence of the Forms (which he accepts) and the Olympian gods (which are at best metaphors based on the gods he defends)—but rather a change in what he thought was necessary to run a city properly. This interpretation is certainly consistent with a Plato who changed his mind over time; but differences between the *Laws* and certain earlier dialogues may also reflect the fact that the *Laws* is presenting what Plato regards as the second-best political system.

In the end, I think that in the *Laws* it is not the case that the good simply is whatever the gods command. But without the order in the universe made possible by the gods (more on this in what follows) there could be no good generally and no standard of virtue in particular. To better understand the important connection Plato sees between the gods and morality, we must look at Plato's arguments for the existence and nature of the gods.

Note that so far Plato has given us a purely consequentialist argument against atheism, i.e. he has argued that the belief in atheism leads to bad consequences. We shall turn to his more direct refutation of atheism shortly.

890b1–891a7

The Athenian and Kleinias agree that the atheist account is not only false, but dangerous for young people. And the danger is not simply 'in cities as public places', but 'in private households' as well (890b2). I assume Plato is saying that atheistic ideas are not simply a public menace—corrupting the youth of a city and thereby the city itself—they are also a threat to the soul of the individual young person himself, aside from any public danger.

How should the legislator of the city of Magnesia reply to such a threat, especially given that atheists have been spreading their ideas for a long time (which suggests a greater threat and perhaps less reason for leniency)? We return to the issue of persuasion versus force, first raised (in Book 10) by the hypothetical impious youth, so to speak, at 885c7–e6. The specific issue is: how to proceed against the atheist. Two options are presented:

(1) Force alone. Threaten all people that they must believe that the gods exist, and as described by law (see 885b4, 890a6), or be punished by death, beating, imprisonment, dishonors, poverty, or exile—depending on the nature of the infraction. The Athenian says that a similar case could be made for what the city believes about 'all great matters' (890b8)—i.e. beauty, justice, virtue. In all such cases one way to proceed would be to tell citizens: believe what the law decrees and act accordingly, or else.

(2) Persuasion (or, more accurately, force and persuasion). This is not an *alternative* to (1) but (at this point) a possible addition: persuading people '*at the same time* that he [i.e. the legislator] establishes the laws for them . . . *adding* arguments to make them as gentle as possible' (890c6–8). Of course, what they are talking about are the preludes to the laws (and specifically the prelude to the law on impiety). It is crucially important to keep in mind that this does not replace force. There will certainly be contexts in which the legislators say to citizens: believe this or else—or else be killed, imprisoned, exiled, etc.

There is of course no mention of a third option: leave the atheist alone to believe whatever he likes. Consider the attitude of Thomas Jefferson (which was not uncommon in Europe and North America during the Enlightenment): 'The legitimate powers of government extend to such acts only as are injurious to others. But it does me no injury for my neighbour to say there are twenty gods, or no god. It neither picks my pocket nor breaks my leg' (*Notes on the State of Virginia*, Query 17, 'Religion' (1785)). This outlook is absolutely alien to Plato and the interlocutors of the *Laws* (though the natural philosophers and scientists of the time might have been more receptive to it). But I believe Plato, were he to encounter such a view, would have responded: (1) the legitimate powers of government extend not only to those acts that are injurious to others, but also to those that are injurious to oneself—and in fact the purpose of government is to make everyone (individually and collectively) as good as possible; and (2) atheism and other impious beliefs may not directly involve the picking of our pockets or the breaking of our legs, but (a) they harm the souls of those who hold them, and

(b) this damage can *lead* such people to pick pockets, break legs, and much worse. (It is beyond the scope of this commentary to discuss the relative merits of the Platonic and Jeffersonian positions.)

Kleinias immediately supports the second option: persuasion (and force). The legislator, he says, should assist 'the ancient law's argument' (890d4) concerning the existence and nature of the gods. (See the textual note on 890d4.) 'Ancient' is Kleinias' assessment, not the Athenian's (nor Plato's); the actual law they are developing is radically different from the ancient (i.e. Olympian) outlook. Kleinias says that they should show that law and art are 'by nature or by something not inferior to nature', since law and art 'are offspring of reason (*nous*)' (890d6–7). Kleinias seems confused—perhaps because of the differences between the atheistic and Platonic accounts—about what counts as 'by nature'. The point, he seems to be saying, is that law and art are the product of reason and the gods, which makes them by nature or (if nature refers purely to the natural world, say) by something that is not inferior to nature (as is the case according to the atheistic conception; i.e. they are the product of human invention).

In response to Kleinias the Athenian raises two concerns:

(1) How difficult it is for crowds to follow such arguments. (I take *chalepa . . . sunakolouthein logois* (890e1–2) to mean 'difficult [for people in a crowd] to follow arguments'. Some editors and translators (e.g. England (1921: 2. 459) interpret the line such that the difficulty refers not to the audience's understanding but to the speakers' presentation of their ideas—'difficult to address crowds, with arguments'. But I think my reading is supported by *chalepa . . . akousein* ('difficult to listen to') at 891a3.)

(2) The great length of such arguments.

Kleinias' response follows the 'usual chiastic arrangement' (England 1921; 2. 459)—that is, he responds first to the second point, and then to the first:

(2′) We put up with lengthy discussions about drunkenness and music (in *Laws* 1–2), so we should not mind doing so about the gods—a much more important topic. And he adds later that length is not a problem if such arguments are beneficial.

(1′) The importance of written law, and particularly of setting down in writing the laws and the preludes to them:

(a) It ensures that the laws will remain completely the same. (On the importance of keeping laws stable, and on changes to the laws, see especially *Laws* 6.769a7–e2, 772a6–d4; 7.797a7–798e7; and Bobonich (2002: 395–408).)

(b) It provides for all time an opportunity for questioning, inquiry, and examination (*elenchus*). People who are unable to follow arguments in support of the laws initially can return often to examine them.

Although the Athenian will agree with Kleinias' conclusion ('we should do as he says', 891b1), it is interesting that these claims about writing and philosophical inquiry were put into the mouth of Kleinias, not of the Athenian.

First, although Plato's audience would surely think of the Socratic *elenchus* here, there is no reason to think that Kleinias would have heard of such a thing; and whatever precisely Plato has in mind, the laws of Magnesia will not allow the kind of *elenchus* among private citizens that we see, for example, in the *Euthyphro* between Socrates and Euthyphro. Given what Plato says later in *Laws* 10, it appears that the inquiry that Kleinias is talking about will take place within an individual's own mind, or with some official in a government sanctioned context.

Second, Kleinias' claims about writing seem to clash with what Plato has written in the *Phaedrus* (274b6–277a5) and especially in the *Seventh Letter* (341a8–345c3) about the limitations of writing. For example, the *Seventh Letter* states: 'no one having reason (*nous*) will ever dare express his thoughts (or 'what he has reached through reason', *ta nenoêmena*) in [language], especially in an unalterable form, as is the case with written outlines' (343a1–4). In the *Phaedrus*, Phaedrus says that writing is an image or phantom (*eidolôn*) of 'the living and animate account (*logon*) of the man who knows' (276a8–9). Writing's relation to philosophical discourse parallels the relation of image to reality. (On the connection between *Phaedrus* 274b6–277a5 and the views on writing expressed in the *Laws* see

Bobonich (1996; 269–71). There is a long-standing debate over
the authenticity of the *Seventh Letter*, though I think it may well
be genuine. Caskey (1974) contains a brief survey of the relevant
secondary literature; Annas, who argues for suspending judgment
on its authenticity, offers good advice on how to view the letters
(1999; 74–7).)

We should not assume that in the *Laws* Plato has completely
moved away from the concerns he expressed about writing in these
other works. Praise of writing appears in the *Laws* because Magnesia
is second best, and, related to this, because the rule of law is second
best, behind the rule of philosopher-kings (see *Laws* 5.739b8–e7
and *Statesman* 293a6–297e5). In this second-best context written
law is praiseworthy—and it's fitting that Plato put this praise into
the mouth of the second-best person in the *Laws*.

891a8–b7

There are two issues worth addressing in this brief section: the
limited role of the taciturn Megillus, and (again) the need to present
arguments for the existence of the gods.

Megillus is the most laconic of the three interlocutors of the *Laws*,
and that is certainly evident in Book 10, in which he speaks twice (a
total of nine Greek words)—both times in this section, and in each
case a pithy affirmation of what someone else says (first Kleinias,
then the Athenian). Why does Plato have him speak *here*? They are
about to launch into the arguments for the existence of gods—the
most important part of *Laws* 10—so it is likely that Plato wants
to underscore the unanimity of the two points Megillus agrees to:
(1) arguments for the existence of the gods, despite their length, must
be presented; and (2) the legislator is the one who should present
these arguments.

But why does Plato have him speak *only* here? First, Megillus
is a Spartan, and Spartans are known for their pithiness. Second,
although neither Kleinias nor Megillus is a philosopher (and both are
less philosophically acute than, say, Adeimantus and Glaucon in the

Republic), Kleinias is nevertheless more philosophically adept than Megillus. Perhaps Plato is saying that in this, the most philosophically (i.e. metaphysically and theologically) profound part of the *Laws*, men like Kleinias will be able to following the arguments only so far, whereas men like Megillus will not be able to follow them at all. What this implies about who in Magnesia will be able to follow what is hard to assess, except that there will likely be some citizens who won't be able to follow such arguments (even granting that the citizens of Magnesia will receive a better education than either Kleinias or Megillus received).

In response to Megillus the Athenian adds—almost as an aside— that if it were not for how widespread the impious arguments are, there would be no need to append arguments about the gods to the city's laws concerning impiety. This seems to imply that ideally the arguments for the existence of the gods need not be a part of the rational education of citizens—the education necessary for molding properly religious citizens. The purpose of such arguments is reactive: to ward off the impious ideas in those cities in which they arise.

Earlier Plato said that the writings presenting the impious ideas do not exist in 'your' cities (that is, in Sparta and the cities of Crete) (886b10–c1). Now he's saying that impious ideas are 'sown among all of mankind' (891b2–3). Is he contradicting himself? And if these ideas don't exist among the Spartans and Cretans, wouldn't it follow (given what Plato just said) that they would not need to bother with arguments for the existence of the gods? But Magnesia is a Cretan city, and all the laws (and preludes) they are now discussing are supposedly for this city.

The way out of this thicket of problems is to note the difference between writings and ideas (or arguments). The *writings* that present impious ideas may not exist among the Spartans and Cretans (and hypothetically among the Magnesians), but certain impious *ideas* do (or would). Atheism and deism might arise among a very small number of people who have never read or even heard about these outlooks; but more important—and most widespread of all—traditional theism (that the gods exist, but are appeasable through sacrifice and prayer) will likely be rampant among the Cretans and Spartans, and therefore among the colonists of Magnesia as well.

But then why bother with arguments for the existence of the gods, when all that's needed are arguments showing that the gods are just and thus would not do what is unjust in exchange for bribes? As much of the rest of *Laws* 10 will make clear, Plato believes a successful defense of the goodness of the gods depends on a more fundamental defense of their existence and precise nature.

891b8–891e3

Plato summarizes the essence of the atheist position: The four elements—bodies or matter generally—are the first things and are thus thought to exist by nature. According to the atheist, 'nature' applies to what has priority metaphysically or cosmologically. The four elements, being the earliest things, are most of all by nature; but so are the heavenly bodies and all kinds of combinations of matter. And soul, on this view, eventually comes to be out of the elements. It is, or is made of, or is some complex combination of, the basic constituents of matter. Note that none of this implies that soul, for the atheist, is *not* by nature. It certainly is, precisely because it can be explained in terms of matter. What does not exist by nature, on this view, what is contrasted with the natural, is what exists by *art*. According to the atheist this is the key difference: The products of art, and of reason generally, are primarily the result of the activities of the human mind, and not of the nature, capacities, and movement of matter.

His next move is to highlight the crucial distinction between two fundamentally different metaphysical outlooks: what we can call the primacy of matter and the primacy of soul. The atheist holds the former, the theist the latter. In fact, the primacy of matter is the *source* of the 'unreasonable (*anoêtou*) opinions' (891c7–8) of those who investigate nature. They have their priorities wrong: the priority (temporally and ontologically) of matter to soul.

Plato has simply underscored this distinction. But does the atheist have a strong case for maintaining this view of reality? For 'it is no small matter' (891d1)—in fact, it's quite a good thing—if it turns out that those who defend impious ideas do so not well but poorly. And the Athenian suspects that the atheist maintains his belief without sufficient support. Plato's approach will not be to prove directly that the primacy of matter is false, but—what comes to the same thing—to prove that the primacy of soul is true.

At this point the Athenian hesitates to go any further, mentioning the need to handle 'unfamiliar arguments' (891d6). Kleinias assumes that the cause of this hesitation is what they discussed earlier, namely, that this will take them too far outside actual legislation and into lengthy philosophical arguments. His reply here is an echo of his former reply: getting the issue right—proving that the proper conception of the gods is indeed correct—should be their primary concern. But it will become clear that the cause of this hesitation is not (or not simply) what Kleinias assumes. In the next section the Athenian is concerned about his interlocutors' ability to follow complex reasoning, and that is most likely the source of his hesitation.

Note that the Greek here—specifically 891e1–3—is difficult to make sense of, though not too much is on the line. For two different ways of interpreting the passage see England (1921; 2. 461) and Saunders (1972; 97–8).

891e4–892d3

Plato next describes the error of the atheist, reiterating that ideas have caused them to be impious: 'arguments that produce the soul of the impious' (891e7–8). His first attempt is confusing—in effect, he says, 'they say that the first is last and the last is first'. Here is the passage, with brackets and italics for clarification: 'what *is* [in fact] the first cause of the generation and destruction of all things [i.e. soul] is *not* first [according to the atheist] but has come into being later, while what *is* later [i.e. matter] is earlier [according to the atheist]' (891e5–8). On the debate over whether the claim that soul is 'the first cause of the generation and destruction of all things' is limited to the ordered universe see Mohr (2006; ch. 8) and the discussion below on 896b1–2.

This misunderstanding about the priority of soul is the cause of, and the key to understanding, the atheists' rejection of the belief in the gods. Plato elaborates on their misunderstanding, which concerns the following (related) issues:

(1) *What soul is*. For example, atheists mistakenly think that soul is a special kind of matter, or arises out of a combination of matter.
(2) *What power soul has*. For example, atheists mistakenly think that soul can allow animals to find food and humans to do arithmetic and write plays but it cannot create or move planets.
(3) *Soul's generation*. For example, atheists mistakenly think that soul comes to be from matter, and is a result of the natural and chance attributes and actions of matter.

Plato mentions what he claims are three facts that the atheist does not understand about soul's 'generation' (and in fact rejects): (a) Soul is among the first things. Plato here leaves open whether anything else is prior to soul (e.g. reason); but the important point is that soul is one of the first things, not one of the last (as the atheists claim). (b) Soul is prior to body. (c) Soul, more than anything else, governs the changes and transformations of material bodies. There may be certain things the nature of which soul cannot determine or control—for instance, what soul initially had to work with in creating the cosmos (e.g. the receptacle of the *Timaeus*, from which the demiurge creates the material world). But for the most part, and primarily, the physical world is governed by soul.

Plato has so far asserted what he thinks is wrong with the atheistic position, but he has yet to *argue* for theism or the priority of the soul. Instead, he next lays out what he believes are important implications of the atheist being wrong:

(1) What is 'related to soul' would 'necessarily come into being before what belongs to body' (892a8–b1).

(2) Opinion, supervision, reason, art, and law—the highest parts or attributes or manifestations of soul—would be prior to bodies and their attributes ('hard things and soft things and heavy things and light things', 892b5–6).

(3) The relationship between art and nature would have to be reconceived. Plato believes that if soul has primacy over matter, then art (*technê*, the intellectual capacity or virtue) is not some recent development in human culture (as the atheist thinks); it too must be prior to matter. And this is no small thing: 'the great and first works and actions'—which I take to refer to the formation of the cosmos—'would be those of art' (892b6–7).

(4) The usage of the word 'nature' (*phusis*) would have to be revised. Atheists call the four elements and the heavenly bodies and living things 'natural' because these were all among the first things, and according to them can be contrasted with what exists by art—man-made things, which obviously arrived relatively recently from the point of view of the history of the universe. This does not mean that Plato will reject the designation 'nature' for matter, heavenly bodies, the bodies of living organisms, etc. He seems to agree with the atheist that 'nature' should refer to what are among the first things, including the material constituents of physical reality and the rest. He differs from the atheist in where he fits art and reason and the other attributes of soul generally into this scheme: if 'soul is among the first things to have come into being, then it may well be most correct to say that *it especially* is by nature' (892c3–5). (See Carone (1994; 276–7).)

In his explication of what he sees as the major implications of the atheist being wrong, Plato may be guilty of an invalid, and anthropomorphic, inference. (See especially points 1–3). For even if it were true that soul is prior to body, this would not imply that every part or activity of soul would be prior to every attribute of body. Yet he seems to assume that if he can show that soul is prior to body, then he can also conclude that every (human) function of soul is prior to all matter and every material attribute: for example, soul is prior to body, therefore opinion is prior to softness.

Plato ends this section of text by underscoring that this engagement with the atheist is not some esoteric academic exercise, but that there is a great deal at stake. He has sketched two radically different views—atheism and a proper conception of theism—and claimed that they are based on two sides of an important and frequently misunderstood dichotomy: the primacy of soul versus the primacy of matter. He says that the view he has sketched and called correct can be considered true ('This is how things are', 892c5) *if* (and only if—that's the force of 'but not otherwise', 892c6–7) someone can demonstrate that soul is prior to body. He has placed the burden of proof where it properly belongs: squarely on the shoulders of the theist.

892d4–893b5

The Athenian says the three of them must 'guard against a completely deceitful argument' or account (i.e. atheism). The 'guarding against' that he speaks of is not the protheism (anti-atheism) argument itself (which, we are reminded, involves demonstrating the priority of soul to body); rather, he has in mind a precaution they should take *before* laying out such an argument. He says that it would be ridiculous to take on something great (defending theism) only to fail at something relatively small; namely, seeing to it that the person best equipped to argue for theism (and only the best person) actually undertakes the task.

In what follows, the Athenian simply assumes that he is the best (and of the three present the only one) qualified to take on the greater task. But to demonstrate why he alone should do so (at least at first), he employs an analogy with a river crossing.

Fording a river

1. The best qualified—the most experienced at river crossing and the youngest—should first make the attempt alone, and test the waters.

2. The reason for this precaution: the safety of the older men, but also to spare them any embarrassment.

3. The implication is that the river is fordable for the best qualified. The question is whether it is fordable for the other two—in which case the best qualified will then help them across—or whether it is not fordable for them (no matter what help they receive). It seems that for the older men, making it across on their own is not a possibility.

Arguing for theism

1'. The best qualified—the wisest, the one most adept at philosophy—should first attempt to go through the case for theism alone. (As England points out (1921: 2. 463), the analogy does not imply that the Athenian must be the youngest of the three interlocutors, though he may be.) Since dialogue is the key to philosophical activity for Plato, this means the Athenian will engage in a dialogue with himself.

2'. The reason for this precaution: primarily the greatest possible success in defending theism, but also to spare the other men any embarrassment.

3'. The implication is that the Athenian *can* argue for theism. The question is whether the argument is 'fordable' for the other two—that is, whether they can follow the argument for theism, with the Athenian's help, or whether they simply cannot grasp the argument. But Plato tells us that the argument they are about to encounter is 'probably not fordable given your strength' (892e6–7), and it's unclear whether that means the other two cannot grasp the argument without the Athenian's help, or that they cannot grasp it at all. (Cf. *Republic* 6.506d1–e3, where, prior to discussing the Form of the Good, Socrates tells Glaucon and Adeimantus that he must leave them behind.)

However we take the last point of this analogy, it is clear that the Athenian must do all of the hard work intellectually. In what follows this passage Plato seems to present Kleinias (and perhaps Megillus, though he is silent) as understanding the arguments, with difficulty, but this understanding takes the form of mere assent.

There is no genuine contribution from Kleinias or Megillus to the discussion of atheism, there are clear signs of confusion and difficulty in grasping the material on their part, and there are major doubts about how deeply they can be said to have understood the issues the Athenian discusses and the arguments he presents. This is not surprising, given the difficulty of what the Athenian covers. Megillus is silent throughout the entire discussion; Kleinias occasionally speaks, sometimes to agree with the Athenian, but often to express his confusion (see e.g. 894b2, b5, d7, d9, e3; 895c3; 895d3, d7, d12). Towards the end of the attempted refutation of atheism the Athenian says: 'Kleinias, you have listened to the arguments brilliantly' (898c9). This exchange is a good indication not only of the passive nature of Kleinias' intellectual participation throughout much of *Laws* 10, and especially during the discussion of the most difficult philosophical issues, but also of the Athenian's (and Plato's) positive appraisal of it. Plato would likely claim that Kleinias and Megillus were persuaded by the Athenian's arguments for the existence of the gods and thus the falsehood of atheism, but, again, it is an impoverished conception of persuasion.

Kleinias and Megillus readily agree with everything the Athenian says about taking over the argument. As a last bit of business before turning to the theistic argument itself, the Athenian invokes the aid of the gods 'at the demonstration of their own existence' (893b2–3). Cleary calls this 'benign circularity' (2001: 130).

893b5–894e3

The ten kinds of motion

1. Preliminaries (893b5–c4)
The Athenian—as he said he would—enters into a dialogue with himself. He first asks which of the following hold (cf. Aristotle, *Physics* 8.3):

(1) Everything is stationary, nothing is in motion. (The Eleatic outlook.)

(2) Everything is in motion, nothing is stationary. (The Heraclitean outlook.)

(3) Some things are in motion, and some things are stationary.

The Athenian accepts view (3). He surely has in mind our common-sense observation of the world, including celestial objects, though this description would also fit the Platonism of the *Republic*, for example, according to which the Forms are motionless (each Form like an Eleatic One) and the physical realm is in some sense a Heraclitean flux. (On Plato's position being 'between' Parmenides' and Heraclitus' see *Theaetetus* 179e2–181a3. On the view that in the *Republic* and some other dialogues Plato regards the physical world as Heraclitean see Irwin (1977).)

The Athenian introduces the concept of place (*chôra*), in which 'the stationary things are stationary and the things in motion are in motion' (893c2–3). He then asks: 'some would presumably do this [i.e. move] in one spot while others would do this in many?' (893c4). He has left behind what is motionless; the following discussion concerns only things that move. He begins by presenting eight kinds of motion—though it is not at all clear that he has done so until he tells us he has.

2. The first eight kinds of motion (893c5–894b8)

a. Motion in one location (i.e. circular motion) (893c5–d6)
This refers not simply to moving spheres (e.g. a celestial object's rotation) but to any object that is moving around an axis but, in doing so, is staying in one place (e.g. a conical piece of wood turning on a lathe).

Plato writes in somewhat cryptic Greek that the objects moving in a circular motion 'have the power of standing still in the middle (*ta tên tôn hestôtôn en mesô; lambanonta dunamin*) and to move in one place, just as the circumferences of circles said to stand still revolve' (893c5–7). The line is ambiguous. England translates it: 'those which have the gift of immobility at their center', and interprets it to mean that 'their centre never changes its position in space' (1921: 2. 464). I take Plato to be saying that an object moving in a circular motion has the capacity (a) to remain motionless at its center *and*

(b) to revolve at its circumference. (I'm not sure what 'and to move in one place' adds, as it essentially repeats the 'move in one spot' from a line earlier. But, like 'said to stand still' in the line about the revolution of the circumferences of circles, it stresses the fact that these objects are moving while staying in the same place.) What intrigues Plato here is the seemingly paradoxical nature of circular motion: it moves while it stands still, and the center point—which is fixed in space—does not move, while every point not on the axis does. (Cf. *Republic* 4.436c9–e6.)

But Plato is intrigued even more by the following 'paradox':

> in the case of *this* rotation, the largest circle and the smallest go around at the same time, and such motion distributes itself to the small and the large proportionally (*ana logon*), being less or more according to proportion (*kata logon*). This is why it [i.e. circular motion] has become a source of all sorts of wonder: at the same time it imparts to large and small circles slowness and swiftness in harmony, an occurrence that one would expect to be impossible.   (893c8–d5)

Take, for example, a carousel in motion, and suppose there is a horse close to the outer edge of the carousel, and a unicorn parallel to that horse and close to the center. The unicorn and horse seem to be moving together in harmony, and in a certain sense one could say they are traveling at the same speed—e.g. ten rounds per minute. And yet the unicorn is moving more slowly than the horse, because the horse is traveling a greater distance than the unicorn in the same time. In this way, concentric circles move with 'slowness and swiftness in harmony'. It seems impossible, Plato says, but it is not; hence the wonderment.

Plato's discussion of circular motion is generally more expansive than the other forms of motion. This must have something to do with the fact that he will later be comparing circular motion to the motion of reason. England (1921; 2. 464) writes that 'Plato must have had some special reason for enlarging on this peculiarity of circular motion', and plausibly suggests that in discussing circular motion Plato 'has the motions of the heavenly bodies in mind' (cf. Skemp (1942; 100–1)). This is likely (cf. *Timaeus* 38c2–d6); but note that wonder over circular motion was not, in antiquity, reserved for the motion of celestial objects (see Aristotle?, *Mechanica* 847b15–21).

b. Motion in many locations (893d6–e1)
Two sub-kinds of motion fall under this class:

(1) Gliding: a motion by which the moving object continually changes to another place, while 'possessing a base of one point' (*basin henos kektêmena tinos kentrou*, 893d8–e1). (I take it Plato is using 'point' loosely to refer to whatever point of contact an object has with the surface over which it is gliding, whether a spinning top moving smoothly over a marble surface, or a stone block gliding on ice.)
(2) Rolling: a motion by which the moving object continually changes to another place and continually changes its point of contact.

That Plato mentions gliding and rolling alone suggests that he has in mind the motion of objects across a surface, which leads one to wonder how he would classify the motion of celestial objects around the earth. Is it gliding or rolling or yet some other form of motion in many locations? (See Skemp (1942; 101).)

c. Separation and combination (893e1–5)
I present this confusing passage in its entirety:

Each time they [i.e. moving objects] encounter (*prostugchanta*) each other, they are split apart (*diaschizetai*) by the ones standing still (*tois hestôsi*), whereas with the others that come and are borne from the opposite direction, they combine (*sugkrinetai*) and become one thing intermediate between the two (*mesa kai metaxu*) [in nature].

We learn later that there are two kinds of 'motion' described here:

(1) *Separation (or splitting apart).* In the next section Plato refers to this splitting as separation (*diakrinomena*, 893e6). In the case of separation, an object moving in many locations collides with an object that is standing still (presumably either completely motionless or perhaps moving in a circular motion), and one or both of the objects split apart (i.e. break into pieces). (It is unlikely that he is saying that the two objects split apart—i.e. don't combine

but rather move away from each other—as separation seems to involve some one thing becoming many, not two or more things ricocheting off of each other and not combining. But much is unclear here.)

(2) *Combination.* In the case of combination, a moving object collides with another object moving from the opposite direction, and the two become one, its nature somewhere between the natures of the two original objects.

In the *Parmenides* combination is associated with coming to be one, separation with coming to be many (156b4–5).

A couple of questions the answers to which are unclear: Why does a moving object colliding with a stationary one cause one or both of the objects to break apart, rather than combine or simply rebound away from each other (like one billiard ball striking a stationary one), whereas when two objects moving from opposite directions collide, they combine (when one might have a greater expectation here of one or both of them splitting apart)? And what happens when two moving objects collide not head-on—i.e. from opposite directions—but, for instance (to use language alien to Plato), at a 45° or 90° angle? Given what Plato says, it seems that neither separation nor combination would occur. Would the result be deflection? Is that a special kind of motion (and if so, why wasn't it mentioned) or does this simply continue to fall under the general heading of motion in more than one location? Plato does not seem to regard the answers to these questions over detail as important in the present context.

In the *Statesman* Plato says that there are two great arts (*megala . . . techna*) that apply to everything (*kata panta*): combination (*sugkritikê*) and separation (*diakritikê*) (282b6–8). He applies them to the art of weaving (282b1–283a7, see also *Sophist* 226b1–227d1) and to political philosophy (306a1–311c8). In the *Sophist* he also applies them to discourse or speech (*logos*) (259e4–6, 262b1–c7). As Wardy writes (1990; 130–1):

One of the most striking aspects of Plato's exposition of this idea is his confidence that combination and separation are to be discerned everywhere, from wool-working to the intermingling and segregation of social classes to the connections and distinctions between concepts. He never qualifies his claims, and it is quite clear that he does not mean them to be taken metaphorically: these phenomena are universal, and to describe both carding and the sorting out of concepts as 'separation' is to use the word literally and correctly.

In the *Sophist* (226d9–227c9) Plato says that every separation is a kind of purification (*katharmos*), and that purification can be divided into purification of the body and of the soul. There are many kinds of purifications of bodies (*ta peri ta sômata polla eidê katharseôn*): the proper purification of 'the insides of the bodies of living beings' is achieved through gymnastics and medicine, the purification of 'the outsides' through 'the art of bathing'; the purification of inanimate bodies is the task of 'the fuller's art and all of the arts of ordering (*kosmêtikê*)'; by which I take it he means the cleaning of clothes and silverware and furniture and carpets, etc.

But what precisely is Plato talking about in *Laws* 10? What he says in this section may somehow include carding wool, cleaning a carpet, purging a disease, and removing dirt from the body through bathing. Yet one suspects that what he has in mind most of all is the fundamental interaction of matter, at the most basic level. (See Skemp (1942; 102–3).) That this is the case becomes clear in the next section.

d. Growth and decay (893e6–7)
Plato writes: 'when they combine there is growth (*auxanetai*), but when they separate there is decay (*phthinei*), for as long as the established state of each thing (*hê kathestêkuia hekastôn hexis*) remains' (893e6–7).

I take 'the established state of each thing' to refer to a thing's essential nature. So what Plato is saying is that when some x *combines* with something else, *x* can be said to grow, as long as the essential nature of x remains the same. Presumably, Plato is referring primarily to natural growth (e.g. an acorn becoming an oak, a child an adult, a person becoming fatter), though what he says could refer to almost anything that becomes larger while remaining what it is. Similarly,

I take decay to refer to cases in which some material is separated off from x, though not to such an extent that x is destroyed—its 'established state' or essential nature remaining intact (e.g. a man growing bald, an apple *beginning* to rot).

It is instructive at this point to consider Plato's discussions of motion in the *Theaetetus* (181b8–d7) and the *Parmenides* (138b7–c1). In both of these dialogues motion is divided into two kinds: (1) motion in place, which is further divided into (a) circular motion and (b) motion in many places; and (2) alteration (*alloiôsis*), i.e. change of quality. The *Theaetetus* provides the following examples of alteration: 'when something is in the same place, but grows old, or becomes black from white, or hard from soft' (181c8–d2). It is natural to ask how this fits the discussion of motion in *Laws* 10, and, most significantly, why alteration seems to have been left out of the *Laws* 10 discussion.

Motion in one location (circular motion) and motion in many locations clearly correspond to the two kinds of motion in location of the *Theaetetus-Parmenides* account. Now alteration may not appear by name on the list of ten types of motion, but it is there; for the next two pairs in the *Laws* 10 list—combination–separation and growth–decay—are both clearly fundamental types of alteration. Later in *Laws* 10 Plato writes of the primary motions of soul (more on these later): 'taking over the secondary-work motions of bodies, they drive all things to growth and decay, separation and combination, and to what follows these: heat and cold, heaviness and lightness, hard and soft, white and black, bitter and sweet' (897a4–b1). Combination can give rise to growth, separation can give rise to decay, and all of these together lead to alterations—e.g. changes from hot to cold, heavy to light, hard to soft.

e. Generation and destruction (894a1–8)

Alteration is change in quality, to use Aristotelian language; it does not involve or include substantial change. The essential nature of the thing that is undergoing an alteration stays the same. But immediately after saying 'for as long as the established state of each thing remains'

Plato adds: 'but if it doesn't remain, there is destruction (*apollutai*) by means of both'—i.e. both combination and separation (894a1). Combination leads to growth, separation to decay, assuming the essential nature of the thing growing or decaying remains the same. If not—if either a combination or separation causes the essential nature of the object to change—then there is destruction. This is a substantial change.

Plato does not tell us how combination or separation can cause destruction, but I take it he must have something like the following in mind. Separation-destruction is pretty straightforward: It is one thing to lose your hair (balding is a type of separation-alteration); it is quite another to lose your head. Decay *is* separation, and decay naturally leads to, or is a sign of, destruction. The slightly trickier case is destruction through combination, since growth (the opposite of decay) is a kind of combination: If x combines with y, and y's established state or essential nature remains the same, x being subsumed by y, then x has been destroyed by combination. Does Plato still have in mind exclusively a moving object striking another moving object coming from the opposite direction, or would, say, one animal devouring another also count as a case of combination-destruction? Is water that is absorbed by a plant's roots and so becomes part of the plant destroyed?

Having covered destruction, Plato turns to the other, opposite, kind of substantial change: generation.

Now when anything comes into being, what is it that happens? It is clear that when the principle (*archê*), receiving growth (*labousa auxên*), proceeds to the second change, and from this to the next and proceeds as far as the third, it provides perception to perceivers. (894a1–5)

The process, as described, is pretty vague:

The principle 'receives growth' (which is the first change) → the second change → the third change → perceptible object(s).

Plato is clearly not concerned (at least not exclusively) with the generation of living things, but with the more basic formation or generation of physical entities themselves. For in the next line he writes: '*Everything* comes to be by changing and transforming in this way' (894a5–6). He does not specify the generation of plants and animals. And this is not surprising, as generation per se better fits the more general applicability of the types of motion discussed so far.

But what exactly is the nature of the generation that Plato here describes? Most have taken him to be laying out some sort of Pythagorean generation of physical reality ultimately from numbers and other mathematical 'entities'. (For such a Pythagorean account see Diogenes Laertius 8.25.) For instance, England (1921; 2. 466) writes:

> Is the *archê* something or nothing? This description of *genesis* is not meant to be a historical account, but a logical deduction from Plato's doctrine of space. It is a kind of geometrical allegory. Geometry postulates a thing 'without parts or magnitude' (Arist. *Met.* A 992a21 [...]. The *first* transformation by which this grows [...] is its elongation into a (still imaginary) line; the second [...] is the extension flatwise of the imaginary line into an imaginary surface. With the third transformation [...] we pass into the region of sensible objects, for now *thickness* is added to length and breadth; the transformed *archê* 'furnishes perceivers with perception'... (See also Skemp (1942; 105).)

Something of this sort might well be what Plato has in mind, though I don't know if he would claim either that it is a mere logical deduction or that the point, line, and surface are simply imaginary. Aristotle does at various places attribute something resembling this to the Platonists. (See *Metaphysics* A.9.992a10–22, M.8.1984a29–b2, M.9.1085a31–b4, N.3.1090b20–7, and perhaps *De Anima* 1.2.404b16–30.)

On this interpretation, Plato is saying something like the following:

> The principle (a point) 'receives growth' (the first change, the point becomes a line) → the second change (the line becomes a plane) → the third change (the plane becomes a solid) → perceptible object.

This may be the correct approach to understanding this passage. But it is worth considering the possibility that Plato here has in mind basically the same conception of the generation of the four bodies (earth, air, fire, and water) presented in the *Timaeus* (53a2–55c6). (By contrast, Skemp claims that while in general the *Laws* 10 account of motion is 'a convenient recapitulation of what has gone before in the *Timaeus*', this passage (894a1–5) gives us 'something that goes beyond the *Timaeus*' (1942; 97, 104).) According to a 'likely account' (*eikota logon*), as it is called (53d5–6), the craftsman (*dêmiourgos*) takes a number of a certain type of triangle (always with a right angle) and puts them together to make this or that equilateral polygon (a square or triangle), a number of which are put together to make a perfect solid (e.g. a cube or tetrahedron); and with an accumulation of these solids we have perceptible earth, air, fire, or water. The triangle, Plato writes, is 'the principle (*archên*) of fire and of the other bodies' (53d4–5). Here is a sketch of which triangles lead to which shapes and ultimately to which basic bodies. (For a brief discussion of how triangles are put together to make the various perfect solids see Zeyl (2000: pp. lxvi–lxix, 45–7 nn. 62–7). The account in Cornford (1937: 210–19) is also useful. On the precise nature of these perfect solids see Mohr (2006: 117–20).)

Isosceles triangle (sides 1: 1: $\sqrt{2}$) → square → cube → earth
Scalene triangle (sides 1: $\sqrt{3}$: 2) → equilateral triangle → octahedron → air
Scalene triangle (sides 1: $\sqrt{3}$: 2) → equilateral triangle → tetrahedron → fire
Scalene triangle (sides 1: $\sqrt{3}$: 2) → equilateral triangle → icosahedron → water

I think this is consistent with the *Laws* 10 model:

(1) The first change: the principle (a triangle) 'receives growth'; i.e. it is formed from three lines and/or utilized by a soul (the craftsman).
(2) The second change: triangles are put together to form a particular equilateral polygon (a triangle or square), which will become the face of one of the above mentioned solids.

(3) The third change: polygons are put together to make perfect solids.
(4) An accumulation of many perfect solids yields, depending on the type of solid, perceptible earth or air or fire or water.

Take the cube (the simplest example):

(1′) The first change: the principle (a right-angled isosceles triangle with sides 1: 1: $\sqrt{2}$) 'receives growth'; i.e. is put together by the craftsman.
(2′) The second change: two such triangles (of the same size) are put together to form a square. (It is likely that Plato has in mind two triangles here, as that would make the account of the formation of earth better parallel the formation of the other elements; but note that at *Timaeus* 55b3–7 the square is constructed out of *four* such triangles.)
(3′) The third change: six such squares are put together to form a cube.
(4′) Perceptible objects: when enough of these cubes have accumulated, there is earth that can be perceived by the senses.

This interpretation can still be classified as a Pythagorean attempt to build the physical world out of mathematical entities, but one that makes better sense of the text than the 'point → line → plane → solid' interpretation, especially in light of the account in the *Timaeus*.

In the *Timaeus*, after saying that the triangle is the *principle* of earth, air, fire, and water (53d4–5), Plato adds: 'Principles yet more ultimate than these are known only to the gods, and to any man they may hold dear' (53d6–7). This principle, prior to the triangle-principle of the elements, likely refers to self-moving motion and soul (see *Phaedrus* 245c6–e4), and ultimately to (a) god(s) or the demiurge or reason (*nous*). (There may be some connection between these passages from *Laws* 10 and the *Timaeus*, and a very cryptic passage in the *Second Letter* 312d2–313a6.)

Whichever interpretation of this tricky passage is correct, Plato is leading up to the idea that this crucially important form of motion, generation, like all other forms of motion, would be impossible without soul and self-moving motion. But the soul is no part of the first eight (in fact, nine) kinds of motion, and thus was left out of the account of generation—which began with what is, on Plato's account, the most basic principle aside from soul (though if I'm right, soul is implied in the idea of 'the principle obtaining growth').

3. The ninth and tenth (or first and second) kinds of motion
(894a8–e3)
The Athenian temporarily resumes the dialogue with Kleinias, saying that there are two kinds of motion yet to be described: 'those two for the sake of which virtually our entire present investigation is undertaken' (894b3–4). He reminds Kleinias that the present investigation is 'for the sake of soul' (894b6). With this in mind, one kind of motion alone is in fact the focus of Plato's attention—self-motion and its priority to all other kinds, since the whole point is not simply to describe the soul (and the kind of motion characteristic of it) but to demonstrate the *primacy* of soul over body or matter.

These are the remaining kinds of motion:

(9) That motion capable of moving others but incapable of moving itself; it moves by another and is changed by another.
(10) That motion capable of moving itself and others. It is responsible for the change and motion of all beings; it is in harmony with all action (or doing) and all experience (or being done to). It employs the previous eight motions—combination and separation, growth and decay, etc.—in causing other things to move. Finally, as we have seen, it is connected to soul (but it is not yet clear in what way).

The scholiast claims that these two kinds of motion are 'psychic' whereas the other eight are somatic (see Post (1944; 299)). But in fact Skemp is right to consider the ninth kind of motion a 'genus' of which the first eight are each a 'species' (1942; 99) (cf. Lewis (1870; 185) and Stalley (1983; 170)): they are all different kinds of motion that can cause other things to move but which (on Plato's view) cannot themselves initiate their own motion.

On the ninth and tenth motions (soon to be promoted to the second and first respectively) see *Timaeus* 46d7–e2.

Having described the two remaining kinds of motion, Plato next evaluates them (and especially the tenth). He says of self-motion: it is the strongest and the most effective; it excels in myriad ways; all other forms of motion are inferior to it; it is first in generation and in strength. The gist of all of this praise, as we shall see, is that self-motion is (1) the first in generation—nothing could come before it, nothing is prior to it in time or in being—and (2) the most powerful or efficacious, in that qua mover nothing is able to accomplish or move as much. Ultimately, it is responsible for all motion. (Note that this evaluation has yet to be defended.)

In light of this evaluation the Athenian tells Kleinias (and Megillus) that he has made two errors: labeling self-motion tenth (when it should be first) and labeling that motion which is capable of moving others but not itself ninth (when it should be second). This seems a good point to provide, by way of summary, a list of the ten kinds of motion.

1. Self-moving motion
2. Non-self-moving motion
3. Circular motion
4. Motion in many locations
   (a) Gliding
   (b) Rolling
5. Combination
6. Separation
7. Growth
8. Decay
9. Generation
10. Destruction

At 894c7 Plato refers to self-moving motion (before it was promoted) as 'pretty much the tenth' kind of motion; a few lines later, at 894c10, he speaks of the 'approximately ten motions'. (At *Timaeus* 34a2 he says the number of motions is seven.) Why the ambiguity? Perhaps because the ten overlap in various ways (3–10 all fall under 2; the sets of opposites—3 and 4, 5 and 6, 7 and 8—can all refer to the same motion, from different perspectives; see the Hippocratic *Regimen* 1.4). And perhaps there are options as to how to classify the motions—for example, gliding and rolling could each be considered a kind of motion in its own right, or a sub-kind. The point is that the precise number of the different kinds of motion does not matter. What matters is the essential difference between self-moving motion and non-self-moving motion, and especially the *priority* of the former.

894e4–895b8

Two Arguments for the Priority of Self-Moving Motion

1. The first mover argument (894e4–895a4)

If we hold that one thing changes another, and this other yet another, forever, will one of these changes ever be first? And how will that which is moved by another ever be first among the things that are altered? For that's impossible. But when something having moved itself alters another, and this other another, and in this way thousands upon thousands of things being moved come into being, what will be a principle of all of their motions except the change from what has moved itself?   (894e4–895a3)

The first part of the argument rules out the possibility of an infinite regress in the series of causes (i.e. motions or changes). Take a causal series: . . . l → m → n . . . Must there be a first cause? Plato implies or assumes that there must be. (See Stalley (1983; 171–2) and Cleary (2001; 130).) Of course, for many, this is *the* issue. But for Plato the question is not whether there *is* a first cause, but *what* the first cause is. And that brings us to the second part of the argument, the aim of which is to rule out the possibility that the motion that can move others but not itself is the first mover. This is an easy task given the terms of the argument: how can something that is by its nature moved by another be a first mover? So the only possible first cause or mover in the universe is self-moving motion, and thus it is the ultimate cause of the myriad things that come into being.

We can present the argument a bit more formally as follows:

1. There must be a first mover.
2. If there is an infinite regress of motions, then there is no first mover.
3. Therefore, there cannot be an infinite regress or series of motions.
4. The first mover must be either a self-mover or a non-self-mover.
5. The first mover cannot be a non-self-mover.
6. Therefore, the first mover must be a self-mover.

(On this argument see Mohr (2006; 175).)

I find this argument even more unpersuasive than most versions of the cosmological argument, though it is worth comparing to the first two 'Ways' of Thomas Aquinas (see *Summa Theologicae* 1.2.3) and it may have the distinction of being the earliest version of the cosmological argument (if we do not count Kleinias' from early in *Laws* 10). One could respond: (1) Plato cannot simply assume or assert that there is no infinite regress, as that amounts to circular reasoning (see Martin (1990; 97, 99, 102–6)); and (2), looking ahead to the particular self-mover or starting point that Plato has in mind (soul or *nous*), even if it is granted that there must be a starting point—that there cannot be an infinite regress (and certainly not an infinite regress of explanations), as we must begin somewhere—why can't the starting point simply be physical reality and the motions that inhere in physical reality by its very nature? (On this last point cf. Theophrastus, *Metaphysics* 2 (11)). We get Plato's ultimate answer to this question later (895c1–896a5), when he identifies self-moving motion and soul.

2. The argument from a hypothetical standstill (895a5–b7)
Plato immediately presents another argument that seems to address some of the concerns I have raised.

If somehow everything were to come together and stand still, just as most of those men venture to say, which motion of the ones we spoke of would necessarily be the first to come to be among them [i.e. all things]? Surely the one that moves itself. For it ['the one that moves itself' or 'all things'] would never be changed (*metapesê*$_i$) by another that is prior, since there is among them [i.e. all things] no prior change.   (895a6–b2)

For the most part the argument is straightforward: Assume hypothetically that everything (all physical reality) becomes motionless (and assume that the state of rest itself needs no explanation; see Stalley (1983; 171), Cleary (2001; 131), and Mohr (2006; 176)). If that were the case, which type of motion would be the first to begin moving again? Clearly, self-moving motion; for all the other types of motion—all those inhering in physical reality—cannot themselves initiate motion. They could start moving again only if some other motion—the self-moving motion, ultimately—were to move them.

The major textual difficulty here is the subject of *metapesê*$_i$. England claims that it is ultimately 'all things' (*ta panta*): 'The subj. to *metapesê*$_i$ is the *auta* (*autois*) of a8, and that is *ta panta* (a6)' (1921; 2. 471). But I find better and more natural the other possible subject: self-moving motion ('the one that moves itself'). Self-moving motion must be the first to appear, since there is in all of physical reality ('all things') nothing that can initiate change, and certainly not anything that can initiate change prior to the motion of 'the one that moves itself'. Plato takes the argument to show that self-moving motion is prior in time and in being to all other forms of motion and in fact to all of physical reality: it is 'the source of all motions, and the first to come to be among what was standing still and to exist among what moves' (895b3–5).

There are a number of replies that one could make. For example, Plato's opponents could reject the idea that if (*per impossibile*) all motion were stopped it would start again. They could argue that if the natural motions inhering in physical entities (miraculously and impossibly) halted there is in the universe nothing that could start the universe moving again. Or they could reply that there is within every basic constituent of physical reality by its nature a specific capacity for motion and change (i.e. each is in effect a self-mover of sorts), and that therefore the material world could simply begin to move again—once whatever hypothetical miraculous force that stopped things in the first place was withdrawn.

It may have been such possible objections that led Plato to insist that the hypothetical situation behind this argument cannot be considered a fanciful one by his atheistic opponents, since many of them, in their cosmologies, postulate just such a situation. (As far as Plato is concerned, it *is* purely hypothetical, because he does not believe it is possible for everything to come to a complete stop—at least not without everything being destroyed. See *Theaetetus* 153d2–5 and *Phaedrus* 245d8–e2.)

Plato writes that '*most* of those men' (i.e. the atheists or natural philosophers generally) 'venture to say' that all things come together and stand still (895a7). This is strange, because not only does the evidence suggest that most of them do not maintain this, it is difficult to come up with more than one or two who might fit Plato's description.

One possibility might seem to be the Eleatics, who denied the existence of any change (and thus of any movement). There is some similarity in language: Plato writes, 'If somehow everything were to come together and stand still' (*ei staiê pôs ta panta homou genomena*, 895a6), which is comparable to Parmenides DK 28B8.5–6: 'since it is now all together one' (*epei nun estin homou pan hen*). But it is unlikely that Plato had the Eleatics in mind—or if he did, he was off the mark—because they do not claim that all things come to a stop, but that all motion is (and always has been) impossible.

Rather, Plato is no doubt thinking of philosophers who postulated a cyclical cosmology, according to which at some point in the cycle all things come together to form a homogeneous one, at which point motion might be said to temporarily come to a halt. The most plausible candidates are Empedocles and Anaxagoras.

Empedocles believes there is a cycle in which all things—ultimately the four elements (earth, air, fire, and water) and the two forces (Love and Strife)—are constantly moving between the point at which Strife is in total control and there is a complete separation of the four elements, and the point at which Love is in total control and all four elements are completely mixed together. He writes: 'All these never cease continually interchanging, at one time through Love all things going together into one (*Philotêti sunerchomen' eis hen hapanta*), at another time each being moved apart by the hatred of Strife' (DK 31B17.6–8). Further, Empedocles might have held that there is in this cycle a beginning from a standstill. Aristotle reports:

> It is not reasonable to make generation come from [bodies] that are separated and moving. This is why Empedocles sets aside [the possibility of] generation in the time of Love, for he could not have established the heavens by building it out of separated [elements] and making them combine through Love; for the cosmos *is* composed of elements in separation, therefore it must come from what is one and combined.   (*De Caelo* 3.2.301a14–19)

One could argue that according to Empedocles every time the cycle hits the point at which Love is in total control there is no change or motion, and that the generation of different parts of the universe begins again. If this were the case, Empedocles would provide the perfect example of what Plato is talking about. Of course, Empedocles could argue that at the moment Love is in full control motion has not *fully* stopped, because the instant this happens Strife begins to re-exert an influence, and as a result the four elements immediately begin to separate again. But then Plato is objecting to just this idea: that some material force like Strife (if it is a material force) could be the initiator of motion—could be a first mover. (It could do this, on Plato's view, only if it were a 'psychic', rather than a material, force.)

Plato might also be thinking of Anaxagoras, and there is here an even greater similarity of language: Anaxagoras writes 'all things were together' (*homou chrêmata panta ên*, DK 59B1) and 'while all things were together' (*pantôn homou eontôn*, DK 59B4). Further, he believed that there was a time before which the universe was in motion (i.e. was rotating), and it seems to follow that all things were at a standstill and then began to move: 'And reason (*nous*) controlled the whole rotation, so that it began to rotate in the beginning' (DK 59B12). But Anaxagoras attributes the beginning of motion to reason (*nous*), which seems to be precisely what Plato wants to say (whatever Plato's dissatisfaction with Anaxagoras' cosmic *nous*; see *Phaedo* 97b8–98d2). Moreover, it is not at all clear that Anaxagoras thinks there is a *cycle* of coming together and separation, such that all things will once again stand still.

The first mover argument and the argument from a hypothetical standstill should both be considered in conjunction with the argument for the immortality of the soul at *Phaedrus* 245c6–246a2. Mohr (2006; 176–7) argues that both arguments count against the view that according to the *Laws* there was a pre-cosmic flux.

895c1–896a5

The Athenian gets Kleinias to see the relationship between self-moving motion and soul via the concept of living:

(1) Possessing the capacity for self-moving motion is what living is.
(2) Possessing (or being) a soul is what living is.
(3) Therefore, possessing (or being) a soul and possessing the capacity for self-moving motion are identical.
(4) Therefore, soul is the capacity for self-moving motion.

In the course of making this point Plato says that when self-moving motion (or soul) comes to be in earth or water or fire, it (the soul-earth and/or-water and/or-fire combination) is living. And he makes clear, perhaps oddly, that the matter the self-moving motion might reside in can be separate or mixed. It is clear from the Greek that 'separate' or 'mixed' refers to the matter—the earth, water, and fire. So Plato is presumably saying that soul can enter earth 'separated' (i.e. not mixed with anything) or water 'separated' or fire 'separated', or it can enter some mixture of the elements.

Now in the case of mixtures Plato must mean (at least primarily) animals and plants: soul residing in certain combinations of elements. But in implying that soul can reside in fire or earth by itself, he is likely talking about celestial objects: the sun is a huge ball of fire (unmixed?) with soul in it; the moon is a huge ball of earth (unmixed?) with soul in it. Can water—or air, for that matter, which Plato does not mention here—have soul in it? Perhaps it did when soul formed the cosmos originally. Do the tides move regularly because soul is *in* these large bodies of water? Plato does not tell us such things specifically, though he does say that 'all things are full of gods' (899b8), and such a view is certainly consistent with what Plato is arguing here.

Having established the basic logical relationship between soul and self-moving motion, Plato drops 'living' for the time being, and expands on the relationship. To do so, he makes the following distinction:

(1) the name (*onoma*) of the being;
(2) the definition (*logos*) of the being;
(3) the being (*ousia*).

Plato says that we can give the name of something and ask for its definition, or give the definition and ask for the name, and in both cases we are referring to the same being. (See also *Laws* 12.964a6–8.)

The name and the definition are relatively straightforward; the being is the difficult-to-grasp concept. Is Plato referring to particular entities or attributes, the essence of some kind of entity or attribute, the Forms, or what?

Plato provides the following example (which I believe he gives to the Athenian, not Kleinias—see the textual note on 895d8–e8). Take the fact that some numbers, like many other things, can be divided into two equal parts. What are the name, definition, and being of this?

(1) name: 'even';
(2) definition: 'a number divisible into two equal parts' (895e3; cf. Euclid, *Elements* 7 (def. 6));
(3) being: the quality or capacity that some numbers have of being divisible into two equal parts.

In the case of (3) Plato doesn't tell us what the being is, but I believe this is implied. It is what both the name and the definition refer to. For instance, take the number 18. Clearly, the being that has just been named ('even') and defined ('a number divisible into two equal parts') cannot be, say, the eighteen rabbits in my garden; nor is it the number 18 itself (the Form 18, if there is such a thing, or the mathematical—what resides between the Forms and physical existence; see *Republic* 6.510b4–511a2). It must be that in reality to which the name and definition refer: the quality that 18 possesses (and shares with other numbers, like 4 and 632) of being divisible into two equal parts (perhaps the Even Itself, if Plato believes such a Form exists).

Now Plato is not here interested in mathematics, but in soul, to which he applies the above division into name, definition, and being.

(1) name: 'soul';
(2) definition: 'motion capable of moving itself';
(3) being: soul; Soul Itself; the capacity for self motion (?).

The being of soul does not, as I see it, refer (primarily) to *my* soul or *your* soul or the soul responsible for the self-generated movement of the sun, but to the capacity for self-movement itself—such capacity being embodied in you and in me and in (that which moves) the sun. That in reality actually is soul. Of course, we do not yet know what exactly this refers to. Is it the Form of Soul or the essence of soul or an abstraction from all the individual souls, or what? Plato is unclear about this in the *Laws*.

We get some help from the *Seventh Letter* (342a7–e2) in clarifying what Plato is saying. (Recall that the authenticity of the *Seventh Letter* is a subject of debate.) The author writes that for each being (*tôn ontôn hekastôi*), three things are necessary if knowledge of it is to be acquired (items 1–3 below). After laying out these three, he expands the list to include five items that could all be referred to in discussing some being:

(1) name (*onoma*);
(2) definition (*logos*);
(3) image (*eidôlon*);
(4) knowledge (*epistêmê*) (or other cognitive states by which some being is grasped);
(5) the being itself.

He writes: 'fifth one should put (the being) itself (*pempton d' auto tithenai dei*), which is the knowable and truly real being (*ho dê gnôston te kai alêthôs estin on*)' (342a8–9).

Here, too, an example is provided from mathematics.

(1) name: 'circle';
(2) definition: 'the figure whose extremities are everywhere equally distant from its center' (cf. *Parmenides* 137e1–3 and *Timaeus* 33b2–7, and Euclid, *Elements* 1 (def. 15));
(3) image: drawing of a circle (which can be rubbed out) or round object turned on a lathe (which can be destroyed);
(4) knowledge (*epistêmê*) and reason (*nous*) and true opinion (*alêthês doxa*) concerning circles;
(5) the circle itself (*autos ho kuklos*).

He says that images are unlike the circle in that they can be destroyed whereas the circle itself cannot. He also says that the first three items all refer to the circle itself. (All of this language strongly suggests that the circle itself is the Form of Circle.) Of the items in (4), he writes that they do not exist in words (as in 1 or 2) nor in physical shapes (as in 3) but in souls. The fact that they exist in souls also sets them apart from 'the nature of the circle itself' (*auto tou kuklou tês phuseôs*) which is not soul- or mind-dependent. Of the three items in (4), reason is closest to (5) and true opinion furthest from it.

The author of the *Seventh Letter* meant this set of distinctions to apply to all beings (see 342d3–e2), and so (if the author was Plato or accurately represents the views of Plato) it applies to our case in *Laws* 10, i.e. to soul. In speaking of the name, definition, and being of soul, Plato is giving us items 1, 2, and 5 from the *Seventh Letter* list. We are not given an image of soul, perhaps because it is not possible for people like Kleinias and Megillus to obtain knowledge of soul (not to mention grasp it with reason), which Plato states emphatically requires items 1–3. What Plato can lead Kleinias and Megillus to is, at best, right opinion about soul, and ultimately about the gods. (The legislators of Magnesia, I take it, can expect to lead most Magnesians at least this far.)

Finally, applying the scheme from the *Seventh Letter* to the discussion in *Laws* 10 of the name and definition of soul implies that the being in the latter is soul itself (not any particular ensouled being)—this is no surprise. But could it be the Form of Soul?

896a5–d4

The discussion of the definition of soul constitutes a sufficient demonstration of the priority of soul; i.e. that soul is 'the first generation and motion of what exists, what has come to be, and what will be, and further of all of their opposites' (896a6–8). Soul generates or brings into existence the rest of existence (this will have to be qualified somewhat), and, as a corollary of this, it is the first mover. As first cause and mover, it is responsible not only for what has come into being and is coming into being, but for everything yet to be.

What does Plato mean in adding 'and their opposites'? The opposites of (1) what exists, (2) what has come to be, and (3) what will be, are: (1′) what is going out of existence (rather than what does not exist, which doesn't make sense), (2′) what has gone out of existence, and (3′) what will go out of existence. (See England (1921; 2. 473–4).) As we have seen, soul is the first mover or cause behind all motion, including decay and destruction.

There is an important ambiguity behind much of the discussion, here and elsewhere, of the priority of soul. Does Plato hold that soul is absolutely prior to everything, including reason (*nous*) and the Forms? Skemp even claims: 'The question that Plato in *Laws* X neither answers nor encourages young men to ask is whether the ultimate *archê kinêseôs* [principle of motion] is *psuchê* or *nous*' (1942; 108) (his own views on these issues are found in his ch. 8). This is very unlikely, though what precisely the relationship is between soul and *nous* is unclear (but see Menn (1995; chs. 4, 6)). Plato's main concern in the *Laws* is to demonstrate the priority of soul to matter or body; but is soul in fact prior to all material things and even to matter itself? One might think the answer is 'yes'; but a more precise answer—especially if what he says in the *Timaeus* is applicable here—is: soul is prior to all material things, and to matter insofar as it has any qualities at all (motions, length, width, strength, etc.) and is not simply the pure potentiality of the receptacle of the *Timaeus* (see 48e2–51b6, 52d4–53b5). Nothing Plato says in *Laws* 10 rules out such a doctrine, though he does not explicitly present such a view.

Kleinias agrees with the Athenian on the priority of soul ('perhaps slightly overshooting the mark', Menn (1995; 37)), stating that soul is the *oldest* of all things, being (or having come to be, *genomenê*) the principle (*archê*) of motion. (They had said that soul is *older* than body; see 892a7–b1, 896a5–7.) The aorist participle *genomenê* can and probably does—in this context, coming from Kleinias—simply mean 'being' (rather than 'having come to be'), though Plato leaves open the idea that soul, too, has come to be. (See Hackforth (1965; 441–2.) Later, the Athenian says that 'soul has come to be [*gegonenai* (perfect active infinitive)] prior to body' (896c1–2).)

After soul, the self-moving motion, is 'the motion that comes to be in one thing because of another, but that itself never causes anything to move by itself' (896b5–7). It is 'second, or however many numbers farther down someone would wish to count it' (896b7–8). This confirms that the second item in the list of motions is or includes all of the other motions (nos. 3–10), for they are all motions that come to be in something—some body—on account of something else (another body or, ultimately at least, on account of soul or *nous*). This secondary motion is a change of soulless or inanimate (*apsuchou*) body. Physical matter or body itself is not capable of self-moving motion.

Plato next makes the following inference: soul is prior to body temporally and logically; therefore, soul is prior to body with respect to rule: 'soul rules, while body is ruled, according to nature' (896c2–3). One could object that this inference is invalid; after all, Alexander the Great was younger (i.e. not prior in time) to myriad people that he ruled. But I believe Plato's unstated argument would have been something like this: soul brings the physical world into existence, and moves and shapes physical reality, and not the other way around; so in that sense soul can be said to rule body—it 'governs' the nature of the physical world.

I take 'according to nature' to refer to the idea that since by nature soul is prior to body in time and in being, so it rules over body by nature. And, whereas Alexander the Great's rule over massive numbers of people (many of them older and wiser) is rule by force and not by nature, by nature the older should rule over the younger, even among humans. (See *Laws* 3.690a7–8, b4–5.)

The next inference Plato makes is (more) dubious. He in effect argues as follows:

1. Soul is older than body.
2. Therefore, 'the things of the soul [are] older than the things of the body' (896c6–7).

He provides the following examples: 'Habits, moral characteristics, wishes, calculations, true opinions, supervision, and memory would have come into being prior to length of bodies, width, depth, and strength' (896c9–d3).

Plato appears to commit the fallacy of division (claiming that what is true of the whole or group must therefore be true of every part of the whole or member of the group), for he seems to be arguing as follows:

1. Soul is older than or prior to body.
2. Therefore, every part or aspect or manifestation of soul is older than or prior to every part or aspect or manifestation of body.

For even if one accepted the claim that soul is temporally prior to body—that some conscious self-mover and cosmic orderer existed prior to the formation of the cosmos—it would not follow that memory, say, and supervision and moral characteristics must *all* exist prior to the coming to be of bodies. Plato has given us no reason to think that these could not and did not come to be only alongside or after the appearance of certain physical entities—i.e. animals and especially humans. In any case, he assumes that the gods have such attributes.

I expect Plato would respond to this objection by claiming that if soul *is* prior to body then at least some functions of soul (e.g. the most essential) would have to be prior to the essential attributes of the body. Further, though he should not simply assume that every function of soul must exist prior to the attributes of body, he could confidently conclude (given the prior discussion) that surely *reason* must be one such essential attribute and that that could account for some of 'the things of the soul' that he mentions.

If Plato is guilty of the fallacy of division, this is not some trivial logical slip. For if he cannot mend the gap in his reasoning then his attempt to argue not only that there are gods but that they care about humans and are just—the core of his refutation of deism and traditional theism—is undercut.

896d5–e7

The Athenian next argues that since soul is 'the cause of all things' (896d8) it must necessarily be the cause of the good and the evil and all such evaluative sets of opposites. His point is not as facile as this might sound. His main concern is not that the soul is the cause of all things and therefore obviously of good and bad things. Rather, he is employing the point he made in the previous section; namely, that as soul is prior to body, so are the things of the soul (including moral characteristics) prior to physical characteristics.

It is somewhat surprising to hear that soul is the cause not only of good things, but of things that are bad or vicious or evil (*tôn kakôn*) (cf. *Republic* 3.379c2–7). We soon learn that soul is the cause of the good by having reason (*nous*, 897b1, c4), and the cause of the bad by lacking reason (*anoia*, 897b3, 898b9). Plato seems here to be primarily concerned with cosmic good and evil: good and evil as they are found in the universe generally, including the movements of the heavenly bodies. Carone (1994; 288–90), however, argues that evil soul is found not (or not primarily) in the cosmos but in humans.

Plato discusses these same or related issues in other later works (see especially *Theaetetus* 176a5–b8, *Timaeus* 47e3–48b3, and *Statesman* 269c4–270a8), and his views as stated in *Laws* 10 are in some respects similar. But his discussion here is unique in claiming that the cause of the evil or bad is *soul*. In the *Theaetetus* the good is said to be with the gods, whereas evil has a mortal nature and hovers around 'this place' (i.e. earth). In the *Timaeus* the good is associated with reason (*nous*) whereas the bad is associated with necessity (*anagkê*). And in the *Statesman* the good, orderly movements of the universe are the result of divine guidance, whereas the bad, disorderly (or backward) movements are the result of god letting go, and are associated with the nature of body (*sômatos phusis*, 269d6–7). It is interesting that in the *Statesman* the Eleatic Stranger (the main speaker) says that 'one must not say . . . that two gods turn it [the cosmos] whose thoughts are opposed to each other' (269e8–270a2).

On the debate over how (or whether it is possible) to reconcile the *Laws* 10 view that soul is 'the cause of all things' (896d8)—'the cause of all change and of motion in all things' (896b1–2; cf. 891e5–6)—with the *Timaeus-Statesman* view that there exists disorderly motion not caused by soul see Vlastos (1995*b*), Easterling (1967), Clegg (1976), and Mohr (2006; ch. 8). Aristotle was perhaps the first to see that something was amiss (see *Metaphysics* 12.6.1071b37–1072a3).

The next point Plato makes is that 'since soul manages and resides in all things that anywhere are in motion', it follows that 'it also manages the heavens' (896d10–e2). He argues as follows:

1. For anything that is in motion, soul resides in it and manages it.
2. The heavens are in motion.
3. Therefore, soul manages the heavens.

The problem is Premise 1. Plato has (claimed to have) proved that soul is the source of all motion and is prior to body; but it does not follow from this that soul (a) resides in and (b) manages anything in motion. With respect to (a) Plato in fact will later leave open whether soul resides in or has some other relationship with the sun (898e8–899a4). And with respect to (b) Plato claims to have demonstrated that the soul is the source of motion. But does this imply that soul *manages* all things that move?

This is important for the case that Plato later wants to make against the deist. The deist claims that the gods do not care about human beings. Contra deism, Plato is going to try to show not only that there is a god, but that god is good and manages the heavens accordingly. Plato has not made this case yet, and doesn't do so here. But he could argue as follows:

1. Soul is the cause of all motion.
2. Soul is the cause of all orderly motion.
3. To the extent that there is orderly motion in the heavens, soul can be said to manage the heavens.
4. Therefore, soul manages the heavens.

As Merlan notes (1960; 94), 'soul' in the singular occurs twenty-two times in *Laws* 10.891c–896d (see his n. 34 for a list). In light of this, the following sudden question from the Athenian is surprising: 'One soul or more than one?' The Athenian answers for both of them: 'More'. That is to say, 'no fewer than two' (896e4–5). But he does not give up on his use of the singular 'soul' (see 896e8, 897b1). I think this shows that it is relatively unimportant for Plato (in this context) whether we say that there are two (or more) souls. As England correctly points out (1921; 2. 475):

In the course of innumerable discussions to which this passage has given rise this *aitia kakias* [cause of evil] has been called a 'world-soul,' and has even been raised to the dignity of a full-blown Devil. Such titles are seriously misleading, and are at variance with the context and drift of the passage.

Who has raised the cause of evil 'to the dignity of a full-blown Devil'? Arguably Plutarch: see *On the Generation of the Soul in the Timaeus* 6–7 (*Moralia* 1014d–1015f), and *Isis and Osiris* 48 (*Moralia* 370e–371a).

Merlan writes: ' "One soul", "two souls, one good, another evil", "one soul good, many evil ones", "many good souls, one evil", "many good and many evil souls"—all this is incomparably less important than the priority of the "psychical" over the physical' (1960; 95). Whether 'soul' is used in the singular (sometimes with reason, as a cause of good; sometimes without reason, as a cause of evil) or the plural (soul-with-reason and soul-without-reason) is mere terminology. The important point is that soul or souls is or are the cause of good and evil and other such evaluative sets of opposites. (On the different ways of conceiving of evil soul in *Laws* 10 see Carone (1994; 283–8).) But behind good soul(s) is reason (*nous*), and, as Menn stresses, 'what is certainly one is *nous*, the virtue that the celestial soul or souls possess' (1995; 18).

Finally, why does the Athenian answer for both Kleinias and Megillus? Probably because the questions, and the answers to them, are beyond their intellectual abilities.

896e8–897b6

After raising, in the previous section, the issue of the number of souls—and establishing that there are at least two—Plato immediately returns to the singular *psuchê* (896e8) which, as England points out, refers to ' "soul," "psychic force"—not "*a* soul" ' (1921; 2. 476) (see also Lewis (1870; 32)). This underscores that how we count the souls in the universe is not terribly important.

Plato wants to present in more detail the way in which soul is prior to body, and specifically the way in which the motions of soul are prior to the motions of body. Soul wishes, investigates, cares for or supervises (*epimeleisthai*, 897a1), deliberates, believes, rejoices, etc., and in so doing directs all things in the universe. These are the 'primary-work motions' (*prôtourgoi kinêseis*, 897a4)—the motions of soul, which have priority over bodily motions in ordering the universe. (Note that *prôtourgoi* is *hapax legomenon*.) As we have seen, such motions are those associated with 'the things of the soul'; namely, 'Habits, moral characteristics, wishes, calculations, true opinions, supervision, and memory' (896c9–d1).

Plato is not denying that physical bodies have powers or motions that inhere in them by their natures (see 889b5–6). Bodies have potentials, including potential motions, that limit what soul can do with and to them. 'Not even the gods can fight against necessity' (Simonides fr. 4 Diehl). Plato quotes or paraphrases this line at least four times (*Laws* 5.741a4–5; 7.818a7–b3, d8–e2; *Protagoras* 345d5). What Plato denies is that physical bodies can *initiate* motions and ultimately explain the order in the universe. Bodies can do work, but it is a secondary kind of work. They can be moved, and thereby move other things, and their natures determine in part how they move and are moved (and how they move other things). But bodies cannot initiate their own movements, or sustain them or direct them. (Plato coins another term to describe *these* motions: 'secondary-work [*deuterourgous*] motions' (897a4–5). *Deuterourgous* too is *hapax legomenon*.)

It makes sense to view the primary-work motions as forms or manifestations of self-motion—the first motion in the list of ten described earlier—whereas the secondary-work motions are forms of the second motion on the list: non-self-moving motion (the capacity to move others but not oneself). The primary-work motions 'take over' (*paralambanousai*, 897a5) and make use of the secondary-work motions of bodies, and thereby direct all of the natural processes that occur in the world (which are described by the other eight motions on the list)—the examples he gives here being growth and decay, and separation and combination (897a6). In so doing, soul causes and directs the physical qualities that appear in the world: 'heat and cold, heaviness and lightness, hard and soft, white and black, bitter and sweet' (897a7–b1). Soul makes use of these qualities too for its purposes as it manages the universe.

Much is unclear here, especially the precise meaning of 'take over' and the nature of the secondary-work motions (or that in reality on which they are based) *before* the primary-work motions put them to use. (For contrasting views see Easterling (1967) and Mohr (2006; 177–80).) But I think Plato must have something like the following in mind. Consider fire. It has the nature it does, including the kind of motion it is capable of. Fire heats and burns (those are kinds of motion), and given its nature it can cause things to melt, steam, boil, topple, flee, etc. But fire cannot come into being on its own. As we have seen, soul must (using reason and choice and a desire for the good, etc.—all primary motions of the soul) put together scalene triangles (sides 1: $\sqrt{3}$: 2) to form equilateral triangles, and equilateral triangles to form tetrahedrons, which go to make up fire. Further, bits of fire could not on their own have massed together to form the sun, and then move about the earth in a regular orbit, at just the right distance and the right speed to produce the beneficial seasons, etc. Soul is required for all of this, but it does all of this with fire, which has the properties it does (in some sense independently of soul).

One peculiarity in the list of the primary-work motions is a set of opposites: 'believing correctly and falsely' (897a2). This set is clearly connected to the idea that there are at least two souls: one the cause of the good, the other the cause of the evil. Soul that is good will believe correctly, soul that is evil will believe falsely. The following pairs are more complex: 'rejoicing and feeling pain, being bold and feeling fear, hating and loving' (897a2–3). Unlike the 'believing correctly'/'believing falsely' pair, it is not the case that good soul will always rejoice, be bold, and love, whereas evil soul will always feel pain and fear and hate. For example, good soul will rejoice or feel pain where that is rational, while bad soul will in each case do the opposite.

Plato proceeds to tell us the difference between good soul and bad soul. Soul with reason (*nous*) 'guides all things toward what is correct and happy', whereas soul without reason (*anoia*) 'produces in all things the opposite of these', i.e. what is incorrect and unhappy (897b1–4). I assume that correctness and happiness at the cosmic level have something to do with orderliness of motion and everything being for the best or with a view to the best, as defined by reason, whereas incorrectness and unhappiness mean the opposite. Plato believes all of this will have some connection to correctness and happiness at the human level as well.

In describing good soul—soul with reason—Plato writes the following cryptic words: *theon orthôs theois*, which I have rendered ' "god" correctly for the gods' (897b2) (see the textual note on 897b2). I speculate that what Plato is saying is that reason (*nous*) is correctly called 'god' when it refers to the soul-with-*nous* that directs the cosmos. Take for example the sun (which is traditionally thought to be a god—in fact, the chorus of Sophocles' *Oedipus Tyrannus* calls it 'the foremost god of all the gods', 660–1; cf. *Laws* 12.950d2–3). The sun itself can be called 'god', but so can the *nous* or soul-with-*nous* that directs the sun; and in fact it is most correct to use 'god' in this latter case (cf. 886d6–7 and 899a7–10). (On the broad use of the term 'god' in the *Laws* see Hackforth (1965; 440).) *Nous* is what makes the gods gods. If reason is 'god' when it is applied to (what are traditionally thought to be) gods, when should reason *not* be called or considered 'god'? When it refers to the reason of an individual human. A human soul with *nous* is not a god, though at its best it may be called godlike or said to be acting like a god (see *Laws* 4.716c1–d4, *Theaetetus* 176a5–b2, *Republic* 10.613a7–b1, Annas (1999), and Sedley (2000)).

I think Morrow correctly identifies the key ambiguity in *Laws* 10 (and elsewhere) about the relationship between reason (*nous*), soul, and god:

Nous, or Reason, is the prime factor in the ordering of the world—so Plato declares both in the *Timaeus* and in the *Laws* (966e)—and this is in the highest sense the divine. On the other hand, Nous can only function as a cause operating in the world when in alliance with a soul. Whether Plato's God, then, is thought of as impersonal Reason, or as a soul in which reason operates with a supremacy impossible to any created soul, is a question that we cannot answer with certainty. (1960; 483–4)

Menn (1995), in part building on Hackforth (1965), offers some powerful arguments for the view that for Plato reason (*nous*) *is* the prime factor in the ordering of the world (to use Morrow's language), though it makes use of souls as mediators in this ordering.

Reason, or soul-with-reason, is at the cosmic level a god. Soul-without-reason does exist in humans, to be sure, but does it exist at the cosmic level, and if so, what is it? Plato entertains this possibility in the next section, though in the end he seems to hold that such a thing does not exist. As I explained in the previous section of the commentary, he does not have in mind anything like a Devil.

897b7–898c9

Plato has established that soul moves the cosmos and all that is in it, and that there are different kinds of soul—good and bad. The next question is: 'which kind of soul (*psuchês genos*) should we claim is in control of the heavens and earth and the whole cycle?' (897b7–8). Carone takes this as evidence for her view that there is no evil cosmic soul: 'It is clear from the argument at 896d–898c that an evil cosmic kind of soul was just a mere *hypothesis*, which Plato posed as an alternative to the good soul at the beginning, but only to reject it' (1994; 289). I think it is possible, but not certain, that this reading is correct. Again, Plato is simply not clear.

I take 'the whole cycle' (*pasês tês periodou*, 897b8) to refer to what Plato will soon call 'the entire (*sumpasa*) course and movement of the heavens and of all the beings therein' (897c3–4). The alternative between good and evil soul is described as follows: 'The one prudent and full of virtue, or that which possesses neither' (897b7–8). Plato often connects prudence (*phronêsis*) with reason (*nous*) (for examples, see Menn (1995; 16)).

What follows is especially difficult terrain, and Plato underscores the strong lead that the Athenian will be taking throughout this section:

AS: Do you want us to answer these questions as follows?

K: How?

AS: We should say: . . . (897c1–3)

And the Athenian proceeds to answer for them.

Plato believes that whether the movements of the heavens as a whole and of the celestial objects taken individually are the product of good soul or bad soul should be decided as follows: If such motion has the same nature as the motion of reason (*nous*), then one ought to conclude that the best soul 'supervises the whole cosmos' (897c6–7). But if the heavens move 'in a frantic and disorderly way' (897d1) we should conclude that this motion is the result of the evil soul.

This sounds pretty straightforward, as if all that were involved were the strict application of some standard. And it would be straightforward if not for the difficulty of answering the question: 'what nature does the motion of reason have?' (897d3). The Athenian says: 'This question, friends, is difficult to answer prudently, which is why taking me on now to help with your answer is just' (897d3–5). (England takes 'to answer prudently' to mean 'to describe with complete understanding' or 'with scientific accuracy' (1921; 2. 477). Morrow believes this would ultimately require a discussion of the mathematics and astronomy of Eudoxus and Archytas, which is beyond the comprehension of Kleinias and Megillus (1960; 482–3).) But whether because this issue is difficult per se, or difficult to explain to men like Megillus and Kleinias, the Athenian says they should not try to answer the question directly, which he compares to 'looking into the sun' (897d8–9). (On the difficulty of looking at the sun being analogous to certain kinds of cognitive problems or limitations see *Republic* 7.515d9–516a3.) So instead of discussing the motion of reason, 'they' will discuss an image (*eikona*) of the motion of reason (or the motion of an image of reason). (For Aristotle's criticism of this sort of analogy see *De Anima* 1.3.407a2–32.)

This of course is reminiscent of the Sun Analogy at the beginning of *Republic* 6 (505d1–e5). Socrates, Adeimantus, and Glaucon have reached the point where it is time to discuss the Form of the Good and how it is grasped. But that is impossible—at least for Adeimantus and Glaucon—and so Socrates suggests that they instead discuss an 'offspring of the Good', namely the sun, and how it is perceived. This, we are told, is analogous to the Form of the Good and the mind's grasp of it. In *Laws* 10, however, I think the connection between reason and its image (more on that shortly) is closer or more direct than is the connection in *Republic* 6 between the Form of the Good and the sun.

So what is the image of reason (or the motion of reason)? The Athenian says we must look to the list of ten motions produced earlier. Again, he underscores the limitations of Megillus and Kleinias: 'I'll come up with our common answer' (897e6).

Note that in much of what follows (from 897e11–898b9) Plato uses—apparently interchangeably—two kinds of word for motion (*kin-* words and *pher-* words). I have not distinguished between them in my translation.

The Athenian quickly isolates two of the ten kinds of motion: motion in one location (i.e. circular motion) and motion in many locations. (See the above commentary on 893c5–e1.) Since circular motion is necessarily moving 'around some midpoint', like a wheel turning on a lathe, it must have 'the greatest possible kinship and likeness to the orbit of reason' (898a3–6). Why? Because, Plato claims, reason and circular motion have a number of significant characteristics in common (898a7–b1). They each move:

(1) in relation to the same things/according to what is the same (*kata tauta*);
(2) in the same way (*hôsautôs*);
(3) in the same place (*en tô; autô;*);
(4) around the same things (*peri ta auta*);
(5) toward the same things (*pros ta auta*);
(6) according to one formula (*logon*) and one order (*taxin*).

When confronted with this list Kleinias says: 'What you say is most correct' (898b5). But this reveals more about his intellectual limitations than it does about his wisdom. For there are at least two basic and difficult interpretive questions regarding this list: How should we apply it to the circular motion (or axial rotation) of a sphere? (In fact, this could apply to the motion of any round object, like a wheel, around a midpoint or central axis, but it is clear that Plato is most interested in the motion of a sphere about its axis, as this has the most applicability when discussing the motion of the cosmos generally.) And how should we apply it to the motion of reason? Unfortunately, Plato gives us few leads with which to answer these questions.

We begin with motion in one location, i.e. circular motion or axial rotation. (The best discussion of this to date is Lee (1976; 74–6).) Let us look at each characteristic in turn, as it applies to motion in one place.

(1) moves in relation to the same things

With most translators, I take this to refer to regularity or uniformity generally. Plato begins with a basic characteristic: regularity as opposed to irregularity. As Lee describes it: 'The main sense is probably that it proceeds at the same steadfast and unvarying rate, without stops or starts or interruptions; however, uniformity in all conceivable respects is probably also connoted by these words [i.e. *kata tauta*] (especially as they are intensified by the following feature), the other items [i.e. 2–6] picking out various aspects of this pervasive uniformity' (1976: 74). Cf. *Timaeus* 36c2–3.

(2) moves in the same way

This is not so much an intensification of #1 (as Lee claims) as it is an implication. For this refers to one form of the regularity of circular motion: it *always* moves in a circular motion. That is, the circular motion or motion in one place is not one part or stage of the motion. Lee thinks that what is being emphasized here is the fact that this motion moves 'in the same way throughout'—i.e. throughout the sphere (1976; 74)—and he may be on to something. Plato's point could be that not only is the sphere, say, itself moving in a circular motion around a midpoint or axis, so is every part of the sphere. If this is Plato's point, it makes #2 less facile than it otherwise would be.

(3) moves in the same place

This immediately suggests motion around some one point or axis, but as that seems to be the main sense of #4, Plato most likely has something else in mind. Lee suggests—correctly, I think—that

Plato is referring here to motion 'within the same limits', which
'rules out such cases as the spinning of a square' (1976; 74).
The midpoint or axis itself is fixed, so the spinning sphere (or
wheel or whatever) is not moving through space (beyond its own
dimensions). Lee says pretty much the same thing, but then adds,
oddly: 'Nonetheless, the present requirement does not in fact entail
that the body should be turning at a fixed point in space, as
Timaeus 40A6–B2 is sufficient to show; there each star's rotary
motion around its own axis is described as motion *en tautô$_i$*, even
though all these bodies are also given a second, lateral (or 'forward')
motion through the heavens' (1976; 75). But I think that the
perfect case—the one Plato is comparing to reason—is one that
does not move through space (i.e. 'laterally' through the heavens),
and this applies only to the spherical motion of the entire cosmos
itself. The other celestial objects are imperfect instances of this kind
of motion, as they move in the same place (around an axis) *and*
through space.

(4) moves around the same things

Plato makes explicit what has been clear all along, that circular
motion is constant motion around one point or axis. Lee suggests
that Plato made this explicit to connect 'the spatial use of the
prepositional *peri* (turning about or around the same point) with
the intentional or cognitive use of the preposition (thinking about
the same topic[. . .])' (1976; 76). In other words, Plato is looking
with one eye on the application of these characteristics to the motion
of reason.

(5) moves toward the same things

Plato probably means that what is moving moves constantly in the
same direction. It does not switch direction in moving around its
axis. Again, this is another manifestation of the general regularity
described in #1. He might also have in mind always having the
same goals, though I'm not quite sure what that would mean in this
context.

(6) moves according to one formula and one order

Lee maintains that this point adds 'nothing substantial to Plato's previous specifications of his physical analogue for *nous*' (1976; 76). But it is likely that Plato does intend some further specification of the general regularity already discussed; for instance, he may be referring to the specific dimensions of the spherical object and the speed at which it moves around its axis. More deeply, although this is a physical analogue for the motion of reason, Plato may be reminding us of the ultimate source of such *logos* and *taxis*, namely soul, which is prior to body. So perhaps Plato is here pointing ahead to the purpose or goal of some instance of circular motion—or to the fact, as he sees it, that such motion always has a purpose or goal, which is evident owing precisely to the order and formula and regularity generally. (But see Lee (1976; 78).)

We must now try to take this list and apply or compare it to the motion of reason. (See Lee (1976; 77–84), though he is less useful here—understandably, as these are murkier waters.) Dorothea Frede (2002: 91) notes: 'In his argument he assumes an analogy, not an identity, between the rotation of the heavens and the procedure of reason. Where the *Timaeus* postulates an identity between the two processes the *Laws* takes care to establish a mere resemblance (897e: *eikôn*).' This is essentially how the *Timaeus* connects reason and circular motion: 'He [i.e. the demiurge] bestowed two movements upon each of them [i.e. the gods]: one was motion in the same place (*en tautô$_i$*) and in relation to the same things (*kata tauta*), by which they would always think the same things (*ta auta*) about the same things (*peri tôn autôn*)' (40a7–b1). Cf. Xenophon, *Memorabilia* 4.4.6–7, according to which Socrates always says the same things (*ta auta*) about the same things (*peri tôn autôn*), whereas Hippias never says the same things about the same things—instead he always tries to say something new (*kainon ti*).

The above tells us that whatever else we can say about the application of the list to the motion of reason, it must involve constantly thinking the same thoughts about the same things.

(1) moves in relation to the same things

By analogy with the previous list, this refers to regularity in general—though here the regularity is cognitive or 'noetic', not physical. The *Timaeus* passage just quoted suggests that 'in relation to the same things' (*kata tauta*) has something to do with the content of reason, but it is unclear what, as the object of reason is dealt with in #4 below.

(2) moves in the same way

This is hard to discern, though it would seem to refer to the fact, as Plato sees it, that reason involves one, unchanging form of noetic or cognitive or psychical motion. Further, by analogy with the previous list, perhaps Plato believes that reason is always the same and the same throughout; though what exactly that would mean I am not sure. Perhaps the point is that ultimately, or at its best, *nous* involves an immediate intuitive grasp, not requiring or mediated by any deductive or inductive processes.

(3) moves in the same place

Further manifestation or explication of the regularity of reason. What reason knows, understands, apprehends, and thinks does not change. And the objects of reason do not change.

(4) moves around the same things

This refers to the *objects* of reason (whatever they may be), and to the fact that they never change. Just as the sphere of the entire world, for example, moves forever and always around the same axis, so reason thinks always of the same thing.

(5) moves toward the same things

I'm not sure what Plato has in mind here. What would it mean for reason not to change direction, other than that it does not start thinking different thoughts and/or about different things, or in some other way become irregular. Plato's intention could be to stress that reason is consistent in its 'motion' and never does what is irrational, or changes its mind (so to speak). Perhaps Plato means that reason always has the same goals (e.g. the goodness of the cosmos), though I'm not quite sure what precisely this would mean.

(6) moves according to one formula and one order

Plato is here claiming that reason always moves (i.e. acts cognitively) in a way that is rational and with a view to what is good or correct or best. Reason is the establisher of *logos* and *taxis* par excellence.

So much of this is speculative, because Plato is not concerned with articulating all of the details of the nature of reason and how it functions, but with showing that good soul—i.e. soul associated with reason—and not its opposite, is responsible for the motion of the heavens. This is why Plato next turns, without seeming to care about loose ends, to the motion 'akin to complete lack-of-reason' (*anoias... hapasês*, 898b9). Such motion, he writes (898b6–9), *never* moves:

(1) in the same way (*hôsautôs*) (corresponds to #2 on the other list);
(2) in relation to the same things/according to the same (*kata ta auta*) (corresponds to #1 on the other list);
(3) in the same place (*en tautô_i*) (corresponds to #3 on the other list);
(4) around the same things (*peri tauta*) (corresponds to #4 on the other list);
(5) toward the same things (*pros tauta*) (corresponds to #5 on the other list);
(6) in one place (*en heni*) (not part of the other list, as this is a defining feature of that motion);
(7) in an arrangement (*en kosmô_i*) or in an order (*en taxei*) or in some formula (*en tini logô_i*) (corresponds to #6 on the other list).

That this list does not match the order of the other two may be Plato's (mildly humorous) way of indicating the disorder represented by this kind of motion.

A motion that never moves in any of these ways is not one of the ten kinds of motion mentioned earlier. It is a haphazard mix of all or some of them. For such a motion is completely erratic and chaotic. What does this imply about complete lack-of-reason? That it is inconsistent, irregular, contradictory, lacking in focus and lacking in sense—in other words, completely irrational. Reason is the opposite.

The Athenian reminds Kleinias and Megillus that they have already demonstrated the priority of the soul: particularly, that soul 'leads everything around' (898c2)—including the orbit of the heavens. The question now is, Which soul leads everything around: the best (that which possesses reason) or the opposite (that which lacks reason)? But by this point in the dialogue the answer seems pretty obvious: good soul. Kleinias responds: 'it isn't pious to say anything other than that soul—one or more—having complete virtue leads things around' (898c6–8). The answer is obvious because the universe is orderly, consistent, predictable, and not erratic or disorderly—cosmos, not chaos. There is implied here a sort of argument from design.

It is worth noting a connected passage from the Platonic work *Epinomis* (which is probably not by Plato, but may be close in time to the *Laws*, and is, as its title indicates, an addendum to the *Laws*):

When soul reaches the best decision in accordance with the best reason (*noun*), the result, which is truly according to reason, is perfectly unalterable. Not even adamant could ever be mightier or more unalterable. Truly, three Fates preserve whatever has been decided through the best counsel by each of the gods, and guarantee that it is brought to pass. Humans should admit as evidence of the reason [or rationality, *noun*] of the stars and this entire movement of theirs, the fact that they always do the same things, because they are doing what was decided an astonishingly long time ago and do not change their decision back and forth, sometimes doing one thing and at others doing something else, wandering (*planasthai*) and changing their orbits. This opinion of ours is the exact opposite of what most people believe—that because [the stars] do the same things and in the same way they do not possess soul. The crowd has followed the fools in supposing that the human race is intelligent (*emphron*) and alive because it undergoes change, whereas the divine is unintelligent because it remains in the same orbits. But in fact anyone could have adopted views that are finer and better and dearer, and could have understood that whatever always acts in relation to the same things (*kata tauta*), in the same way (*hôsautôs*) and because of the same things (*dia tauta*), is because of this to be regarded as intelligent. Such a person could also understand that this is the nature of the stars, the finest of all things to behold, and further that moving through their march and dance, the finest and most magnificent dance there is, they bring to pass what all living things need. (982b8–e6, trans. from Cooper (1997), rev.)

The implication is that it is obvious that the cosmos moves in a way more like circular motion than it does erratically—rationally, not irrationally.

Why doesn't Plato say that the motions observed in the heavens are mixed—that they are *predominantly* akin to the motions of reason, but that there is also some evidence of the other, or at least that the motion of the heavens is not fully moved by reason or characterized by spherical motion in every way? This would seem to offer a better explanation of natural phenomena like the retrograde motion of planets, the erratic motion of shooting stars, etc. I suspect he denies this because doing so makes the analogy, and thus his argument, stronger. In any case, Plato denies the retrograde motion of the planets—that the planets are in fact wanderers (from *planasthai*, to wander). In *Laws* 7 he writes:

Best of men, this belief (*dogma*) about the moon and the sun and the other stars—that they sometimes wander (*planatai*)—is not correct, but the complete opposite is the case. For each of them traverses the same path, in a circle—not many [paths], but always one—though each appears to move in many. (822a4–8)

On this controversial passage see Heath (1913; 181–9).

In this section of the *Laws* Plato is most of all interested in the motion of the cosmos itself, and there is nothing erratic or less than perfectly rational about that. The fixed sphere of the stars reflects the perfect circular motion of the cosmos. Other celestial objects can be examined individually, and their motion could be said to be predominantly directed by good soul.

Note that although this is actually part of Plato's response to the atheist, he is clearly looking ahead to the other two impious beliefs, the refutation of which requires not simply the priority of soul but of good soul, which orders the universe rationally.

Finally, it is also important to note that Plato is not simply concerned here with the proper conception of the cosmos. In the *Phaedo* Plato writes that the souls of the wicked are 'compelled to wander' (*planasthai*) in the afterlife, and 'they wander' (*planôntai*) until they are 'again imprisoned in a body' (81d7–e2). In the *Laws* too he associates the motion that does not wander with virtue, though he focuses on political implications or applications, as is made clear in *Laws* 12 (962c8–963a4). There Plato says that the Nocturnal Council must possess complete virtue or virtue in its entirety (*pasan aretên*), which means that it must 'not wander (*planasthai*) and aim at many things, but looking to one thing, always aim all things, like arrows, at this' (962d2–5). But the legal customs (*nomima*) of other cities wander, because the different parts of legislation in each city look to different things. In many cases the definition of justice in a city is whatever allows some people to rule, whether or not they are good rulers. For other people, whatever makes them wealthy is the proper basis for legislation. Still others are moved by the desire for the free life. And the ones *considered* the wisest look to a combination or mix of these aims. But the Athenian and his interlocutors agree that all the laws of the city they are forming must always look to one thing: virtue. This is one way in which Magnesia is ruled by and consistent with reason (*nous*).

898c9–899c1

The Athenian—expecting and receiving an affirmative response—asks: If soul leads around sun and moon and the other stars, then doesn't it lead around each one? If Plato here means that since the entire cosmos is moved by soul, therefore each celestial object within it must (directly or indirectly) be moved by soul as well, then whatever else one might think about his views, one could not fault the inference. But Plato likely has in mind a more robust inference; namely, that if the entire cosmos is moved by soul, then each celestial object within it must *directly* be moved by soul as well. Yet even if we were to accept that soul directs the universe, why not take this to mean that it simply orders the circular motion of the entire cosmos? Why assume that soul must also micro-manage, so to speak, the motion of each individual celestial object? In any case, this micro-management seems to be what Plato intends (or at least it is one possibility, given what he will say about how soul moves the sun). He now focuses on one celestial object, the sun, and how it is led by soul. This is only an example, for he says that what he'll say about the sun 'obviously applies to all of the stars' (898d6–7).

Plato assumes the sun is moved by soul—he would claim to have established that—but what he needs to do now is say something about *how* soul directs the motion of the sun. He says that everyone sees the sun, but no one sees its soul. That should not concern us, however, because everyone can see a living creature without seeing *its* soul, 'whether living or dying' (*oute zôntos oute apothnê¡skontos*, 898d10–11). (On why *apothnê¡skontos* should be rendered 'dying' and not 'dead' see Saunders (1972; 99).) We do not see soul in a living thing, and we don't see it leaving the body when a living thing is dying (which, according to traditional stories about the soul, it must do). In fact, Plato would claim, we have every reason to expect that soul is all around us; but soul—whether soul that directs the sun or the soul of a human being—cannot be perceived through the senses. It is intelligible (*noêton*) through reason alone. One purpose of the following discussion of how soul moves the sun is precisely to show in what way one can speak of soul without reference to the evidence of the senses.

Plato asserts that soul must lead or direct the sun in one of three ways (898e5–6). He first presents the three ways (898e8–899a4), and then gives a briefer summary of them (899a7–9). A bit later, applying what he says about the sun to all celestial objects, he gives a highly condensed version of the ways soul might direct celestial objects, in which the second way seems to be omitted, or combined with the third (899b6–7).

Here are the three possibilities:

1. Soul resides within (the chariot of) the sun, so that the sun is a living thing.
2. Soul is outside of the sun, and uses some kind of matter ('a body of fire or some kind of air', 898e10–899a1) to push the sun 'by force' (*bia*ᵢ, 899a2).
3. Soul, 'being itself void of body' (*psilê sômatos*), guides the sun with 'some other extremely amazing powers' (*dunameis allas tinas huperballousas thaumati*, 899a2–4).

Plato says that soul moves the sun either (1) from the inside, making the sun a living being, or (2) from the outside, using matter and mechanistic or material forces, or (3) in some other miraculous or simply unknown way. (He also describes the third way in these terms: 'however or in whatever way' it does it, 899a9.)

These are the key questions: What precisely does Plato have in mind in each case? Who held such views of the movement of the sun and other celestial objects? And which view, if any, can be ascribed to Plato? (According to Jaeger (1948; 142) all three were positions defended by various people in the Academy, with Plato probably holding the first view.) As we shall see, Plato did not seem terribly concerned about answering these questions, perhaps because answering them was not necessary in the context of a discussion with Kleinias and Megillus.

Some passages in the *Timaeus* suggest that Plato might have held the first view: There we are told that the demiurge assigned a soul to each star, and 'mounted each soul in a carriage, as it were' (41d8–e2). (We'll shortly be considering a different view from the *Timaeus*, so perhaps this one is metaphorical.) Further support for Plato holding the first view, but not the second, is found in the *Critias*. There Plato tells the following story:

But, as they [the gods] received what was naturally theirs in the allotment of justice, they began to settle their lands. Once they had settled them, they began to raise us as their own chattel and livestock, as do shepherds their sheep. But they did not compel us by exerting bodily force on our bodies, as do shepherds who drive their flocks to pasture by blows, but rather, by what makes a creature turn course most easily; as they pursued their own plans, they directed us from the stern, as if they were applying to the soul the rudder of persuasion (*peithoi*). And in this manner they directed everything mortal as do helmsmen their ships. (109b5–c4; trans. in Cooper (1997))

Some of the language Plato uses here—'exerting bodily force on our bodies' (*sômasi sômata biazomenoi*, 109b7–c1)—is similar to language he uses to describe the second position: 'by force pushes body with body' (*ôthei bia; sômati soma*, 899a2). One might argue on the basis of this passage that Plato would not have subscribed to the use of such physical 'force' in his cosmology had there been alternatives, which he clearly thought there were. Further, the fact that Plato seems to omit view 2 from his final summary of these options (899b6–7), or at best conflates views 2 and 3 there, suggests that this was not his own position. Finally, Plato tells us that this was the position of others ('as is the view of certain people', 899a1–2), which is language he arguably would not have used if this were his own position. Menn argues that view 2 is emphatically not Plato's own (1995; 77 n. 14), and he is probably right, though demonstrating the incorrectness of view 2 is not Plato's concern in this section of *Laws* 10. Further, it is not ruled out by the discussion of primary-work and secondary-work motions, the language of which is sufficiently wide open to be consistent with soul using matter to push celestial objects 'by force'. According to Lewis, the second 'hypothesis' regards the motion of the sun 'as under the direction of an external angel, or *Daimôn*, having a material yet highly ethereal body, and making use of a sort of impulsive motion' (1870; 234). Though the use of the term 'angel' is typical Lewis, he may be right generally, in which case Plato would not be objecting to this possibility at all.

The third position is especially interesting because some scholars have claimed that it refers to Aristotle and his view (defended in *Metaphysics* 12.7) that the unmoved mover moves celestial objects through being the object of desire. (For example, see Jaeger (1948; 142) and

Düring (1966; 187).) But the suggested chronology is extremely implausible, and even if he had been aware of this position of Aristotle's, I think it unlikely that Plato would have chosen this opportunity to mention it. As Lloyd writes: 'the passage at *Laws* 898e f. is so obscure and inexplicit that one may justifiably protest against Düring's confident assertion that Plato is there "obviously thinking of . . . *Metaph.* 1072b3"' (1968; 165). The third possibility is actually not a specific view at all, but in effect 'none of the above': any mysterious or otherwise unknown way in which soul might move the sun and other celestial objects.

In fact, one could plausibly argue that Plato's own position falls under this heading. In the *Timaeus* he describes the relationship between soul and the entire cosmos:

Applying this entire train of reasoning to the god that was yet to be, the eternal god made it smooth and even all over, equal from the center, a whole and complete body itself, but also made up of complete bodies. In its center he set a soul, which he extended throughout the whole body and with which he then covered the body outside. And he set it to turn in a circle, a single solitary heaven . . . (34a8–b7)

On this picture of celestial motion the sun is part of the body of the universe, which itself is a living thing, and moves as a result of its motion—neither being itself a living thing (as in view 1) nor it seems being pushed by material force (as in view 2). (See Menn (1995; 77 n. 14).)

This much is clear: which view is correct (according to Plato) is not as important as the crucial fact, as he sees it, that if one accepts that soul is in some way behind the movement of the sun and other celestial objects (and the connected arguments Plato presents about soul and the cosmos), one must accept that the soul that moves the heavens is *good* soul.

Not only must one accept the goodness of the soul that moves the universe, 'All men ought to regard this soul as a god (*theon*)' (899a9). Kleinias adds that only someone who has reached 'the ultimate in lack-of-reason' (*to eschaton . . . anoias*, 899b1) would fail to do this.

Plato proceeds to stress this, and to return the discussion from the motion of the sun back to the universe as a whole. Good soul, he says, does order the entire universe, and in so doing moves the sun and other celestial objects, and thereby causes the years and months and seasons. Thus they—the soul or souls that move the celestial objects—must be gods. Note the continued ambiguity over the number of souls: 'soul or souls' (899b4).

Plato seems to be saying that the soul that moves the sun is a god; and in addition the soul or souls that move the other celestial objects must be considered gods as well. So the problem of the number of souls translates into a similar problem concerning the number of gods. But this is no problem at all, as we have seen. Whether it is one soul that moves the cosmos and all of the celestial objects in it, or a number of souls, does not really matter to Plato. The important point is that this soul or souls is or are prior to body, and is or are to be considered a god or gods. Since in the *Laws* Plato is concerned with keeping his views as much as possible connected to traditional conceptions of the gods, he would likely say that even if it turns out that there is only one good soul that is causing all of the heavenly motions, we ought to continue thinking that there are many gods in the world. Soul qua mover of the sun would be one god, soul qua mover of the moon would be another, etc.

Plato concludes this section by asserting that no one should disagree with the claim that 'all things are full of gods' (*theôn einai plêrê panta*, 899b8). This of course is a famous line attributed to Thales. Aristotle writes in the *De Anima*, in virtually identical language, that 'Thales thought all things are full of gods' (*panta plêrê theôn einai*, 1.5.411a7). It is fitting that towards the conclusion to his case against atheism—much of which has been aimed at the natural-philosophy tradition—Plato quotes the father of that tradition. But Plato is giving Thales' words a new meaning. Just as Plato said Socrates was disappointed with Anaxagoras for *claiming* that *nous* (reason) moved the world, but without holding a robust enough view of this, so Plato is here implying that Thales may have held that the universe was full of gods, but what he meant by that was largely flawed or insufficient. For, like the other Ionian scientists, Thales did not believe what Plato has argued for in *Laws* 10: that the universe is full of gods who actively, consciously (we would say) order the universe with a view to what is best.

899c2–d4

Plato concludes his refutation of atheism with a challenge to the atheist: demonstrate the error of the view that soul is prior to body (i.e. that soul is 'the first genesis of all things' (899c7)) or be persuaded by the theistic position and live accordingly, i.e. 'live believing in the gods' (899c9).

This raises some questions. Is the challenge meant to be issuing from the three interlocutors and directed at any atheist? Or is it something the rulers of Magnesia will make to Magnesian atheists? If the second is the case—as I think it must be, given that much of this discussion is a prelude to the laws of impiety—then which Magnesian atheists are intended? All of them, including non-philosophers (like Kleinias and Megillus), who could conceivably reject the existence of god, or simply young Magnesians with a capacity for philosophy? If this is a challenge that would be made by the laws or rulers of Magnesia, as is likely, who would be allowed the opportunity to respond to it? And, of course, who will determine whether an atheist's attempt at demonstrating the errors of the argument for theism succeeds or fails?

Many of these questions will be answered when we get to the discussion of the actual laws on impiety, at the end of *Laws* 10. But the problem inherent in having theist rulers deciding on the merits of arguments for atheism and against theism will remain.

One last question of more immediate interest is this: Is it enough that an atheist (or potential atheist) comes to accept that soul is prior to body and thus theism is true? The wording of this passage might seem to imply that it is. But in fact we know that this is not sufficient, because Plato has indicated before that in addition to atheism there are two other impious views concerning the existence and nature of the gods: deism and traditional theism. Plato next turns his attention to deism—the view that the gods exist, but do not take thought for humans.

As a postscript to the discussion of atheism, let me note that toward the very end of the *Laws* Plato summarizes (and emphasizes) the essential points of the case against atheism (12.966d9–e4, 967d4–e2). He writes that there are two views that lead humans to believe in the gods and to be pious with respect to them: (1) the primacy or priority of soul; and (2) the orderly, rational motion of celestial objects.

III. DEISM (899D5–905D7)

899d5–900d4

This section consists primarily of the Athenian's opening statement to the deist—'the one who believes that the gods exist, but that they don't think about human affairs' (899d5–6). Note that the assumption is that this statement is addressed to a *young* man (900c1), for reasons that were indicated earlier and will be explained in greater detail later.

Deism is presented as a mixed impious belief. Its source is part bad and part good: 'poor reasoning (*alogias*) and an inability to condemn the gods' (900a8–b1). Let us look at each part in turn.

(1) *Poor reasoning.* Plato mentions two possible unsound arguments, either or both of which may have led a particular person to hold that deism is true.

(a) The mistaken view that evil people can be happy. What is the poor reasoning here? Plato must have something like the following in mind:

    i. If the gods supervised human affairs, evil people would never be happy.

    ii. Evil people sometimes *are* happy.

    iii. Therefore, the gods do not supervise human affairs.

Plato believes this reasoning is poor because, he claims, the second premise is false. He says that evil humans are often *presented* as happy by the Muses, and that they are said to be so 'according to all kinds of accounts' (899e3–4); but this view is in fact false. (It is interesting to hear him say that the Muses are actually wrong. Whatever the source of religious truth, it is not Muse-inspired poets. Cf. *Ion* 533c9–536d3.) I think he is here referring to the common opinion people have about evil and happiness, and one of the sources of that opinion; namely, legends which portray evil people as successful. (For examples of this and the next kind of poor reasoning see *Republic* 2.364a1–365a3 and *Gorgias* 471a1–d2.)

This first deistic argument is fairly straightforward—it asserts that happiness and evil can coincide in the same person. Someone who held this view might give the following kind of example: a man who is successful because he is an excellent surgeon, but who is evil in that he beats his wife and neglects his children. There need be no causal relation between the two; there is no suggestion that the evil is in fact the *cause* of the person's success or 'happiness'. I believe the second example of poor reasoning deals with claims of a more causal relationship between evil and happiness.

(b) The mistaken view that evil can cause or contribute to happiness.

Or perhaps you see humans nearing the end of old age, leaving behind grandchildren in high honors, and now you are disturbed observing in all these cases . . . that there are some who have engaged in many terrible acts of impiety, and *through these very acts* (*di' auta tauta*) have gone from humble beginnings to tyrannies and pre-eminence. (899e4–900a6)

In this case a person rises from a low stature to positions of great power, and even beyond his life his wealth and power are passed on to his children and grandchildren; and yet it was precisely the evil on his part—e.g. unscrupulous business dealings or political maneuvering—that led to the acquisition of this success and power. The argument here is similar in structure to the previous one:

    i. If the gods supervised human affairs, evil could never lead to happiness.

ii. Evil does sometimes lead to happiness.

iii. Therefore, the gods do not supervise human affairs.

Plato does not present any further arguments for his views here, though he has discussed earlier in the *Laws* his conviction that there can be no genuine happiness—no matter how much wealth, health, strength, or beauty one possesses—without virtue (see 1.631b3–d2 and 4.715e7–717a3). Perhaps the best presentation of the opposing view is contained in the Ring of Gyges story, which Glaucon tells at *Republic* 2.359b6–360b2. In the famous fragment from Euripides' *Bellerophron* (fr. 385 Mette) Bellerophron argues against the existence of the gods on the grounds that tyrants prosper, and small pious cities are defeated by more powerful impious ones. In Euripides' *Cyclops* Odysseus says, in his prayer to Hephaestus and Sleep, before his attempt to blind Polyphemus, that if Odysseus dies at the hands of the Cyclops, people will have to conclude that chance (*tên tuchên*) is a spirit, and that the spirits (presumably the traditional gods) are weaker than chance (599–607).

(2) *Inability to condemn the gods.* According to Plato, owing to the poor reasoning just described, the deist does not believe that the gods care about or supervise human affairs. But the deist could have come to an even worse conclusion based on what he believes regarding the happiness of evil humans. He could have come to reject the existence of the gods entirely (though Plato doesn't mention such a conclusion here); or, and this does interest Plato, he could have concluded that not only do the gods neglect human beings, they are in some way actively responsible for human evil. This inability to condemn or blame the gods for human evil is the result, Plato says, of 'some kinship (*suggeneia tis*) with the divine that leads you to what is of the same nature (*to sumphuton*)' (899d7–8). (See also the reference to 'kinship' (*suggeneian*) at 900a7–8 and *Protagoras* 322a3–5.) With whom is Plato contrasting deism? I think it must be traditional theism—the third impious belief that Plato wants to refute. For the traditional theist believes that the gods can be swayed by prayer and sacrifice to overlook human evil, and in fact reward it, which is an *active* sanction of evil not implied in deism. This must be what Plato is referring to. And if that's the case then deism is not worse but better than traditional theism—it has more affinity with the divine. So there is something in the

deist that prevents him from attributing to the gods a more active role
in human evil. What is this affinity with the gods? I think the *Timaeus*
helps here:

Concerning the most sovereign part of our soul, we should think in this
way: that god has given this [part of the soul] to each of us as a spirit
(*daimona*); indeed, we claim that this resides in the top of our bodies, and
raises us up from the earth toward what has a kinship (*suggeneian*) with us
in heaven, as if we were not an earthly plant (*phuton*) but a heavenly one.
(90a2–7)

Our kinship with the gods is possession of this spirit—the best part
of a human's soul. (On spirit (*daimon*) used in the *Laws* to refer to
something within each person see 5.732c4 and 9.877a3–6.) So it seems
Plato is saying that the spirit—i.e. reason (*nous*), the best part of the
human soul—in the deist is akin to the divine and thus keeps him from
attributing anything positively evil to the gods. But what is it about
the deist's reason that prevents him from holding the wrong view? It
must be the idea that the gods are incapable of evil. The deist believes
(mistakenly, says Plato) that there are limits to the gods' power—an
inability or ignorance (but not indifference) that prevents them from
ensuring that the virtuous (and only the virtuous) are happy. But deists
are incapable of going beyond this and attributing evil to the gods. Yet
if Plato is saying that it is their reason (*nous*) that prevents deists from
going astray in this way, isn't that simply another way of saying that the
alternative view is irrational? I think that's the case—that Plato wants
to claim that the concepts 'god' and 'good' are intimately (or we could
even say logically) connected, and so anyone who holds that the gods
are capable of being vicious or acting in any way contrary to virtue is
irrational. (See Lewis (1870; 253).) This is an indication of just how
bad the third kind of impiety is.

   Deism occurs in the mind of a youth whose reason is sufficient to
prevent him from believing that the gods are capable of evil (or that
the gods do not exist), and yet whose reasoning is flawed enough to
conclude that evil men can be happy. What the Athenian wants to
do in the remainder of the space he dedicates to deism is ward off or
defeat (*apodiopompêsasthai*, 900b5) this impious belief through argumentation. (Plato's three other uses of the term *apodiopompeomai*—two
of which are in *Laws* 9—suggest something akin to exorcism and/or

purification. See *Laws* 9.854b7, 877e8–9 and *Cratylus* 396e3. See also LSJ s.v. and Lewis (1870; 245–9).) He believes he can do this by connecting the case against deism to the one against atheism. The Athenian reassures Kleinias and Megillus that if they cannot handle the argument—ford the river—'I will take over from you two, as I did just now, and take [you] across the river' (900c2–4).

The Athenian adds:

> But perhaps it would not be difficult to prove this at least, that the gods supervise small matters no less than the especially big matters. For presumably he heard and was present at what was just said: that, being good with respect to every virtue, the supervision of all things is perfectly appropriate to them.   (900c7–d3)

But even if we grant that the gods supervise all things, that does not entail that they would necessarily give everything the same amount of attention (which 'supervise small matters no less than the especially big matters' seems to imply). At most it means that the gods won't neglect or overlook anything, which is not the same as giving everything the same attention. So the Athenian seems to overstate the case. (See the textual notes on 900c8 and 900c9.)

900d5–902b3

The Athenian begins to present his argument against the young deist (singular), so it is surprising that he opens as follows: 'So, after this, let *them* examine with us in common what virtue of the gods we meant when we agreed that they [i.e. the gods] were good' (900d5–6). Why 'them'? Probably because in much of his refutation of deism Plato is actually addressing both the deist and the traditional theist (see 901c8–d2).

Plato's aim in this section is to move from the gods' goodness to their possession of virtue, and from their virtue to the idea that they must supervise everything and neglect nothing.

The virtues he mentions are courage, moderation, and reason—three of the four traditional virtues (if we count reason and wisdom as roughly the same). Conspicuous by its absence is justice. Scholars who seek esoteric readings of the text could have a field day here (and I leave them to it). Plato surely believes the gods are just; in fact, that is a crucial part of his argument against traditional theism. But although it may be surprising that he did not at least mention justice here, I suspect he left it off the list because, as becomes clear, in the present context he is most concerned with the virtues that prevent an agent from being lazy and neglectful and overly concerned with luxury. Moreover, Plato might not think he needs to mention justice if having the other three virtues guarantees that a person is just.

Plato next points out that the virtues are noble whereas their opposites—the vices—are shameful. This may appear too obvious to be worth mentioning or stressing, but, as the *Euthyphro* makes clear, this would not have been so obvious for someone taking the traditional stories about the gods seriously (see *Euthyphro* 6b7–c1, 7b2–8b6). On this traditional view some human actions could be held to be noble by some gods and shameful by others, and Plato is making clear that he does not regard this as a possibility. (Shortly, he will even quote Hesiod in support of his position that the gods must be consistent with respect to good and evil.)

The gods have nothing to do with vice: 'neither the great nor the small of such things dwell among the gods' (900e7–8). I take it the Athenian uses these words to make clear that even though the gods are not neglectful of anything, however small, that does not mean they must have some connection with vice, however small or low and however much vice is found among human beings (about whom the gods are concerned).

Having established a general connection between the gods and virtue, Plato gets more specific: 'neglect and laziness and luxury' (900e10) are to be attributed not to virtue but to its opposite, vice. Which vices specifically? No doubt the opposites of the three virtues he mentions; namely, cowardice, being immoderate, and lack-of-reason. And lest people think that the traditional gods whose stories they were raised on share in some way with these characteristics, Plato quotes part of a relevant passage from Hesiod. Here is the line from *Laws* 10.901a3–5: 'Would everyone who is luxurious and negligent and lazy be according to us the sort the poet says are most "like stingless drones"?' (*kêphêsi kothouroisi malista eikelon*, a4). The part in quotes is from *Works and Days*:

> Hunger and the lazy man are always together,
> But both gods and men resent (*nemesôsi*) the lazy one,
> Who lives like stingless drones (*kêphênessi kothourois eikelos*) . . .
>
> (u. 302–4).

Plato uses this passage as added evidence that the gods reject laziness and the rest. One could argue that the gods may not admire laziness in humans, and may even command humans not to be lazy, but that they themselves could nevertheless be lazy. The gods, one could argue, are above or beyond the good and evil they have constructed or ordained for humans. But Plato maintains that 'the god should not be said to have just the sort of character that he himself hates' (901a7–8). Plato does so because he assumes that the gods are consistent; moreover, he will soon stress that what is good applies to all moral agents (i.e. to both gods and humans). So no god can possess any vice or, therefore, any of the characteristics that are offspring of vice, like laziness and neglect. Plato builds on this.

Both gods and humans can be treated alike—i.e. as moral agents—because they both possess reason. And if (*per impossibile*) a person possesses reason and 'his reason (*nous*) supervises the great things but neglects the small ones' (901b2–3), what could explain this? There are only two possible explanations:

1. *Ignorance:* The agent mistakenly thinks that it makes no difference to the whole (i.e. whatever is being supervised considered as a whole) if he neglects the small, as long as the great things are properly supervised.
2. *Vice:* The agent recognizes that it makes a difference if he neglects the small, but he does so anyway, through indolence (*rha$_i$thumia$_i$*) and luxury (*truphê$_i$*) (901c1).

One might add a third possible explanation; namely, that the agent neglects the small because 'it's *impossible* to supervise all things'

(901c3). But the Athenian says that this is not an explanation, because if it is impossible for an agent to supervise something, then the issue of *neglect* does not arise. (A human who does not supervise the movements of Jupiter is not neglecting that planet's orbit.) Later, Plato will assert that 'the gods do whatever is possible to mortals and immortals' (901d8–9). This is not necessarily divine omnipotence, but he clearly thinks it includes the supervision of all things. (More on the gods' capabilities in the next section.)

Plato continues: There are two reasons only why the gods would neglect small things (like humans); namely, ignorance and vice. But the gods cannot be vicious or ignorant; therefore, they cannot neglect the small things. Therefore, they cannot neglect humans.

The Athenian says: 'Now let the two of them answer the three of us' (901c8). He is addressing both the deist and the traditional theist. I take it that the Athenian addresses the deist and traditional theist only once *directly*, and afterwards simply discusses, with Kleinias (and a silent Megillus), what they would say. I translate the relevant passage as follows: ' "First, do you both claim that the gods know and see and hear everything, and that nothing of which there are perceptions and knowledge can escape them?" Is this the way these things are said to be (*legetai*), or how?' (901d2–6). (See the textual note on 901d5.) The anticipated affirmative answer is meant to rule out the possibility of ignorance mentioned above.

What we get at this point appears to be traditional Socratic *elenchus*. That is, the Athenian is not relying on any deep metaphysical argument, but seems to be attempting to get the deist and traditional theist to reject their positions on an issue—in this case, the possibility of divine neglect through ignorance—using views that they themselves hold. But the Athenian claims that both the deist and traditional theist maintain 'that the gods know and see and hear everything'. Would your typical traditional theist be likely to believe this? The Olympian gods, and especially Zeus, are sometimes described as possessing knowledge of everything (see Lesher (1992; 105)), though some of them are surely ignorant of some things at some times—for example, Zeus when he is asleep (see *Iliad* 14.352–60). As for deists, it is possible that Xenophanes believed that god had knowledge of everything (see DK 21B24–25), but it is unlikely that, for example, Thales or Anaximander—both arguably deists—held such a view. It is probably the case, however, that Plato is thinking of the views of the deist and traditional theist *who have heard the preceding refutation of atheism. They* would surely agree, Plato is saying, that the gods know everything.

After dispatching the possibility of ignorance, Plato turns to vice. He appeals not to the majority, but to unanimity: 'we five [the Athenian, Kleinias and Megillus, and the deist and traditional theist] have agreed that [the gods] are good—in fact, best' (901e1–2). If the gods are good, they are virtuous and cannot do anything inconsistent with virtue. It follows that the gods will not do anything—in this case, neglect the small—through indolence and luxury, for 'laziness is an offspring of cowardice, and indolence an offspring of laziness and luxury' (901e6–7; cf. the Hippocratic *Law* 4: 'cowardice indicates powerlessness'). Just as cowardice (*deilia*) is a parent to laziness (*argia*), being immoderate (or intemperance)—lack of *to sophronein*—can be seen as a possible parent to luxury (*truphê*), given that Plato mentions moderation at the beginning of this section (900d7). Plato seems to be arguing as follows: If neglect of the small is not caused by ignorance, then the cause must be indolence (or sluggish indifference, *rha_ithumia*). What would cause indolence in a soul? Laziness or idleness (*argia*, from *a* + *ergon*) combined with luxury. (I imagine that without exposure to luxury—and in turn a love of luxury—one could hate work without becoming indolent.) But laziness is the offspring of cowardice (excessive fear of hard work, competition, failure?), and if by 'luxury' Plato means not simply the availability of or access to luxury, but a strong desire for the easy, luxurious life, then it is likely that Plato could say (though he doesn't here) that luxury is the offspring of being immoderate. But cowardice and being immoderate are vices—they are the opposites of courage and moderation—and the gods cannot be vicious. 'None of the gods, then, is negligent from laziness and indolence, for presumably none shares in cowardice' (901e9–10).

We can set the argument out as follows:

1. Only indolence could lead the gods to neglect the small (having ruled out ignorance).
2. Indolence appears in a soul characterized by laziness and (the desire for) luxury.
3. Laziness is a product of cowardice, and the desire for luxury is a product of being immoderate.
4. The gods, who are good and virtuous, cannot be cowardly or immoderate.
5. Therefore, the gods cannot be lazy or desire luxury.
6. Therefore, the gods cannot be indolent.
7. Therefore, the gods cannot neglect the small.
8. Therefore, the gods supervise the small.

The Athenian could now end this part of the discourse by asking the deist (or traditional theist) whether he thinks the gods are ignorant or vicious, and he will do so; but first we encounter the follow problematic passage:

So what is left, if they do neglect the very small things in the universe: either they do this knowing that it is absolutely necessary † to supervise none† of these things, or—what is left, except the opposite of knowledge? (902a1–4)

Not only is the repetition of 'what is left' (*to loipon*, a1, 4) odd, the passage does not seem to make sense. We would expect the Athenian to say that if the gods *do* neglect the universe, they must do so from ignorance or vice (which we now know is impossible). That is, we should expect him to say 'knowing that it is absolutely necessary to *neglect none* of these things' or 'knowing that it is absolutely necessary to *supervise these things*'. But what he says—if we follow the manuscripts—is that if the gods do neglect the universe, they must do so because they know that it is necessary to supervise none of the small things (a hitherto unheard-of possibility), or they do so out of ignorance.

This passage is much more problematic than most editors and translators seem to think. For not only does it leave out the issue of vice entirely—or it presents the issue in a very strange form—it also introduces another (bizarre) possibility; namely, that the gods *know* that it is unnecessary to supervise small things. But this does not connect to anything that has come before, nor does it map well against the question he proceeds to ask the deist and traditional theist (at 902a6–b2; more on this shortly).

I suggest that the passage at 902a1–4 is a repetitious and mangled attempt to summarize the alternative which Plato eventually presents to the deist (and traditional theist). Plato probably intended to say something else than what is captured by the manuscript reading; namely: If the gods do neglect the small things, they do this (1) *despite* knowing that they should supervise them (in which case they act out of vice or weakness of will (*akrasia*)), or (2) out of ignorance. So I think there must be a problem with the text, and particularly this line (from 902a2–3):

> *gignôskontes hôs to parapan oudenos tôn toioutôn epimeleisthai dei*
> knowing that it is absolutely necessary to supervise none of these things

See the textual note on 902a3 for discussion of how one might emend this line, though none of the suggestions is entirely satisfactory.

After this problematic passage Plato has the Athenian ask the deist (in the Greek, the return to the singular is obvious):

> So which is it, very best of men: Should we put you (*se*) down as saying that the gods are ignorant and through ignorance neglect what ought to be supervised, or that they know what they ought to do, as the basest of humans are said to do: they know it is better to act otherwise than how they are acting, but don't do so, because they succumb to pleasures or pains? (902a6–b2)

(On *akrasia* in *Laws* 10 see Mayhew (2007; 104–10).) Kleinias, answering for the deist, not surprisingly responds: 'How could that be?' (902b3).

902b4–903a9

Deists claim that the gods are not concerned with human affairs—apparently because they think humans are too small for the gods to deal with (as opposed, say, to the orbit of Jupiter). Plato argues that even if it were the case that the affairs of humans are small (when considered in the context of the entire universe), that would make no difference.

He gives two related reasons for this: First, *if* humans and their affairs were small, they would be the very best of the small, and are certainly not insignificant (like a random pebble, a drop of dew, a speck of dust). For humans possess soul, and they are 'the most god-revering (*theosebestaton*, 902b5) of all animals'. Plato makes a similar point in a passage from the *Timaeus* (41a7–42a3) worth mentioning here. The Demiurge has just created the gods, and next turns to humans. To ensure that the latter are inferior to the gods (for example, they will be mortal), he leaves it to the gods to create the humans (rather than create them himself). The humans are made of the same material as the gods (the soul of the world), so they have comparable intellectual capacities (most significant, they too possess reason). In a complicated section of the passage apparently involving the migration of the souls from the stars to the earth (the details need not concern us), the souls are placed into bodies and become 'the most god-revering (*theosebestaton*) of animals' (42a1). Our passage in *Laws* 10 echoes this one, and makes clear that the gods could not be indifferent to such beings. For humans are god-revering, and this trait is directly linked to that aspect of their nature that connects them to the gods.

Second, 'all mortal animals are possessions of the gods, as are the entire heavens' (902b8–9; see also 906a7, *Phaedo* 62b8, *Critias* 109b7), and—great or small—the gods would not neglect such possessions (whose special nature has just been discussed). For the gods 'are the most solicitous and the best' owners (902c2–3). We have already been given some support for this claim—the gods are not ignorant or immoral, and so could not neglect their possessions owing to ignorance or vice—and Plato provides additional reasons for this assessment. I take the *gar* at 902c3, in 'For (*gar*) let us consider the following', to be introducing an argument for the claim that the gods are the most solicitous and best owners (see England (1921; 2. 489)); specifically, an argument from perception and power.

Plato states that perception and power are by nature opposites: In the former case, what is small is more difficult—that is, it is more difficult to perceive small objects than large ones. In the latter case, what is small is easier—that is, it is easier to carry, control, and supervise the small than the large. (Plato actually refers to the small and few [*tôn smikrôn kai oligôn*], 902c11. I take it that humans are few in comparison to the whole of existence, and the fewness of humans is to be contrasted with the expanse of the world as a whole. But for ease of discussion I refer in what follows to the small alone.) I can see a full moon more easily than an individual pebble, but I can move and control the latter much more easily than I could the moon (which I cannot control at all). So, Plato concludes, it cannot be the case that the gods are capable of controlling and supervising the orbits of celestial objects and the seasons on earth, but are incapable of controlling and supervising human affairs.

What if someone tried to turn this argument against Plato, and argue that the gods are *capable* of supervising humans and their affairs, *if* they noticed them; but they don't, since the small are harder to perceive than the large? Plato would have an answer available: Recall that in the last section the interlocutors agreed (whether with good grounds is another question) that 'the gods know and see and hear everything, and that nothing of which there are perceptions and knowledge can escape them' (901d2–5).

Having established that the gods *can* supervise both the large and the small things in the universe, Plato attempts to bolster his case by arguing that in fact the supervision of both are interrelated—that the supervision of the large requires or is supported by the supervision of the small. So if the gods are concerned with the supervision of the whole universe—and the deist would not deny *that*—then they must be concerned with the supervision of the small. The two examples that Plato gives with any detail are the doctor and the stonemason: 'If a whole [patient] is assigned to a doctor to treat, and [the doctor] wants and is able to supervise what's big, but neglects the small parts, will the entire [patient] ever fare well for him? . . . [T]he stonemasons claim that large stones do not lie well without small ones' (902d2–e3). Plato also mentions captains, generals, household managers, and 'certain statesmen' (*tisin politikois*, 902d8). Now each of these is plausible enough, as each must directly or indirectly micro-manage the smaller parts of what he controls. For instance, a doctor who claims concern for the whole patient but neglects an infected toe or an inflammation in the ear on the grounds that these are small matters will not fare well (nor will his patient). (Why does Plato mention *certain* statesmen? I suspect he wants to include here only those statesmen who are concerned with the good of the whole city, and not those who rule with an eye exclusively to their own well being or that of their own class.)

Plato deduces that since this principle—in supervision, a concern for the large *requires* a concern for the small—is true for 'mortal craftsmen' (902e5–6), and since the gods are superior to mortal craftsmen, therefore this principle must be true for the gods as well. But not only is this a non sequitur, it is hard to imagine how this principle would apply to the gods' supervision of the universe. A stonemason may well need both small rocks and big rocks to make a wall secure; but in what way would the gods *need* humans to properly see to the orbits of celestial objects or the different seasons on earth? (*Pace* England, who calls the comparison to the stonemason 'a singularly apt analogy' (1921; 2. 489–90).) Further, as Mohr has argued, this line of reasoning implies that Plato holds that evil people are used, and in fact required, by the gods in seeing to the good of the whole:

the Demiurge supposes the whole which he constructs of parts that are both good and bad is better than a whole of only good parts. . . . In the *Laws* evil does not exist over and against and in spite of the Demiurge [as Plato says it does in the *Timaeus*], but is adapted just as it is directly into his design. (2006; 200–1)

I cannot imagine Plato held this view explicitly—at the very least there would seem to be some tension between it and his view that the gods cannot be responsible for evil—but his lack of clarity over how precisely the divine stonemason is to use the little rocks as well as the big ones, with a view to the good of the whole universe, leaves him open to this implication.

Plato ends this section with a summary of his argument against the deist. He concludes by reiterating that the gods are *able* enough, *wise* enough, and *willing* enough to supervise both the large and the small. Or, to put it negatively, they are not incapable of supervising humans, or ignorant of humans, or lacking in character such that they would neglect humans. But, again, Plato tells us little about what form this care takes. In fact, Frede concludes—based in part on the dearth of details in Plato's account—that 'Care for the individual thus amounts to no more than the pattern of retribution that is established by the "divine King" for everyone' (2002; 94). I doubt that this is all there is to what Plato is advocating (surely the benefits of sunshine and the different seasons are part of what the gods do for us), but it is surprising and frustrating how little Plato tells us.

The last line in the argument against the deist contains a minor textual issue. See the textual note on 903a7.

The Athenian has finished presenting philosophical arguments against deism, but he is not finished with the deist.

903a10–905d2

The Athenian has enabled the hypothetical deist to see the errors of his ways, 'by forcing him, with arguments' (*toi biazeshtai tois logois*, 903a10). But this apparently is not enough—at least not for every possible deist who might arise in their city. So they will also need 'some mythic incantations' (*epôidôn ... muthôn ... tinôn*, 903b1–2) to make this persuasion complete or completely effective.

Bobonich holds that these 'mythic incantations' actually represent further *argument* for deism (2000: 385). I think Dodds is right that they are not rational, though are 'made to serve rational ends' (1957; 212); see also Morrow (1960; 485).

But if the previous arguments were persuasive—so much so that they count as force (cf. Gorgias, *Encomium of Helen*, 8–14)—why the need for a myth, which Plato should not expect to be as powerful as philosophical argumentation? They are needed precisely for those people (especially the young) who cannot understand or respond to serious philosophical discourse. (Cf. *Laws* 2.659c9–660a8, and note especially the 'incantations of the souls', *epô¡dai tais psuchais*. See also 664b3–c2, 665c2–7.)

The need for myth here is similar to the need for the Myth of Er at the end of the *Republic* (see 10.614b2–621d3). Having presented a philosophical argument for the connection between virtue and happiness (especially in Book 4), an argument later bolstered by the metaphysics of the Platonic Forms (in Books 5–7), Plato still feels the need to tell a tale of reward and punishment in the afterlife. I assume Plato thinks this is needed not only for the likes of Kephalus, who in *Republic* 1 makes clear the connection he sees between justice and a concern for his fate in the afterlife and who leaves the discussion before he hears any philosophical argumentation (see 1.328b5–331d10), but also (and primarily) for the children who will benefit from hearing such tales as they grow up.

Note that having said that the deist was *forced* by arguments Plato now writes: 'Let us persuade the young man, with arguments' (*peithômen ton neanian tois logois*, 903b4). But the 'argument' or account that follows is a complex myth about the gods who rule the universe (and are called, or compared to, rulers, craftsmen, a game-player, and a king), and how they move souls from one incarnation or place to another.

The gods put together the universe (*tou pantos*) with a view to the good—'the safety and virtue'—of the whole. This includes or involves each 'part' of the universe: 'each part, to the extent that it can, does and has done to it what is fitting' (903b6–7). Plato recognizes that there will be limitations on what can be expected from each part ('the extent that it can'), and makes clear that each part will be expected to do and endure what is best not for itself but for the universe as a whole.

Rulers oversee every aspect of the activities and experiences of every part, to the smallest detail and for all times. 'Rulers' refers to the gods, but may also include spirits as well (see *Phaedrus* 246e4–247a4, *Statesman* 271d3–e4, *Laws* 5.747e3–5, 10.906a7, and *Epinomis* 984d2–985c1). Carone (1994; 291) argues that 'rulers' also includes humans (see also England (1921; 2. 491)), but that is unclear.

Plato reminds the deist that he ('stubborn man') is one of these parts, and that even though it is a very small part 'it always strains to look toward the universe' (903c1–2). It is interesting that Plato is not here saying—as we might expect him to in trying to persuade the deist—that the gods are watching over every single person (cf. *Gospel According to Matthew* 6.25–34). Rather, he says that there is something in the deist—perhaps that share of reason (*nous*) that makes him a deist and not an atheist—that strains to consider itself part of a universe ordered by god and (the implication is) is willing to do its part. The deist has forgotten (this is either a polite way of saying he never knew, or it refers to the soul in an earlier incarnation) that 'all generation' (i.e. everything that comes to be) 'comes to be for the sake of this: that a happy existence may belong to the life of the universe; and it does not come to be for the sake of you, but you for the sake of it' (903c3–5). The deist focuses so much on himself—on how he has fared compared to other, less deserving people—that he has forgotten that everything that happens (and will happen, e.g. in the afterlife, to himself and to the less deserving, but apparently successful, people) aims at the happiness of the universe as a whole. (See *Philebus* 54c1–11 for a similar statement about generation.)

Every artist and craftsman (e.g. a doctor) does the same as the divine craftsman who crafted the universe: 'he makes a part straining for what is best in common, for the sake of the whole, and not the whole for the sake of a part' (903c7–d1). On the importance of this principle in medicine see for example the Hippocratic *Regimen* 1.2 (and, again, *Laws* 902d2–6). I take it that the point Plato is making is that a doctor, say, in treating a damaged leg, is not concerned with the welfare of that limb but with the patient as a whole (and would thus sacrifice the leg if necessary for the survival of the whole person). Plato clearly believes this same principle applies to the political art, and, though he does not discuss it in detail here, he does take the opportunity in this myth to make a crucially important point of Platonic political philosophy; namely, that the whole (whether universe or city) is more important than the part, including those parts that are individual human beings. (See *Republic* 4.420b3–421c6 and *Laws* 5.739b8–e7.) (On Aristotle's critique of this aspect of Platonic political philosophy see *Politics* 2.5.1264b15–24 and Mayhew (1997: 123–7).)

It may sound as if Plato is preparing the way for a doctrine of renunciation: accept your fate, and the fact that you may have to be sacrificed for the sake of the happiness of the universe. But he would claim that this is not the case, if you consider the big (eschatological) picture: 'you are irritated, not knowing how what concerns you turns out best for the whole *and for you as well*, in virtue of the power of your common generation' (903d1–3). This is clear enough from one perspective: the deist does not see how what is best for the whole is also best for him—and thus the complaint about divine neglect. But why is this owing to 'the power of your common generation' (and what is that)? And is Plato saying that when I see an immoral man achieving a success that has escaped me (e.g. his business is flourishing, while my crops have failed this season) I should simply recognize that this must, from some cosmic perspective, be good?

Plato explains what he means in the next few lines. He is not saying that the way things are in this one life must be best for the deist. It is only by going beyond this life and looking at how the universe and everything in it are organized—at what in fact the gods do with us—that the deist (and anyone else) will see clearly that the universe, organized in the best way possible as a whole, is also best with a view to each part. I also think, though this is less clear, that the 'common generation [or origin]' refers to the common generation of human souls and the special connection human soul has to the soul that organized the universe.

So how is it that the best arrangement for the universe as a whole is also good for each part—i.e. each human soul? Through the movement of individual souls to that place in which they belong, after each incarnation.

Since soul is always put together with bodies—sometimes with one, sometimes with another—and undergoes all kinds of changes through itself or through another soul, no other function is left for the game-player except to transfer the character that is becoming better to a better place, and the one becoming worse to a worse place, according to what is appropriate to each of them, such that each is allotted its proper fate.   (903d3–e1)

There is a lot to unpack here. First, in saying that soul is always put together with bodies, I think Plato is using 'always' (*aei*) to mean 'constantly', for he cannot mean that all soul is always embodied. Second, 'sometimes with one, sometimes with another' refers to a series of incarnations that an individual soul might pass through. (More on this shortly.) Now England (1921; 2. 492) takes 'changes through itself or through another soul' to refer to the important distinction made earlier in *Laws* 10 between self-moving motion (motion capable of moving itself) and non-self-moving motion (motion capable of moving others but not itself), but this is unlikely. Instead, I would suggest:

(a) *Changes through itself.* Shifts in character brought about by the individual soul itself—what one does oneself in one's lifetime to become virtuous or vicious (or more or less virtuous or vicious).

(b) *Changes through another soul.* Aspects of character which result from the influence of parents, educators, statesmen, etc.

The second of these might also include changes to soul owing to the gods moving a soul from one location to another (more on that shortly), but such 'psychic transfers' seem to take place after, and to take account of, the changes to soul referred to here.

Soul is put together with body, and in this embodied state the human, from birth to death, undergoes changes—develops a virtuous or vicious character (or something more complex or mixed). The gods do not need to see to this. It works naturally; that is, certain thoughts, behavior, associations, etc. simply do result in the development of a certain type of character. Hence 'no other function is left for the game-player'. What the gods must do—like a game-player moving pieces on a board—is, at the death of a person move that soul to the ethically appropriate place. An important part of this story—explicit in the Myth of Er—is that the person, and not any god, is responsible for what happens in the afterlife. See *Republic* 10.617e4–5: 'Responsibility is the chooser's; god is not responsible' (*aitia helomenou; theos anaitios*). See also *Laws* 904b8–c3.

At this point in the myth Kleinias asks for a clarification, and what he gets instead is one of the densest, most impenetrable passages in the *Laws*: 903e3–904a4. Crombie writes: 'It seems to me that it is anybody's guess just what this passage means' (1962; 384 n. 1). The best discussion of this passage to date is Saunders (1973), and he calls it 'Mumbo-Jumbo' (p.232). Before I plunge in with my thoughts, it will help to indicate at the outset that the Athenian takes Kleinias' question, 'How do you mean?' (and thus Plato intended the question) to refer to the 'game-player' having only one function and therefore a relatively easy time with the management of souls. Note the opening and closing lines of the problematic passage, which I quote in full:

The way in which the supervision of the universe by the gods would be easy—this is what I seem to be explaining. For if someone, failing always to look to the whole, were to mold all things by changing their shapes—for example, having ensouled [or 'cold'] (*empsuchon* [or *empsuchron*]) water come from fire, and not many things from one or one from many—then once they [i.e. all things] have taken part in a first or second or third generation, there would be an unlimited number of transformations in the arrangement of the cosmos. But in fact it is marvelously easy for the one who supervises the universe. (903e3–904a4)

The major textual issue in this passage is: whether one should accept *empsuchon* ('ensouled') with the manuscripts, or *empsuchron* ('cold') with Stallbaum. It is hard to say, in part because no matter which reading one chooses, the meaning of the text remains difficult and downright odd. But I think that given the context—with the emphasis on souls—and given that *empsuchon is* the manuscript reading, we should accept that. I hope to make some sense of this reading in what follows. (Diès (1956; 173 n. 1) notes that *Epinomis* 985b4–6 supports the manuscript reading. Lewis (1870; 295–6) offers an interesting defense of the alternative.)

The core of this passage is a description of two different views of the kind of universe the gods might work in: an erroneous view which, if true, would render the work of the gods virtually impossibly difficult, and the correct view, which is supposed to explain why the gods' task is in fact relatively simple. The two views can be briefly described as follows:

1. The gods do not look to the whole while molding the universe, such that the universe is chaotic, and, for example, ensouled water can come from fire.
2. The gods look to the whole while molding the universe, such that the universe is orderly, and many come from one and one from many.

As Saunders and others have pointed out, the first of these probably refers to a Heraclitean universe (see Saunders (1973; 240–4), though it may also be fruitful to compare this passage to the Hippocratic *Regimen* 1.4). Consider these two fragments from Heraclitus:

This *cosmos*, which is the same for all, was not created by any one of the gods or by mankind, but it was ever and is and shall be ever-living fire, kindled in measure and quenched in measure.   (DK 22B30)

To souls, it is death to become water; to water, it is death to become earth. From earth comes water, and from water, soul.   (DK 22B36)

The picture Plato is here portraying is of a chaotic universe of flux, where (a) virtually anything can change into anything else, (b) souls and gods emerge or arise out of matter, and (c) the craftsman who molds the universe would, *per impossibile*, have to decide independently on every change, without reference to a plan or order.

The view that Plato endorses is extremely unclear, but in contrast to the Heraclitean one it must represent some kind of orderly, intelligible world in which change occurs according to a specified plan, *logos*, design—with a view to the whole and what is best for it—and (the implication is) where soul does not emerge out of matter, but molds it. Perhaps Plato has in mind something like this picture from the *Timaeus*:

For then it appeared that all four kinds of bodies [earth, air, fire, and water] could turn into one another by successive stages. But the appearance is wrong. While there are indeed four kinds of bodies that come to be from the triangles we have selected, three of them [i.e. air, fire, and water] come from triangles that have unequal sides, whereas the fourth alone [i.e. earth] is fashioned out of isosceles triangles. Thus not all of them have the capacity of breaking up and turning into one another, with a large number of small bodies turning into a small number of large ones and vice versa. There are three that can do this. For all three are made up of a single type of triangle, so that when once the larger bodies are broken up, the same triangles can go to make up a larger number of small bodies, assuming shapes appropriate to them. And likewise, when numerous small bodies are fragmented into their triangles, these triangles may well combine to make up some single massive body belonging to another kind. (54b6–d2, trans. in Cooper (1997))

If this is what Plato is talking about in *Laws* 10.903e3–904a4 (and I suspect that something like it is), then his point is that unlike the Heraclitean chaos, the actual universe is such that only certain types of triangles can fit together to form earth, air, fire, or water; and in the same way earth, air, fire, or water can be broken down into certain types of triangles, which can then become some other kind of material—and all according to an order designed by a soul possessing reason. This is probably what Plato means by (the very cryptic) 'many things from one or one from many': many triangles of a certain kind become water, say, or water becomes many triangles of a certain kind. And having primacy over all of this—and in fact being responsible for this orderliness—are soul and reason (though perhaps Plato is thinking of some version of what Empedocles describes in DK 31B17, 26).

Plato again describes the wrong view, and an already murky passage becomes extremely dense: 'once they [?] have taken part in a first or second or third generation, there would be an unlimited number of transformations in the arrangement of the cosmos' (904a1–3). 'They' probably refers to the parts or constituents of the universe. If any material can transform into any other, chaotically, and soul can emerge out of anything (e.g. ensouled water out of fire, as Heraclitus describes), then within three generations—i.e. within the time that all the parts of the universe have gone through three such chaotic transformations—the number or kind of transformations would be virtually unlimited (cf. Empedocles DK 31A72, B57, 59, 61). In such a universe, were a god to attempt to supervise the movement of souls, it would be an impossibly difficult task. But as it is the cosmos has been ordered with a view to the whole and to what is best for it. The gods and spirits may still be said to be micro-managing the universe, and they are certainly concerned about every part of it no matter how small, but such supervision requires nothing impossible.

Kleinias speaks for all of us when he asks: 'Again, what do you mean?'. Plato continues with the myth. This is what he says 'our king saw' (cf. *Philebus* 29c6–8, where *nous* is called king):

(1) All actions involve soul (in contrast to the wrong view just described).
(2) There is much virtue in action, and also much vice.
(3) Soul with body, having come to be, is indestructible but not eternal. I follow England (1921: 2. 494) in taking this to mean that each of these—soul and body—is indestructible, like a god, and Plato tells us why: 'for there would never have been generation of living beings if either of these two had been destroyed' (904a10–b1). But a soul-body composite is *not* indestructible (and thus not eternal); nor is matter eternal, if it was created.

(4) Whatever in soul is good is naturally beneficial, while the evil is harmful. The connection between the good and the beneficial is built into the fabric of the universe.

In what way is any of this an answer to Kleinias' request for clarification? It explains in part what Plato was trying to describe in the previous paragraph: that the universe is not such that every action (physical and involving the soul) must be undertaken by a god, without any plan—without a view to the whole. All action by its nature has soul behind it—as we saw in the discussion of the ten kinds of motion. If soul put the world together in a certain way—considering the nature of matter but also with a view to the whole—then the 'rulers' of the universe need not oversee every detail of the universe (which is not to say they neglect anything). Further, unlike the wrong view described above, whereby the soul comes to be as part of the physical processes of the world, 'our king' recognizes that soul (apart from body) is eternal or indestructible, and its continued existence is not something that the rulers of the world need to attend to.

The purpose of this entire account is of course to allay the worries of the deist. For what the king or ruler of the world does attend to is the application of what is in effect a law of nature; namely, that virtue is beneficial and evil is harmful. This is what the gods will make sure happens to a soul in the life and/or after the death of any soul-body combination. 'Seeing all this, he presumably designed the position of each of the parts so that virtue would be victorious in the universe, and vice defeated, in the easiest and best way' (904b3–6). With every birth (and presumably with every death) a soul 'must always take a certain place and reside in certain locations' (904b7–8). Why refer to place *and* location? Could one of these refer to the kind of body the soul enters (see *Timaeus* 42b3–d2) while the other refers to whether the soul ends up on earth or in Hades or whatever? No, since only earthbound souls end up in bodies (whether human or animal or plant, if the *Timaeus* conception is operative here). So perhaps these two simply serve to remind us that there are a number of possible places that souls can go.

This relocation of souls to the places they deserve to be is what it is for virtue to be victorious in the universe; this is what the good of the whole universe consists in. If someone were to conclude that this psychical mechanics implies determinism, think again: 'But he leaves the cause for the coming to be of each particular sort of person to the will of each of us. For as one desires, and as one is with respect to soul, so (pretty much in every case) is the sort of person each of us becomes, for the most part' (904b8–c3; cf. 5.731c1–7). This refers to the kind of person one becomes in one's lifetime, and that determines where one's soul ends up after death.

We can now make better sense of the earlier distinction between soul moving itself and soul being moved by another soul (see 903d3–5). A soul moving itself is in part what Plato has just described. By taking the actions we take throughout our lives we determine (in part) what kind of character we come to acquire. (I say 'in part', because what kind of character we come to have can also partially be determined by our parents, the kind of upbringing we have, the nature of the city we live in, etc.) 'So all things that are sharing in soul change, possessing within themselves the cause of the change, and in changing they are moved according to the order and law of destiny' (904c5–8). Depending on how a human soul 'changes' within his or her life—i.e. becomes (more or less) virtuous or vicious—the soul is moved (after death) 'according to the order and law of destiny'. Even here the rulers' task is relatively simple. Once the moral character of a soul is determined, its location is automatically determined as well (and it simply moves, or is moved by the gods, to that location).

Plato next explains that there are roughly three directions in which a soul can move after the death of its body, depending on the progress or regress of its character during that life:

1. Insignificant change in character

'When the change in character is smaller and less significant, there is smaller horizontal movement in space' (904c8–9). When over the course of a particular incarnation there is no change, or there is merely a slight change in character (for better or for worse), then there is a horizontal movement in space. I take this to mean that the soul returns to or remains on the earth, but in a different body and perhaps in another location (hence the horizontal movement). Horizontal is to be contrasted with changes in location that are up (toward the stars?) or down (to Hades and beyond, as we shall see). (In the *Timaeus* Plato writes that a person who has failed to live a good life 'would be born a second time, now as a woman; and if even then he still could not refrain from wickedness, he would be changed once again, this time into some wild animal that resembled the wicked character he had acquired' (42b5–c4). This would count as horizontal change, as used in *Laws* 10, though I do not know that Plato has precisely the *Timaeus* account in mind, which seems to describe what happens to significantly vicious people, see 12.944c4–94562.)

2. *Significant change in character for the worse*

'[W]hen a change is more significant and more unjust, the movement is into the depths and the places said to be below, which people call "Hades" and related names, which terrify them both in dreams while they are alive, and when they have been sundered from their bodies' (904c9–d4). In this section of *Laws* 10 Plato twice mentions the movement of souls that have made a significant change for the worse to places like Hades (904d2, 905a8)—which perhaps indicates that this is an especially important part of the myth, that the souls of vicious people end up in nasty places. This is important in two ways: as a warning to vicious or potentially vicious people, and to allay the worries of the deist, who thinks that the earthly success of vicious people is an indication of the neglect of the gods. Plato is making clear that in the long run it is not. (In *Republic* 3.387b8–c6 Plato condemns this kind of myth, including such terrible names for the underworld, at least as part of the education of the Guardians, on the grounds that it would instill too much fear of death in them, thus making them too soft. He does add, however, that these stories 'are perhaps good with a view to something else'. I suspect that the difference between *Republic* 3 and *Laws* 10 here has more to do with the different contexts—the education of Guardians, in contrast to stories meant to persuade a young deist—than it does with any change in attitude or outlook on Plato's part.)

3. Significant change in character for the better

'But whenever a soul gets a larger share of vice or virtue, owing to its own will and to an increased influence from others, then, by mingling with a divine virtue it becomes exceptionally such; and it undergoes an exceptional change of place and is transported along a sacred road to a better place elsewhere' (904d4–e1). The first clause refers to significant changes both for the worse and for the better, and indicates how such significant changes take place: through a person's own will (and thus choices and actions) and through a person's associations. (I follow England (1921; 2. 497) in taking familiarity (*homilian*, d6) to refer to the association with *people* of a certain character. Cf. *Laws* 9.854b6–c5.) It is a bit odd that Plato should, after describing changes in character for the worse, speak of soul getting a larger share of vice or virtue. We expect him at this point to speak of virtue alone. But that he refers to both virtue and vice does not cause any problems in interpretation. What he says applies to the vicious change he just spoke of (and will mention again) and to the virtuous change which is to be described. I take 'mingling with a divine virtue' to refer to both ways of improving one's moral character: making virtuous choices and undertaking virtuous actions, *and* associating with virtuous people (parents, statesmen, and later friends and acquaintances). This is all divine because all virtue (even in humans) is connected ultimately to the reason (*nous*) not only that individual humans possess but that orders the universe. Cf. the passage in the *Timaeus* according to which the good person 'would at the end return to his dwelling place in his companion star, to live a life of happiness that agreed with his character' (42b3–5), and which shortly thereafter describes the ultimate return of the soul of a good person to an 'original condition of excellence' (42d2).

Plato follows these descriptions with a summary, beginning with a quote from Homer (*Odyssey* 19.43):

'This is the judgment of the gods who hold Olympus', O child or young man, who believes he is neglected by the gods: the one who becomes more vicious is conveyed to the vicious souls, while the one who becomes better is conveyed to the better souls, in life and in every death, to experience and to do what is appropriate for like to do to like.   (904e3–905a1)

I think 'every death' refers to the series of incarnations a soul may go through, though this series need not be endless if a person makes a significant change in the direction of virtue, which seems to end the cycle of incarnations and takes the soul out of a body and away from earth and toward the heavens. It is clear what Plato means by the vicious being conveyed to the vicious *in death*: this is the gods sending the soul of a vicious person to Hades or beyond, where the souls of other vicious people reside (for how long or under what terms we are not told). To reside with vicious people is their punishment. But what does it mean for the vicious soul to be conveyed to vicious souls *in life*? After all, Plato believes (in the *Laws* and elsewhere) that associating with virtuous people is one way to improve one's character, while associating with vicious people normally yields the opposite result. I think Plato is pointing ahead to the punishments for violating the laws on impiety, the most severe of which are not death, but life imprisonment with other incurably impious people (see 909b6–c3; and cf. 5.728b2–c8.)

Plato next presents a reminder and warning that this judgment of the gods is inescapable: it has been written into the fabric of reality and given the highest priority by those who have ordered the universe. (There is a textual dispute here; see the textual note on 905a3). Not surprisingly, Plato stresses not the reward for virtue but the punishment for vice. In effect, he turns the concerns of the deist—that the gods neglect us—into a threat or warning:

For you will never be neglected by this judgment—not if you were so small as to sink into the depths of the earth, or so high as to fly to the heavens—but you will pay them the appropriate penalty, either while you remain here, or after you've been brought through to Hades or been carried over to a place even more savage than this.   (905a4–b1)

The gods do not neglect human beings: there is no escaping divine punishment.

As this is myth, and thus perhaps more poetical and emotionally evocative than normal prose, Plato—in discussing a sinner trying to be 'so small as to sink into the depths of the earth, or so high as to fly to the heavens'—seems to be borrowing imagery from Euripides (see *Medea* 1296–1300 and *Hippolytus* 1290–5).

There is one noteworthy textual issue here, concerning 'a place even more savage' (*agriôteron*). See the textual note on 905b1.

The myth now becomes less myth-like and sounds more like standard argumentation. Plato turns to the deist's argument. As earlier presented, the deist came to be a deist by seeing impious people moving (despite or because of their impiety) from a small lot in life to greatness (899d6–900a6). Plato here (905b1–7) reminds the deist of this reasoning, and points out that what was just said applies to such people, thus defeating the deist's argument.

Again revealing that philosophical argumentation is not enough, Plato next asks the deist:

But bravest of all men, how can you think it's not necessary to know this [i.e. that the impious will be punished in the afterlife]? If someone does not know it he would never see an impression, nor be able to offer an account, of life with respect to both happiness and an unhappy fortune.   (905c1–4)

This resembles philosophy *als ob*: it is not an argument for the nature and existence of the gods, but for why one should proceed *as if* the gods have a particular nature (i.e. that they are not neglectful of human affairs). Plato's last attempt at convincing the deist head-on is to tell him that this belief allows him to make the most sense of the world, and particularly of the fates of happy versus unhappy people.

Plato concludes the myth as follows:

So if Kleinias here and our whole Council of Elders persuade you about this—that concerning the gods you don't know what you're saying—the god himself would assist you nobly. But if you should still need some further argument, listen to us address the third opponent, if you possess any reason whatsoever.   (905c4–d2)

On 'the god himself' (*ho theos autos*) see Lewis (1870; 65). The reference to the Council of Elders is a rare reminder in *Laws* 10 that the Athenian and his interlocutors are discussing a (second-best) city in speech, with the aim of assisting Kleinias (and indirectly the group of other men he will be working with) in the founding of a new colony in Crete. (See *Laws* 3.702b4–d5; cf. 3.691e1–692a3.)

Plato believes that this myth, in combination with the argument against deism that preceded it, should convince the deist of the error of his position, in which case he should see this as divine aid—evidence that the gods do not neglect *him*. (That is the sense and purpose of 'the god himself would assist you nobly'.) If the deist is still not convinced, there is one last chance ('if you possess any reason whatsoever'): listen to the Athenian et al. 'address the third opponent', i.e. the traditional theist (905d1–2). The three men agree that they should next refute 'in every way possible' the view that 'the gods can be appeased by the unjust, if they receive gifts' (905d4–6).

IV. TRADITIONAL THEISM (905d8–907b9)

905d8–906c7

In the *Republic* Plato criticizes what I'm calling traditional theism (see 2.364b3–365a3), and quotes (with some alteration) a passage from Homer's *Iliad* that is an excellent example of what in the *Laws* too he condemns:

> The gods themselves can be moved.
>
> . . . .
>
> And with sacrifices and soothing prayers
> And libations and burnt offerings, humans turn [the gods] around
> With begging, whenever someone has transgressed and done wrong.
>
> (*Iliad* 9.497, 499–501; quoted in *Republic* 2.364d6–e2)

As we shall see, Plato believes the successful case against deism makes it easy to refute traditional theism. (Note that some ancient texts in fact support Plato's project, e.g. *Odyssey* 1.32–4, where Poseidon chastises humans for blaming their ills on the gods.)

He proceeds by asking what sort of beings would the gods need to be if (*per impossibile*) they were to be appeasable by humans. He repeats the question using a strange formulation: 'what or what sort (*tines ê poioi tines*) would they [have to] be?' (905e1–2). Plato is asking: What kind of thing broadly speaking—and then, within that class, what specific sort of thing—would the gods have to be?

Plato first indicates the broad classification: 'Presumably they will necessarily be *rulers*, since they are to manage the entire heavens perfectly (or 'completely', *entelechôs*)' (905e2–3). Since the interlocutors have recently referred to the gods as rulers and kings (see 903b8, 904a6), this makes for an easy comparison. Moreover, rulers are most of all the kinds of persons whom one might think of appeasing—they, more than others, are in a position to be appeased. Plato will next turn to the *kind* of ruler that would be open to appeasement, and then ask if that sounds like the sort of rulers the gods are. (There is a possible problem with the word 'perfectly' (*entelechôs*). See the textual note on 905e3.)

The Athenian asks which (earthly) rulers the gods resemble, and then—perhaps motivated by piety—corrects himself and asks which kind of rulers resemble the gods. The rulers Plato mentions are: drivers of competing teams of horses; captains of ships (most

likely naval captains, given the emphasis on battle or conflict);
rulers of armies; doctors (combating diseases); farmers (combating
the uncertainty of seasons and harvests); and shepherds. England
exaggerates only a little in claiming that all of these involve conflict
between good and evil (1921; 2. 500). In any case, such conflict
becomes Plato's main concern, as the 'for' (*gar*) at the opening of the
next passage makes clear:

For since we have agreed among ourselves that the heavens are full of many
good things, and also of the opposite, and that there is more of what is
not good, this sort of battle, we claim, is immortal and requires amazing
vigilance, and the gods and spirits are our allies, while we are the property
of the gods and spirits.   (906a2–b1)

Carone (1994; 294) is perhaps right to argue that the claim that 'there
is more of what is not good' makes sense only if Plato has humans
in mind, for how could evil outnumber good in the entire cosmos,
which is ordered by good soul? But this in itself need not imply
that Plato views evil cosmic soul as merely hypothetical, because this
passage is part of the 'mythic incantations', which are emotionally
charged and contain appeals to fear. (On there being 'more of what
is not good' see *Republic* 2.379c4–5.)

The gods are similar to the above mentioned rulers in that they
too are rulers in a (cosmic) battle between good and evil. This
perhaps explains why Plato did not include heads of household
in the above examples of rulers; but it is nevertheless surprising
that he did not mention statesmen (though he earlier mentioned a
king). Perhaps because the *Laws* describes a second-best city, and
does not advocate the rule of philosopher-kings, Plato did not want
the presentation of the gods as rulers to be taken as a model for
political rule.

The gods and spirits are like rulers of armies and (naval) captains
in that they are our allies in this battle. This is connected to the case
against deism, in which the gods and spirits are said to help put both
the evil and the good into their proper places. And the gods and
spirits are like farmers and shepherds and drivers of horses in that we

humans are their property (just as a farmer might own the crops, a shepherd the sheep, a driver the horses). That the gods are rulers in this way underscores what kind of rulers they are—he will shortly call them 'absolutely supreme masters' (906b7–8)—and perhaps is meant to reiterate the point made earlier in the case against deism; namely, that the gods are concerned with the good of the whole, not the good of any particular part viewed in isolation from the good of the whole. (Plato does not yet say anything about how the gods are rulers in the way doctors are; but he will get to that model eventually.)

If the gods are our allies in a war between good and evil in the universe, what role do (or even could) *we* play in this war? Bobonich provides the correct answer by connecting this passage to the earlier discussion of deism, and particularly to Plato's claim that 'what concerns you turns out best for the whole and for you as well' (903d1–3). Bobonich (2002; 433) concludes: 'Plato is not suggesting that our ultimate reason for seeking to advance virtue is that doing so is in accordance with god's plan. Rather, god aims at what is best and it is the fact that this goal is best that should also be our reason for pursuing it.' Thus, as he puts it, 'the theology of Book 10 invites the citizen to see fostering virtue as sharing in god's plan for the universe as a whole'.

So Plato claims to have established that the gods are powerful and vigilant rulers in a battle between good and evil. We might expect him to turn now to the nature of an appeasable ruler, but instead he reminds the reader what will lead to victory in this battle, and what will lead to defeat: 'Injustice and hubris without prudence destroy us, while justice and moderation with prudence save us, and these reside in the ensouled powers of the gods, though one can clearly see some small amount of these residing in us as well' (906b1–4). One could take the 'without prudence' to refer to hubris alone or to both injustice and hubris; and one could take 'with prudence' to refer to moderation alone or to both justice and moderation. In each case the latter is likely correct, though not much is riding on this. The important point is one that is made elsewhere in the

Laws: vice destroys us while virtue saves us (see 12.961d1–963a4, 964c6–d8; cf. 5.734c3–e2). And whatever Plato intended in this line concerning the relationship between prudence and the other virtues, he generally takes prudence to be a primary, resulting in justice and moderation, etc., while its lack results in injustice and hubris, etc. (cf. 12.963e1–8).

The model of virtue in this line is an interesting and important one. England is not far off in saying that the virtues are the attributes of the gods themselves (1921; 2. 500). God is *nous* (reason) or *phronêsis* (prudence), wherein the other powers (or virtues) reside. I take this to mean that reason is the primary virtue, while the others depend upon and/or are manifestations or applications of this primary virtue. (Plato is capable of formulating this slightly differently: the gods, he says elsewhere in *Laws* 10, are 'good with respect to every virtue', 900d1–2.) The virtues are or reside in the gods or god, and a small amount resides (or can reside) in humans as well (see Menn (1995; ch. 3)). Note that towards the end of the final book of the *Laws* Plato writes that the members of the Nocturnal Council (the most philosophical institution in Magnesia) must attend to the study of both the unity of the virtues—how four (prudence, courage, moderation, and justice) can be one (virtue) (12.963a6–965e5)—*and* the existence and nature of the gods (12.966c1–968a4). Though Plato does not stress the point, the two issues are intimately connected.

Plato next returns to the issue of appeasement. There is he says no doubt that there are vicions souls who have acquired unjust gain, and further that these evildoers throw themselves down before guardians in the hopes of keeping more than they deserve *and* suffering no harm for their injustice. Plato claims that this is true for different kinds of guardians—for guard dogs, shepherds, gods. He first focuses on gods, and returns to guard dogs and shepherds in the next section.

Plato says these evil appeasers use flattery and prayer. Clearly, he thinks praying for what is unjust and/or to avoid a punishment one deserves is not proper and will reach deaf ears in the case of the gods. But this is not to say that Plato believes all prayer is wrong. On the contrary, he believes it is good to pray to the gods, if what you pray for is consistent with prudence and with what is best. This creates a problem for the conception of prayer in the *Laws* which has received virtually no scholarly attention (but see McPherran (2000)). For if the gods supervise us and always do what is best (with a view to the whole), what genuine use would there be to our prayers? If what we ask for is immoral, irrational, or mistaken, then the gods will not grant us what we pray for. But if what we request is consistent with prudence and the good, then isn't this something the gods will bring about in any case, thus rendering our prayers useless? Though it isn't clear to me what Plato's response would be, it must have something to do with the effect prayer has on the person praying—proper prayer being good exercise at being like god—and perhaps on his children as well. For Plato's statements (in the *Laws*) on prayer see 3.687c1–688c1; 4.709b7–d9, 716c1–718a6; 5.736c5–d4, 741a6–c6; 6.757d5–758a2; 7.801a8–e4, 821c6–d4, 823d3–824a1; 8.841a6–c8; 10.887c2–e7 (and cf. Xenophon, *Memorabilia*, 1.3.2).

In contrast to the vicious men's claim that it is possible to have too much and not suffer, the Athenian and his interlocutors believe that having too much (*tên pleonexian*, 906c3) has different names, depending on the context, but all of them are dangerous and disastrous. *Pleonexia* in the body is called *disease*; in the seasons and the years it is called *plague*; and in cities and political systems (*politeiai*) it is called *injustice* (see also *Symposium* 187e6–188b6). Why does Plato go into this here? Why not simply remind us that such men will suffer in the afterlife, if not in this one? He apparently thinks it is more important at this point to remind us that it is unlikely (if not impossible) that such people will not suffer in life (as they will after death). This is the point of claiming that injustice is the psychological and political equivalent of disease or plague (cf. *Republic* 4.444c2–e1). Further, Plato is here showing how the gods are also rulers in the way doctors are; and this points back to the Book 9 theory of punishment, which is analogous to medicine in many ways (see Saunders (1991; ch. 5)), and ahead to the application of this conception of punishment to impiety at the end of Book 10.

906c8–907b9

Having compared the gods to different kinds of rulers, Plato next turns to presenting the argument or account that must logically be presented by the 'one who says that the gods are always forgiving unjust humans and those who act unjustly, if one distributes to them some of what's been gained unjustly' (906c8–d2). Why does Plato refer to both 'unjust humans and those who act unjustly', which seems redundant? It could be that he wants to make clear that he intends to cover unjust character *and* unjust words and deeds. Or 'those who act unjustly' might include those who are basically just but who commit an unjust act (and then try to pray their way out of it). Note that in *Laws* 9 Plato seems to think that one can commit unjust actions voluntarily, but that one cannot voluntarily *be* unjust (860d1–861a3).

In order for traditional theism to be true, the gods would have to be rulers who resemble the following:

1. Dogs who allow wolves to ravage the flock, in exchange for a share of the kill (906d3–5 is reminiscent of Homer, *Iliad* 16.352–5).
2. Captains who ' "turn from their course by the libation of wine and the burnt offering", and overturn ship and sailors' (906e1–2, in part quoting Homer, *Iliad* 9.500).
3. Charioteers who throw a race for money (906e4–6; Lewis (1870: 72) suggests that we should here think of any case in which the gods help someone win a horse race—as Athena helps Diomedes and wrecks the chariot of Eumelos at *Iliad* 23.382–400).

I think it is no coincidence that Plato in each case quotes or alludes to Homer. Perhaps he wants to show that in attacking the third kind of impiety—what I'm calling traditional theism—he actually has the tradition on his side. Or he may have enjoyed the irony of using Homer to attack traditional theism.

Now if Plato were to say simply that the gods could not act in these ways, his reasoning would be circular. But he is relying on the discussion of the gods that goes back to the beginning of his refutation of atheism, and especially his discussion of deism, which he said on a couple of occasions was addressed to the traditional theist as well. So could the gods that have been described in *Laws* 10—gods that are good, knowledgeable, virtuous, and concerned about the good of the entire universe (including the good of humans)—ever act like these dogs, captains, or charioteers? The Athenian says that to say so would be 'ridiculous' (906d9). Similarly, to the suggestion that the gods might compare favorably to 'the dogs charmed by wolves' Kleinias replies: 'Silence!' (906e11) (cf. *Republic* 6.509a9, and see Lewis (1870; 72)).

Plato asks: 'to us, aren't all the gods the greatest of all guardians and over the greatest things?' (907a1–2). (I follow Pangle (1980; 307) in taking *hêmin* to be an ethical dative meaning 'to us', whereas most other translators take it with *ta megista* to mean 'the greatest things for us', which makes less sense.) It cannot be, he concludes, that 'those who guard the finest affairs, and are themselves distinguished with respect to their virtue in guarding, are worse than dogs and average humans, who would never give over what is just for the sake of gifts given in an unholy way by unjust men' (907a5–9). Kleinias calls this 'an intolerable account', and goes on to say that 'anyone holding this opinion is in danger of being judged—most justly—the most evil and most impious of all the impious' (907b1–4). The Athenian neither agrees nor disagrees, so we cannot tell whether Plato would also rank this impiety as the worst of the three, though he may have. (In any case, see *Laws* 4.716e2–717a3.) The Athenian instead declares that they have sufficiently demonstrated 'that the gods exist, that they supervise us, and that they in no way can be appeased so as to act contrary to justice' (907b5–7).

Perhaps as a reminder that they are having this conversation for the benefit of, and with an eye to, the founding of Magnesia, Kleinias—as if in his role as co-founder of the colony, and speaking for himself and Megillus—replies: 'We, at least, vote for these arguments' (907b8–9).

V. THE LAWS ON IMPIETY (907B10–910D4)

Note that the laws on impiety discussed here do not cover all illegal actions that Plato considers impious, only those *directly* related to the gods and religion. For instance, *Laws* 12 opens with the claim that ambassadors or heralds who fail to convey a message or who convey a false message have committed 'acts of impiety, contrary to the law, against the messages and commandments of Hermes and Zeus' (941a1–8). And much of the *Laws* 9 discussion of homicide is cast in the language of impiety (e.g. 865d3–e6).

907b10–d4

This brief section provides a transition between the prelude to the laws on impiety—the bulk of Book 10, and especially the arguments against atheism, deism, and traditional theism—and those laws themselves, which the Athenian will turn to next. Plato refers here to 'the prelude to the laws on impiety' (*to prooimion asebeias peri nomôn*, 907d1–2).

The Athenian feels the need to apologize for the vehemence and vigor of the prelude, which I take to refer to both the urgent tone of their account at times (despite claims about the need to be gentle or tame), the stress on what is at stake, and the length of this prelude compared to all others. His excuse is their 'love of victory over vicious humans' (907b10–c1). Early in the *Laws* Plato had chastised Kleinias and Megillus for the focus on victory in war prominent in Doric (i.e. Cretan and Spartan) culture (see 1.625c9–632e7). But it turns out that the love of victory per se is not wrong, on Plato's view, so long as the object and the motivation of this love are proper. The proper object is evil humans, and the proper motivation is the concern that if the impious were not defeated *by arguments* they would be emboldened to act according to their impious beliefs—which the Athenian and his companions think would be disastrous.

This apology for or defense of the vehemence of their arguments might also be meant to prepare the way for the vehemence to come: the discussion of punishment for certain violations of the laws on impiety.

For all the vigor and thoroughness of this prelude, however, neither the Athenian nor Kleinias seems to be completely confident, which is perhaps Plato's way of suggesting that success in converting impious youths is not guaranteed, and in fact may be difficult. This makes the discussion of the laws on impiety all the more urgent. The Athenian says that the prelude can be considered well spoken if they 'have made even some small contribution to persuading these men in some way to hate themselves, and somehow to like the opposite character traits' (907c6–d1). Kleinias adds: 'There is hope; and if not, at least the kind of account will not discredit the legislator' (907d3–4), which is very muted optimism. Ast's suggestion (presented by England) is likely on the right track: 'Ast takes the words to mean that the weight of the argument has been such that, even if it failed, no fault could be found with the legislator who used it; the fault would lie with the depravity of the unconvinced transgressor' (1921; 2. 504).

907d5–909d2

The most useful general studies of the laws on impiety in *Laws* 10 are Saunders (1991; ch. 12) and Morrow (1960; 470–96). For a brief but useful account of Athenian impiety law see Parker (2005).

Parker writes of the law in Athens: 'Impiety is likely to have had no defined content: the law will have been of the form "if any individual commits impiety, let anyone who wishes indict him ..." and the prosecutor will then have mentioned in the indictment particular forms of impious behavior'; e.g., mutilating divine images, revealing sacred mysteries, introducing new gods (2005; 65). Plato's aim is no doubt, at least in part, to provide some 'defined content' to a proper law against impiety. (See Morrow (1960; 476).)

The brief preface to the law on impiety (907d5–9) suggests that in (Magnesian) practice the entire law, as written, will have three parts (see Lewis (1870; 75)): (1) The prelude—the bulk of *Laws* 10, i.e. Plato's case against atheism, deism, and traditional theism. (2) The exhortation—'an account that is like an expounder [or interpreter, *hermêneus*] of the laws [. . .] forewarning all the impious to abandon their ways for pious ones' (907d5–8)—which is not provided, but merely given this mention. (3) The actual law itself, with punishments. It remains to discuss (3).

The Athenian introduces the law thus: 'For those who do not comply, let the law concerning impiety be as follows' (907d8–9). Plato may be referring directly to those who do not comply with the exhortation that was just mentioned, but more generally he must have in mind all those who have not been persuaded by the lengthy prelude.

The first line of the law reads: 'If anyone is impious in words or in deeds (*logois eit' ergous*), let the one who encounters this defend [the law] by informing the magistrates, and the first magistrates who learn of it are to bring [the accused] before the court created to judge these cases according to the law' (907d10–e3). On what is meant by 'impious in words or in deeds' see Saunders (1991; 306–8). I take *impiety in word* to refer to any statement or promulgation of impious beliefs. (Saunders thinks it unlikely that the law would include the casual expression of heretical ideas, but I am not so sure.) What is meant by *impiety in deed* is a bit more difficult to pin down. First, the line between word and deed is not clear. For instance, is writing a treatise defending atheism impiety in word or deed (or both)? But then not much hangs on this. The following are certainly instances of impious deeds: temple robbery; activities of the dissembling impious person, mentioned below (908d3–7), e.g. claiming to use magic, plotting by means of mystery rites, attempting to bewitch the gods with sacrifices and prayer (909b1–6); setting up private shrines (909d3–910d4).

In the Greek there is no object of 'defend' (*amunetô*, which takes a dative). I suppose 'the city' (*toi polesi*) is possible, but the best suggestion is the one most often adopted: 'the law' (*to; nomo;*) (see England (1921; 2. 504)). This is supported by the nearby 'avenge the laws' (*timôrein huper tôn nomôn*, 907e5).

Nothing else is said here about 'the court (*dikastêrion*) created to judge these cases' (907e3), but perhaps it is the same court (described in Book 9) which hears capital cases: 'Let the judges for a capital offense be the Guardians of the Laws and the court composed of those selected for merit from the magistrates' (855c6–d1).

As an indication of the importance of the law on impiety, and the danger Plato sees in not prosecuting it, the law adds that any magistrate who hears a report of an impious crime and fails to bring the case to court may *himself* be charged with impiety 'by anyone wanting to avenge the laws' (907e5).

Plato next presents a general statement on punishment for impiety: 'If someone should be convicted, let the court assess one separate penalty for each of those who are impious. Let imprisonment be imposed in every case' (907e6–908a2). This 'someone' is anyone impious in word or deed, including the above-mentioned magistrates. Plato makes clear (in somewhat strange language) that not every impious crime deserves the same penalty. For example, there is no reason why both an impious act and failing to bring the case to court should have the same penalty. Further, as we shall see shortly, not every kind of impiety deserves the same punishment (908b3–4).

If the last line of this passage is to be at all consistent with what follows, Plato must mean that imprisonment is to be imposed in every case *initially*. For the death penalty will sometimes be imposed, e.g. in certain cases of recidivism (908a7–8). Plato later states that the dissembling atheist deserves more than two deaths (908e1–2), but this is not necessarily a contradiction, for Plato seems to believe that although such an atheist is *deserving* of death, there are reasons he nevertheless ought to be imprisoned instead. Tougher to reconcile with the claim that imprisonment ought to be the penalty in all cases of impiety is his later imposition of the death penalty for certain cases of establishing private shrines (910d1). Note that the penalty for citizens convicted of temple robbery is death (9.855e6–7).

There are to be three kinds of prison:

1. A general prison, for nearly all crimes calling for imprisonment.
   (The only exceptions will be criminals sent to the other two special
   prisons.) It is centrally located, in the marketplace (*agora*).
2. The Sound-mind Center (*sôphronistêrion*). The name of this prison
   is almost certainly a playful dig at the school of Socrates in Aristo-
   phanes' *Clouds*, often translated 'the Thinkery' (*phrontistêrion*,
   see l. 94). The Sound-Mind center is located near the meeting
   place of the Nocturnal Council, so that its members can properly
   admonish the prisoners sent to this special prison.
3. The prison for the worst offenders is 'in the middle of the
   countryside, in some empty place that is as savage as possible,
   having as its name some word for punishment [or vengeance,
   timôrias]' (908a5–8).

Lewis comments: 'The first prison was for safe custody; the second
for correction, discipline, or reformation; the third, the prison
of vengeance (*timôrias*), of strictly penal restraint, intended for
examples, and not for the good of the offender' (1870; 76). This
is likely correct with respect to the second and third prisons;
but I believe the first probably aims at 'correction, discipline, or
reformation' as well, though not of the sort requiring the special
instruction and admonition of the Nocturnal Council.

The Athenian next says that there are two kinds of offender (dissembling and honest) for each of the three kinds of impiety (atheism,
deism, and traditional theism), thus generating six kinds of impious
offender. The penalties, the Athenian adds, will not be the same for
all of these. Instead of discussing the distinction between dissembling
and honest offenders generally, he does double duty by discussing in
detail the difference between honest atheists and dissembling atheists.
(This distinction between dissembling and honest offenders makes
clear or emphasizes that wrong belief alone—at least as expressed in
words—is a crime, though less serious than wrong belief together
with vicious character and/or action. See Morrow (1960; 489).)

The honest atheist has a just character, hates vicious people,
loathes injustice, and does not act unjustly. He is full of candor

in speaking about the gods, sacrifices, etc.; he does not disguise his atheism. He is capable of causing some harm—'by ridiculing others [he] would perhaps make some of them such as he is, if he doesn't receive a penalty' (908c8–d1)—but he does much less harm than the dissembling atheist. The honest atheist is impious in word alone, not in act. Perhaps most significant here, he is curable or reformable.

Dissembling atheists have a character that combines a lack of self-control concerning pleasure and pain with 'strong memories and sharp minds' (908c3). The result is men who are beastlike (909a8)—meaning, I take it, that they will do *anything* to get what they want (wealth, and the pleasure that can be secured with wealth), and that they have the cognitive strengths enabling them to do it. Although Plato calls this type of person a dissembler (*to eirônikon*, 908e1–2), this has little to do with Socratic irony. This atheist is not overly modest or prone to Socratic disavowals of knowledge. (On different kinds of irony or dissembling see Diggle (2004; 166–7).) Rather, motivated by money, these atheists are religious frauds, pretending an expertise in sacrifices, magic, etc. And Plato's worry must be that the religion they peddle will not be the proper religion defined in the law code (from which there would be little or no wealth to be gained). From this type of atheist, Plato says, 'are produced many diviners (*manteis*) and men knowing all kinds of magic (*magganeian*); and from this sort sometimes also come tyrants and demagogues and generals, and those who plot by means of private rites, and the machinations of those called "sophists"' (908d1–7). The dissembling atheist—like some sophists, and unlike the honest atheist—will not attack or undercut religion directly and in the open, but cunningly and dishonestly. The dissembling atheist is incurable or incorrigible.

It is obvious that the sophists were motivated by money, but were they dishonest with respect to their views on the gods? Some probably were not (see, for example, the *Sisyphus* fragment of Critias, DK 88B25); but others were less open about their theological views. For example, Gorgias 'defended' the view that nothing exists, including presumably the gods (see *On Not Being*, DK 82B3), while in his *Encomium of Helen* (DK 82B11) he lists the gods as one possible cause of Helen's actions—though even here he might seem to equate the gods with chance and necessity (see §6). Similar contrasts can be found in the ancient evidence on Protagoras (cf. DK 80A23, B4 with Plato, *Protagoras* 320c8–328d2) and Prodicus (cf. DK 84B2 with B5).

There may be many kinds of atheist (subtypes of the ones described), but the two mentioned are the only ones that need to be distinguished in the law in defining the punishments for atheism:

1. The dissembling atheist 'commits faults that are worthy neither of one nor two deaths' (908e1–2), but more (is the implication).
2. The honest atheist 'requires admonition together with imprisonment' (908e2–3).

The Athenian adds, without elaboration, that there are two kinds (dissembling and honest) for deism and traditional theism as well. In fact, in his statement on punishment in the law Plato does not distinguish between atheism, deism, or traditional theism, which underscores the primacy of the dissembling–honest distinction over any other.

Having sketched the punishments for dissembling atheists and honest atheists, the Athenian next presents in greater detail the punishments for dissembling heretics and honest heretics generally. For the latter, he writes the following:

The ones who have come to be impious through lack-of-reason, without vicious anger or character, let the judge place, according to law, in the Sound-mind Center for not less than five years; and during this time let no other citizens meet with them except members of the Nocturnal Council, who are to associate with them for admonishment and for the preservation of the soul. When the time of their imprisonment has come to an end, if any one of them seems to be of sound mind, let him reside among those of sound mind; but if not, and he is again convicted on such a charge, let him be punished with death. (908e6–909a8)

Saunders (1991; 310–12) is excellent on this passage, and I follow him in much of my discussion.

We see here that this passage is consistent with Plato's earlier claim that the honest atheist should receive admonishment and imprisonment. What is most striking about this punishment is the unusual source for this admonishment. As Saunders comments (1991; 311): 'This is a remarkable piece of legislation, sharply different from anything in Athens. Plato is prepared to require high-ranking officials to spend five years—at least five years, in fact—on reintegrating somewhat foolish persons into society.' Note that the word translated 'admonishment' is *nouthetêsis*, which literally means placing or implanting reason (*nous*) in a person. That is what the (very philosophical) members of the Nocturnal Council will (in each case) spend five years trying to do: to move the heretic's mind from a state of folly or lack-of-reason about the gods to a proper, rational state. No details are given, but I assume the person will repeatedly hear the arguments, with full explanation, for the existence and nature of the gods. (Cf. *Gorgias* 513c4–d1 on what it would take for Socrates to convince Callicles—though if someone like Callicles appeared in Magnesia, he would likely be considered incorrigible.)

Associating with good people—and the members of the Nocturnal Council are surely good, the Athenian would claim—is beneficial, and in fact necessary if the prisoner is to become good. (See *Laws* 9.854b1–c5.) Will these prisoners associate with one another? Saunders thinks not: 'Presumably also he may not meet even his fellow-heretics—for such contacts would generate fellow-feeling and tend to confirm them in their heresies' (1991; 310). Saunders may be right; but Plato may instead have held that such prisoners are not unjust, merely mistaken on this issue, and thus some exposure to each other is not a problem. If Saunders *is* right, then he must also be right about their being fed by slaves (cf. 909a2–4, c1–3).

There are at least three other puzzles concerning this passage. First, Plato is vague about the term of imprisonment: 'not less than five years' (909a1–2). I assume that after five years (and no earlier), the prisoner will be reassessed, and based on the reassessment either be released or held in the prison for additional admonishment (or possibly declared hopeless and sentenced to death). Saunders speculates that the vagueness here covers the different kinds of heretic: 'if the third heresy (that gods are bribable) is the worst of all, simple atheism would attract the full five years in prison, the second heresy (say) six years, and the third (say) seven years' (1991; 308). But I see no evidence that deism is regarded as worse than atheism, and some that deism is in fact considered better (see 899d7–8, discussed above).

Second, as Saunders points out, there is a problem with the terms of the prisoner's release.

'If' and 'if not' read as if they refer to the same point in time, i.e., when the possibility of release arises. But they can hardly be; for obviously, 'such a charge' can occur only in society, *after* release. Hence 'if' implies: 'but if he does *not* seem to be of sound mind, he is not released'; in effect his sentence, subject to the minimum period stipulated initially, was an 'indefinite' one, terminable not by a decision of a court but at the discretion of officials. 'If not' will mean, 'if the appearance of soundness of mind proves (after release) to have been deceptive'. The heretic, though released, is on probation.   (1991; 310)

Finally, why is the punishment in the case of recidivism death? Such a person at this point may be declared or considered incurable, but, as we shall see, he is not as bad as the incorrigible heretics, who receive life imprisonment in the most remote prison. Perhaps Plato reasons that if he withstands five years or more of this admonishment from the members of the Nocturnal Council and does not change, then he must be as bad as the others after all. Or perhaps (and more likely, I think) Plato reasoned as follows: Such an atheist cannot be released to the public, for that could harm the city. And he cannot stay at the Sound-mind Center, the purpose of which is to reform the prisoner, which, it has been determined, is in his case no longer or unlikely to be possible. Keeping him there would be a waste of time and (assuming prisoners do have contact with each other) a danger to the others. If he was sent to either of the other prisons he would mix with people who are even worse in character than he is, which is a fate worse than death. (See *Laws* 5.728b2–c8.) And so death it is.

Plato next turns to the punishment for the dissembling heretic. But before stating the punishment itself, he describes this sort of heretic in a bit more detail. (Recall that the earlier description was of the dissembling atheist in particular, not of all three types.)

Despising humans, they lead the souls of many of the living while claiming to lead the souls of the dead and promising to persuade the gods, by bewitching them with sacrifices and prayers and incantations (*epô¡dais*), and so they attempt to destroy utterly individuals and whole households and cities, for the sake of money. (909b1–6)

This describes atheists, deists, or traditional theists who disguise their own views and dishonestly persuade people of something other than what the city dictates they should believe in—this is what is meant by 'lead the souls of many of the living'—and they do so for the sake of money. Who precisely does Plato have in mind here? I take it that what he gives us are examples; this does not exhaust every possible kind of dissembling heretic (for recall that his earlier description of the dissembling atheist included false prophets and magicians, etc.). But here are the two types he does mention: (1) those who claim to be able to persuade the gods through sacrifices, prayers, and incantations; and (2) those who claim to lead the souls of the dead.

On (1), I think Plato has in mind anyone who, fraudulently and for profit, plays on the genuine beliefs of a traditional theist of the honest variety: someone passing himself off as a priest, diviner, seer, magician, etc. who claims to be able to persuade the gods to act in a certain way (contrary to justice) through the use of sacrifices, prayers, or incantations. Not only are such people committing fraud and harming others, they are perpetuating false beliefs.

It is possible that (1) may include (2), the latter being one kind of the former. In any case, on (2), Saunders describes a

particular kind of curse to which he thinks this might refer: 'The
mention of "soul-leading the dead" suggests strongly that what Plato
has in mind includes at least the "bindings" by which one may
seek to harm another by harnessing a dead person's resentments'
(1991; 309).

In *Laws* 11 Plato discusses magic in terms which suggest that its use
is a serious crime and would fall under the category of dissembling
impiety. For instance, he writes:

Another [kind of poisoning], through certain kinds of magic (*magganeiais*)
and incantations (*epô¡dais*) and so-called binding spells, persuades those
who dare to do harm that they *can* do this, and [persuades] others that
they are harmed most of all by those who can bewitch [them]. Now with
respect to all such things, it is never easy to know their nature, nor, if one
could know, is it easy to persuade others. It is not worthwhile to attempt to
persuade the souls of humans who are suspicious of one another with respect
to such things—if they should ever see molded waxen images at doorways
or where three roads meet or at tombs of their ancestors—to be directed
to make light of all such things, as they do not have a clear opinion about
them.   (933a2–b5) (On difficulties with this text see Saunders (1991;
320–3) and England (1921; 2. 554–5).)

That Plato did not include discussion of this in Book 10 suggests
that he does *not* make a distinction between honest magicians (that
is, those who really believe such things, however false they are) and
dissembling magicians (those who know that what they are peddling
is false, but do so anyway for money). He must think they are all
dissembling.

What should we make of the surprising claim that it is never easy
to know the nature of magic and such, and that it is not worth trying
to convince people that there is nothing to it? England interprets
this skepticism as in fact precisely the kind of dismissal of magic
that we would expect of Plato at this point in the *Laws*: 'It gives a
reason for neglecting magic; i.e., it is very uncertain whether there
is anything in it' (1921; 2. 555). Saunders argues that the lack of
certainty in fact applies only to what precisely happens to the souls

of the dead (1991; 321), and he may be right. But I would further argue that Plato does not want people simply to dismiss such magic as irrational superstition, because the fear-based belief in some of these things may have a lot in common with the fear-based belief in the stories about the afterlife that he has recently presented (in answer to the deist), and to push for a rational rejection of the one type of belief (however bad) could lead to the rejection of the other (which is good or useful). And note that the positive attitude toward such beliefs is not unheard of in the *Laws*. For instance, in his discussion of involuntary homicide Plato writes that the killer should 'not underestimate an old saying from the ancient myths'; namely, that the (soul of the) person killed, 'filled with fear and terror' from what has happened, will haunt the killer—unless, presumably, the killer goes into exile (9.865d3–e6).

Let us look finally at the punishment for the dissembling heretic, who Plato claims is incorrigible. It is broken into three parts: (1) the nature of the convict's imprisonment; (2) what should be done with the convict's body at death (this is clearly life imprisonment); and (3) how the children of the convict are to be treated as of the commencement of the parent's imprisonment.

[1] If one of these is convicted, let the court punish him with imprisonment, according to the law, in the prison in the middle of the country. No free man is ever to visit such men, but they will get food from slaves, as arranged by the Guardians of the Laws. [2] When he dies, he is to be cast out beyond the borders unburied; and if a free man should help bury him, let this person be brought to trial for impiety by anyone who wishes. [3] If he [i.e. the convict] should leave behind children fit for the city, let the Supervisors of Orphans care for them as well, as if they were orphans in no way inferior to the others, from the day their father is convicted at trial.   (909b6–d2)

Section (1) is pretty straightforward. The main interpretive problem concerns not its meaning but why Plato did not sentence such people to death (see Saunders (1991: 312)). Clearly, Plato's concern is not with helping these people, but with punishing them for their wrongdoing. I believe that they are placed in this prison, with other heinous heretics, because that is a punishment worse than death. This actually fits well with Plato's death penalty for recidivism in the case of reformable heretics. Saunders thinks that Plato might be 'content to use them as "examples" or lessons, *paradeigmata*, to others, in spite of their being out of sight' (1991; 312); for some support for this view see 9.854e6–855a2 and cf. *Gorgias* 525c1–8. This is the most desolate prison, completely cut off from every other citizen, including family members. (The prisoners' children are to be regarded as orphans.) But citizens of Magnesia are to be raised to regard being sent to this prison as something like going to the most unpleasant parts of Hades—i.e. as a fate worse than death. This can be effective only if the prisoners in fact live. There is even the promise that one's corpse will be mistreated if one ends up in such a place.

Section (2) shows that if ever there arises an *Antigone*-like conflict between familial obligation and civic obligation, the city will side with Creon over Antigone. If someone ends up in this prison, he is a non-person, and should no longer be considered dear to you (even if he is a parent). So if you were to attempt to bury this person, you could be tried for impiety (though it is not clear what kind of impiety you would be charged with, what your sentence would be, etc.). (On Athenian parallels to leaving the dead unburied in such cases see Morrow (1960: 492).)

Section (3) makes clear that such a prisoner is to be regarded by everyone as dead—as having no relatives and no contact with anyone in the city. For the most part Plato rejects the ancient view that the sins of the father automatically become the sins of the children. Yet familial background is not unimportant. He writes: 'If the prisoner should leave behind children *fit for the city*, let the Supervisors of Orphans care for them' (909c6–7). Plato must believe that an incorrigibly impious man might likely have unduly influenced his children, and therefore the offspring of such a prisoner will have to be examined to see if they can be allowed to be part of the general population. (On the Supervisors of Orphans see *Laws* 11.924b8–c6.)

909d3–910d4

Plato ends *Laws* 10 with a set of laws against the establishment, ownership, and use of private shrines. He introduces these laws as follows:

A law should be laid down for all of these people in common, which would make many of them offend less against the gods by deed and by word, and particularly become less unreasonable (*anoêtous*), by not allowing them to deal in the divine (*theopolein*) contrary to the law. Let the following law be laid down for all of them without qualification (*haplôs*). (909d3–7)

The first puzzle to sort out is who exactly Plato has in mind here—who are 'all of these people'. It would be pointless if this referred to all citizens, as that is technically true of every law and would not need to be specified. Further, he thinks that there is a certain group of people who need to be controlled or prevented from committing impious acts, and the laws that follow are aimed at doing just that. Morrow (1960; 492 n. 278) and Saunders (1991; 313) think Plato is referring to those I have labeled 'traditional theist'. That would make sense of 'without qualification' (*haplôs*), in that he would not be specifying only the dissembling type of traditional theist, but both types (to prevent the other type, however honest, from being tempted into impious action). But this seems too narrow, for, as we shall see, these laws are surely also aimed at dissembling atheists and deists. So Plato probably has in mind *all heretics* without qualification, though the laws that he is about to present will likely never need to be applied to honest atheists or deists.

The aim of this law is to cause as many of these people as possible to 'offend less against the gods by deed and by word'. Despite reference to the usual 'word and deed', the emphasis is on impious *action*—on preventing impious worship and sacrifice, etc., which may be why he mentions deed first here. But perhaps it is nevertheless important to mention offending by word, since that may cover all kinds of illegal prayers and incantations. Again, the line between word and deed is not always clear, so it is best to mention both.

Note finally that Plato's aim is to make these people become less unreasonable (*anoêtous*), where possessing *nous* is to share in or be like god.

The law itself seems fairly straightforward: 'Let no one possess shrines in private households (*hiera . . . en idiais oikiais*)' (909d7–8). The key word here is *hiera*, literally 'sacred things', though it certainly can mean 'temple'. In my translation I have rendered *hiera* 'shrines', 'temples', or 'sacred things', depending on the context. First, it seems odd to speak of private temples; 'shrines' is the more accurate English, as Plato is referring primarily to altars set up in the home, or for example in a small, remote spot by a river bed. More difficult is what to make of the opening section of *Laws* 10, where Plato writes that the 'second gravest' of the crimes that remain to be discussed 'affect private sacred things (*hiera . . . idia*) and tombs' (885a1). He must there be referring to those private sacred things—but certainly not shrines—that a citizen *is* allowed to possess. He does not tell us what these are, though earlier in the commentary (ad loc.) I speculated on what might be included. Similarly, in *Laws* 4 he makes clear that there should exist 'private buildings (*hidrumata*) of the ancestral gods', though he adds that people must worship there 'according to law' (717b4–5). It is unclear how this is to be reconciled with the law against private shrines (if it can be).

When it occurs to someone (literally 'comes to someone's reason', *epi noun iê̦ tini*, 909d8) to make a sacrifice, he should go to the public temple and give his offerings to the priests and priestesses. Plato has previously said nothing about priests and priestesses in Book 10 (though they are mentioned elsewhere in the *Laws*, see esp. 6.759a1–e1). I think this is because Book 10 is concerned with what *philosophy* can say about theological issues, with an eye to refuting the three kinds of impiety. The actual rituals of the city's religion are a matter for the political founders, who should of course consult with philosophers on these issues and see to it that the civic religion is consistent with what has been said in Book 10. (For a superb discussion of religion in the *Laws* see Morrow (1960; ch. 8). On priests, priestesses, and other religious officials see Morrow (1960; 413–27).)

Plato ends the initial part of the law against private shrines with a strangely formulated line: 'Let him join in prayer (*suneuchesthô*) along with anyone else he wants to join in prayer with him (*autou suneuchesthai*)' (909e2–3). Plato wants to make clear that even though he is forbidding private shrines (and prayer and sacrifices), one may still come to public temples with one's family or any other 'private' group, and sacrifice and pray with them—so long as one is sacrificing and praying as the law dictates.

Plato next presents the two related reasons why such a law is needed:

(1) Establishing shrines and gods correctly is not easy, but requires 'deep thought' (*megalês . . . dianoias*, 909e4–5); however, the people who customarily take it upon themselves to establish private shrines do not employ deep thought, but act from emotion and irrationally.

(2) The law against private shrines prevents (certain) impious people from committing impious acts in secret.

Let us look at each of these in more detail.

(1) The reference to gods suggests that Plato has in mind not simply the establishment of private shrines, but the invention or perhaps introduction of deities to be worshipped privately; that is, not by the entire city. But figuring out the existence and nature of the proper gods is difficult—the bulk of *Laws* 10 was devoted to it. And although it does not require philosophical wisdom to *understand* this (though good men like Kleinias and Megillus had a hard time following all of the arguments), it does require wisdom to undertake such a task. The same is true for deciding on which gods to worship—which names to give them, etc.—and that cannot be undertaken lightly. This is why establishing temples and shrines, too, must be undertaken exclusively by the founders of the city, preferably having been advised by philosophers.

But which type of person has traditionally set up private shrines (and perhaps worshipped strange gods)?

It is customary for all women especially, and for those who are sick in any way or in danger or distressed (however one might be distressed), or, conversely, when they gain some prosperity, to sanctify whatever is in front of them at the time and to swear to offer sacrifices and promise to found shrines to gods and spirits and children of gods. And because of fears from apparitions seen when awake and from dreams, and similarly recalling many such visions, they make remedies against each of them by filling every house and every village with altars and shrines, founding them in clear places or wherever someone happened to have such experiences.   (909e5–910a6)

The types of people who traditionally establish private shrines—and this is not even counting charlatans and other frauds—are not deep thinkers, but superstitious and overly emotional people, who act on the spur of the moment in response to danger, sickness, distress, on the one hand, or sudden prosperity on the other, or to visions and dreams. Plato says that women are especially of this sort. (This view is not only old, it has proven to be long-lasting. A character in Joseph Conrad's *Nostromo* says: 'God for men—religions for women' (1904; ch. 4).) So, judging by this passage at least, Plato seems to have moved away from the more positive view of women and their intellectual abilities found in the *Republic*. (On women in the *Laws* see Saunders (1995) and Bobonich (2002; 385–9). On the superstitious person in ancient Greece see Theophrastus, *Characters* 16, with Diggle (2004; 349–75).)

(2) Plato writes that an additional reason for the law against private shrines is 'so that the impious won't act deceptively in these matters by founding shrines and altars in private households, believing (*oiomenoi*) they can in secret make the gods agreeable through sacrifices and prayers' (910a7–b3). Surprisingly, it sounds as if Plato has in mind only traditional theists, since dissembling atheists and deists who establish private shrines or engage in other secret religious activities without the city's sanction do not actually

believe they can 'make the gods agreeable through sacrifices and prayers'. This must be an oversight. Recall that he earlier wrote of the dissembling atheist: 'From these are produced many diviners and men knowing all kinds of magic . . . and those who plot by means of private (*idiais*) rites' (908d3–6). Clearly, this sort could make use of and prosper by practicing in secret, and Plato should have included them here as well.

Plato says that allowing the impious to make sacrifices and prayers in secret and against the law increases 'injustice infinitely' and brings 'the reproach of the gods against both the impious themselves and those who (though they are better than them) tolerate them, such that the entire city catches (*apolauê$_i$*) their impiety (in a way justly)' (910b4–7). Private shrines allow the spread of the disease of impiety. (On impiety as an illness or disease see 888b8, 906c2–6, 908c4–5; on *apolauê$_i$* as referring to the spread of disease see Saunders (1972; 103–4).) The spread is potentially unlimited, because, occurring in private, the city—both magistrates and other concerned citizens—is unable to keep it in check. The impious themselves would receive the primary blame, but so would those who, though they do not themselves share in this impiety, tolerate it, thus allowing it to spread. Again we see the appeal (in this case implicit) to citizens to report any acts of impiety (see also 907d10–e5 and 910c4–5).

Plato adds that if the entire city 'caught' this impiety, that would happen in a way justly, because if a citizen commits impiety, or tolerates it, then he deserves the consequences of his actions: the spread of these ideas and so 'the reproach of the gods'. Of course, in another way it would not happen justly—that is, it would not be conducive to the health and goodness of the city, which justice is. The only ones who would not be blameworthy, if this impiety spread, would be the legislators, for they had set down the law against private shrines, including the following law which sets out the proper punishment.

Laws 10 closes with the statement of the punishment for violating the law against private shrines. Plato first divides the possession of private shrines into two kinds:

(1) The childish sort. The injustice is not grave and impious (910c2–3).
(2) The sort of 'act of impiety characteristic of unholy men' (910c7–8).

It is not entirely clear what the difference between the two amounts to. *Pace* Saunders (1991; 315), however, I think that in some sense the difference corresponds to the earlier distinction between honest and dissembling impiety. The first refers to the honest traditional theist who establishes, possesses, or worships at a private shrine, honestly (however foolishly or irrationally) thinking that gods can be won over through sacrifice and prayer. The second refers to the dissembling atheist and deist. This sort *pretends* to believe that there are gods who can be swayed by sacrifice and prayer, and persuades others of this, sets up private shrines, etc., in order to make money. The second must also include the dissembling traditional theist, though it is unclear what such a person would be like. He would have to believe genuinely that the gods exist and can be swayed by sacrifice and prayer, but then be dishonest in how he presents and peddles this to others, motivated by moneymaking.

The punishment for each is as follows:

(1) The Guardians of the Laws 'are to order the private shrines be carried off to the public ones'; those who disobey are to 'be punished until the shrines are carried off' (910c5–7).
(2) The death penalty.

The main concern in the first case is not so much punishment of the offender, but the removal of the private shrine (including, I take it, any forbidden private sacred objects). If the offender does obey, it seems there will be no further punishment. No indication is given as to what would happen if the offender disobeys. Saunders speculates that the penalty would be some kind of fine (1991; 314). This is possible: though fines are not proposed anywhere in Book 10, they are mentioned elsewhere in the *Laws* (see, for instance, in the case of theft, 9.857a2–b3; 11.914b6–c3, 933e6–934a6; 12.941d4–942a4). But it must be the case that if the person persists in disregarding the orders from the Guardians of the Laws, more serious actions will be taken.

The death penalty for this second type is an exception to the earlier punishment proposed for dissembling heretics, which was life imprisonment in the most remote prison (see 909b6–c1). (It in fact contradicts that punishment, *if* the diviners and those who plot by mystery rites are included in the law against private shrines, as I think they would often be.) One might respond that people *can* do those sorts of things *without* setting up private shrines, in which case they would not get the death penalty. The problem is that doing such things *and* setting up private shrines ought to be worse than just doing the former, but recall that the death penalty is supposed to be *better* than a term of life in the most remote prison. So the reason for the death penalty here is likely that of all the acts that a dissembling heretic can commit, establishing private shrines and introducing the worship of new or foreign (unapproved) gods are the most dangerous. Such a harsh punishment underscores this to the citizens—makes clear to them how serious a crime this is—thus increasing its prophylactic force.

The statement of the punishment ends: 'After the Guardians of the Laws judge whether it is childish or not, and bring the accused before the court accordingly, let them impose the penalty for impiety in these cases' (910d1–4). This line is unnecessarily compressed. I take Plato to be proposing the following: First, the Guardians of the Laws will determine whether or not the alleged violation of the law against private shrines is of the childish type. Second, the Guardians of the Laws will bring the accused before the court *accordingly* (*houtôs*, 910d2)—that is, they will send the case to court *if* the act is found to be the non-childish kind (see England (1921; 2. 510)). Finally, if at court the accused is found guilty, then punishment is imposed. (I assume that if the Guardians of the Laws determine that the alleged crime is of the childish sort, some magistrate will determine whether the accused is in fact guilty, and if so order the private shrine be removed—punishing the guilty party if he fails to do so.)

So *Laws* 10 ends not with a bang, but with a whimper. Nevertheless, this ending—with the law prohibiting private shrines—is a fitting one, as it connects the laws on impiety, and thus *Laws* 10 itself, to the deeper political philosophy underlying the entire project of the *Laws*.

In *Laws* 5 the Athenian presents the model political system and the fundamental principle underlying it, and relates the city in speech he and his companions are creating to this model. 'That city and that political system are first, and those laws are best, where this old saying holds as much as possible throughout the entire city: it is said that the things of friends really are common' (739b8–c3). He goes on to describe or summarize the communism of women, children, and property presented in the *Republic*. In this best political system, he says, everything has been done to exclude completely 'what is called "private" (*idion*)' (739c5) from every aspect of life. The political unity strived for is the unity of a living organism, in which every part is in unison and feels pain and pleasure at the same time and with respect to the same things. (Cf. *Republic* 4.423e5–424a3, 5.457c10–466c2, 8.543a1–b6.) Such a city, the Athenian concludes, would be 'inhabited by gods or children of gods' (739d6–7). He says that 'one should not look anywhere else for a model (*paradeigma*) of a political system' (739e1–2), and adds that if the city they have been describing ever came into being, it would be closest to this model, and its unity would be in second place (*hê mia deuterôs*, 739e4).

The prohibition against private shrines not only helps to prevent impiety, on Plato's view, it also contributes to the elimination of the private (particularly in the realm of religion). Moreover, *Laws* 10 generally aims to get the city as close as possible to being a city 'inhabited by gods or children of gods', by identifying the true gods and fixing them in their proper place in the city, and by encouraging citizens to try as much as possible to be like the gods; that is, to possess—or where that's not possible, to act in accordance with—reason (*nous*).

Textual Notes

I list here my departures from Diès, and discuss them below.

	Diès	This translation
890d4	delete νόμῳ (Winckelmann)	νόμῳ (MSS)
895d8−e8	Distribution of lines: *AS* d8−10 *K* d11 *AS* d12 *K* e1−3 *AS* e4−8	Distribution of lines: *AS* d8−11 *K* d12 *AS* e1−3 *K* e4 (Ναί) *AS* e4−8 (*post* Ναί)
897b2	θεῖον ὀρθῶς θεὸς οὖσα ὀρθὰ (see Diès app. crit.)	θεὸν ὀρθῶς θεοῖς, ὀρθὰ (major MSS)
900c8	τούτῳ (Lov.)	τοῦτο (MSS)
900c9	μᾶλλον δέ (Eusebius and Theodoterus)	omit μᾶλλον δέ (MSS)
901d5	λέγετε (O⁴)	λέγεται (MSS)
902a3	οὐδενὸς ... ἐπιμελεῖσθαι (MSS)	†οὐδενὸζ ... ἐπιμελεῖ- σθαι†
903a7	καὶ μάλα (O³, Eusebius IN)	μάλιστα (major MSS)
905a3	θέων (England)	θεῶν (major MSS)
905b1	ἀπώτερον (A³0³)	ἀγριώτερον (A²0³)
905e3	ἐνδελεχῶς (Stobaeus)	ἐντελεχῶς (major MSS)

890d4: νόμῳ. Most editors delete this, changing 'the ancient law's argument' into 'the ancient argument' (see England (1921: 2. 458)). But I follow Einarson (1957: 272–3) and have kept it in, though it does not seem to affect the content.

895d8–e8: There is a noteworthy controversy over who speaks what lines here. The key issue is this: Does the even-number example—the name, definition, and being of 'even'—come from the Athenian or from Kleinias? I follow Burnet (1907) over England (1921: 2. 472) and Diès, and give the example to the Athenian. Although it is possible that these are Kleinias' lines, I think the passage in question is too sophisticated to come from him unbidden (and I find support for this reading at *Laws* 7.818c3–5).

897b2: θεὸν ὀρθῶς θεοῖς, ὀρθά. According to the major manuscripts Plato writes the cryptic words θεὸν ὀρθῶς θεοῖς (which I have rendered ' "god" correctly for the gods') in describing good soul—soul with reason. The Greek is not completely intelligible, but I find none of the proposed emendations persuasive (see England (1921: 2. 476) and the app. crit. of Diès, ad loc.).

900c8: τοῦτο. I see no compelling reason to abandon this reading, which has manuscript support. In any case, the difference is minor: 'prove this' (ἐνδείξασθαι τοῦτο) rather than (if one follows Diès) 'prove to this person' (ἐνδείξασθαι τούτῳ).

900c9: omit μᾶλλον δέ. The manuscript reading is preferable to that of Eusebius and Theodoterus (accepted by Diès):

    (a) MSS: 'the gods supervise small matters *no less than* (οὐχ ἧττον ἢ) the especially big matters'.
    (b) Eusebius and Theodoterus: 'the gods supervise small matters *not less, but more, than* (οὐχ ἧττον, μᾶλλον δέ, ἢ) the especially big matters'.

As I argue in the commentary (ad loc.), Plato's argument, of which this line is a part, is barely consistent with the manuscripts' reading. The reading of Eusebius and Theodoterus, however, does not follow at all. England suggests that μᾶλλον δέ was 'the addition of some early Christian scribe' (1921: 2. 485).

901d5: λέγεται. I translate the line in question: 'Is this the way these things are said (λέγεται) to be, or how?' The λέγεται of the major manuscripts is disputed. Diès and most other editors accept λέγετε (O⁴), which would render the translation: 'Is this the way you (pl.) say (λέγετε) these things are, or how?' If this reading is adopted, then the previous lines would be directed at the deist and traditional theist. Pangle also accepts the major manuscripts here, defending the reading as follows: 'The editors' confidence in this reading overlooks the shiftiness of the Athenian's ascription of speakers in this section' (1980: 534 n. 30). I do not share Pangle's confidence in discerning the Athenian's (or Plato's) 'shiftiness'. Not much rides on this dispute, however, and I believe one ought to accept the major manuscripts whenever possible. In my view, if λέγεται is correct, it is more likely the result not of shiftiness but of the less-than-polished state of the *Laws*.

902a3: †οὐδενὸς ... ἐπιμελεῖσθαι†. As I explain in the commentary ad loc., there is a problem with the passage in which this line occurs. The key line is from 902a2–3. If one follows the manuscript tradition the line should be rendered as follows:

γιγνώσκοντες ὡς τὸ παράπανοὐδενὸς τῶν τοιούτων ἐπιμελεῖσθαι δεῖ

knowing that it is absolutely necessary to supervise none of these things

I translate the line in this fashion, but set between daggers 'to supervise none' (οὐδενὸς ... ἐπιμελεῖσθαι), as I think one of these words must be incorrect.

Ritter's suggested change of ἐπιμελεῖσθαι to ἀμελεῖσθαι might appear to work perfectly:

γιγνώσκοντες ὡς τὸ παράπαν οὐδενὸς τῶν τοιούτων ἀμελεῖσθαι δεῖ

knowing that it is absolutely necessary to *neglect* none of these things

This is precisely the sense we expect. But, as England points out, there is a major problem with this suggestion: 'Ritter is ill advised in proposing to emend ἐπιμελεῖσθαι to ἀμελεῖσθαι (mid.), for there is no such word' (1921: 2. 488). England is almost certainly right. According to the *Thesaurus Linguae Graecae*, ἀμελεῖσθαι appears 55 times (though many of these occurrences are late), five times in the classical period (twice in Xenophon, thrice in Plato). All three of the occurrences in Plato are passive (*Republic* 10.613b2; *Laws* 7.814c3, 10.904e5), as are both of those in Xenophon (*Cyropaedia* 5.5.41, *Spartan Constitution* 10.2). Searches for other necessarily or potentially middle forms (aside from the infinitive ἀμελεῖσθαι) yield similar results.

If the text was not originally ἀμελεῖσθαι, perhaps it was ἀμελεῖν (act., 'to neglect'). Plato wrote ἀμελεῖν at 900b3. A couple of lines before 902a3, at a1, the manuscripts have ἀμελοῦσι (though Eusebius has either ἐπιμελοῦσι or ἐπιμελοῦντες). And a bit later, at 902a7, the text reads ἐπιμελεῖσθαι … ἀμελοῦντες. In this context, I think there was room for corruption of the text at 902a3 from ἀμελεῖν to ἐπιμελεῖσθαι. This, however, is pure speculation.

Another (albeit drastic) solution is to delete οὐδενὸς, which yields:

γιγνώσκοντες ὡς τὸ παράπαν τῶν τοιούτων ἐπιμελεῖσθαι δεῖ

knowing that it is absolutely necessary to supervise these things

The text so emended fits the context of the passage perfectly, but unfortunately this emendation has no manuscript support.

Another hand on one of the manuscripts (O^3) had similar concerns about this passage, and took the opposite approach, attempting to improve things by inserting another negative:

γιγνώσκοντες ὡς τὸ παράπαν οὐδενὸς τῶν τοιούτων ἐπιμελεῖσθαι οὐδὲν δεῖ

knowing that it is absolutely not necessary to supervise none of these things

But not only is this awkward, it is inaccurate: not supervising none of the small things is different from supervising all of them, and the latter is what Plato's argument requires.

If the manuscript reading is correct, then Plato must be considering a case *per impossibile*, and we should take the passage as follows:

either they [i.e. the gods] do this knowing that it is absolutely necessary to supervise none of these things [but that is impossible, as it *is* necessary to supervise them, and so there can be no such knowledge], or—what is left, except the opposite of knowledge [i.e. they are *ignorant* about what they should supervise, and that, too, is impossible]?

Whatever the solution, I think this passage either is evidence of the unpolished state of the *Laws*, or bears the marks of later textual corruption.

903a7: μάλιστα. Here is the last line in the Athenian's argument against the deist: 'We seem to me now to have had a completely reasonable (μάλιστα μετρίως) dialogue with the one who likes to accuse the gods of negligence' (903a7–8). Diès does not accept μάλιστα with the major manuscripts, however, but καὶ μάλα with O³ and Eusebius. The difference is not significant. On Diès's reading we should instead translate 'had a very reasonable (καὶ μάλα μετρίως) dialogue'. But there is no reason to reject the major manuscripts here.

905a3: θεῶν. The dispute here concerns whether to accept θεῶν (genitive plural of θεός, 'god'), or θέων (participle of θέω, 'run', 'hasten') following a suggestion of England. The difference in translation is between 'from this judgment of the gods' and 'running from this judgment'. England's text has θεῶν; but in his commentary on the passage (1921: 2. 498) he writes: 'Is it possible that Plato wrote θέων?'. Diès adopted this suggestion, as did Saunders in his translation (1970: 439). But Saunders later changed his mind and defended the other reading (1972: 101–3); see also Einarson (1957: 273). With Einarson and (the later) Saunders, I find θεῶν preferable.

905b1: ἀγριώτερον. I render this 'more savage'. The major manuscripts and Eusebius have ἀγιώτερον ('more hallowed'), which seems impossible in this context, as Plato is describing a place *worse* than Hades (and ἅγιος in the sense of awe before what is evil or impious is not elsewhere attested in the classical period). Based on marginal suggestions in some manuscripts, most editors and translators have opted instead for either ἀπώτερον ('more remote', accepted by Diès) or ἀγριώτερον ('more savage' or 'more wild'). (See the discussions in England (1921: 2. 498) and Saunders (1972: 103).) I believe ἀγριώτερον makes slightly more sense. This reading gets some support from the fact that Plato later says that the prison which houses the worst offenders is to be built in an empty place 'that is as savage [or wild] as possible' (μάλιστα ἀγριώτατος, 908a7).

905e3: ἐντελεχῶς. I have argued elsewhere (Mayhew (2006)) that one can make a roughly equal case for both the ἐνδελεχῶς of Stobaeus and the ἐντελεχῶς of the mss. I have translated the manuscripts' reading, though without much confidence.

References

Bibliographical note: Laks (2000) is a good article-length treatment of the entire *Laws*; Stalley (1983) is a useful monograph-length thematic introduction. Morrow (1960) and Bobonich (2002) are the two best detailed studies of the dialogue—the former historical in its focus, the latter philosophical. England (1921), a two-volume commentary on the *Laws*, is indispensable for anyone working with the Greek text. (Schöpsdau (1994) and (2003) are the first two volumes—so far covering Books 1–7—of an ongoing German translation with commentary of the *Laws*.) For an overview of *Laws* 10 see Cleary (2001). Morrow (1960: ch. 8) is a lengthy presentation of religion in the *Laws* (on which see also Schofield (2003)). Lewis (1870) is an eccentric (and often dated), but sometimes useful, commentary on the Greek text of *Laws* 10. For more detailed bibliographical information on all aspects of the *Laws* see Saunders and Brisson (2000).

ANNAS, J. (1999), *Platonic Ethics, Old and New* (Ithaca, NY: Cornell University Press).

BETTS, R. (1989), 'The Sophists and Relativism'. *Phronesis*, 34: 139–69.

BOBONICH, C. (1996), 'Reading the *Laws*', in C. Gill and M. M. McCabe (eds.), *Form and Argument in Late Plato* (Oxford: Oxford University Press).

—— (2000), 'Persuasion, Compulsion, and Freedom in Plato's *Laws*', in G. Fine (ed.), *Plato, 2. Ethics, Politics, Religion, and the Soul* (Oxford: Oxford University Press).

—— (2002), *Plato's Utopia Recast: His Later Ethics and Politics* (Oxford: Clarendon).

BURNET, J. (1907), *Platonis Opera V* (Oxford: Oxford University Press).

CARONE, G. R. (1994), 'Teleology and Evil in *Laws* 10', *Review of Metaphysics*, 48: 275–98.

CASKEY, E. (1974), 'Again—Plato's Seventh Letter', *Classical Philology*, 69: 220–7.

CLEARY, J. (2001), 'The Role of Theology in Plato's *Laws*', in F. Lisi (ed.), *Plato's Laws and Its Historical Significance* (Sankt Augustin: Academia).

CLEGG, J. (1976), 'Plato's Vision of Chaos', *Classical Quarterly*, 26: 52–61.

COHEN, D. (1983), *Theft in Athenian Law* (Munich: Beck).

COOPER, J. (1997) (ed.), *Plato: Complete Works* (Indianapolis Ind.: Hackett).

CORNFORD, F. (1937), *Plato's Cosmology: The Timaeus of Plato translated with a running commentary* (London: Routledge & Kegan Paul).

CROMBIE, I. M. (1962), *An Examination of Plato's Doctrines, 1. Plato on Man and Society* (New York: Humanities).

DIÈS, A. (1956), *Platon: Les Lois, Livres VII–X* (2nd edn., 1994) (Paris: Belles Lettres (Budé)).

DIGGLE, J. (2004), *Theophrastus: Characters* (Cambridge: Cambridge University Press).

DODDS, E. R. (1957), *The Greeks and the Irrational*, paperback edn. (Boston, Mass.: Beacon).

DOVER, K. J. (1988), 'The Freedom of the Intellectual in Greek Society', in K. J. Dover, *The Greeks and Their Legacy: Collected Papers, 2. Prose Literature, History, Society, Transmission, Influence* (Oxford: Blackwell).

DÜRING, I. (1966), *Aristoteles: Darstellung und Interpretation seines Denkens* (Heidelberg: Universitätsverlag).

EASTERLING, H. J. (1967), 'Causation in the *Timaeus* and *Laws* X', *Eranos*, 65: 25–38.

EINARSON, B. (1957), Review of A. Diès, *Platon: Les Lois, Livres VII–X*, *Classical Philology*, 52: 271–4.

ENGLAND, E. B. (1921), *The Laws of Plato*, 2 vols. (Manchester: Manchester University Press).

FREDE, D. (2002), 'Theodicy and Providential Care in Stoicism', in D. Frede and A. Laks (eds.), *Traditions of Theology: Studies in Hellenistic Theology, Its Background and Aftermath* (Leiden: Brill).

HACKFORTH, R. (1965), 'Plato's Theism', in R. E. Allen (ed.), *Studies in Plato's Metaphysics* (London: Routledge & Kegan Paul).

HEATH, T. (1913), *Aristarchus of Samos: The Ancient Copernicus. A History of Greek Astronomy to Aristarchus together with Aristarchus' Treatise on the Sizes and Distances of the Sun and Moon* (Oxford: Clarendon).

IRWIN, T. (1977), 'Plato's Heracliteanism', *Philosophical Quarterly*, 27: 1–13.

JAEGER, W. (1948), *Aristotle: Fundamentals of the History of His Development*, trans. R. Robinson (Oxford: Oxford University Press).

KIRK, G. S., RAVEN, J. E., and SCHOFIELD, M. (1983), *The Presocratic Philosophers*, 2nd edn. (Cambridge: Cambridge University Press).

KRAUT, R. (1992), 'Introduction to the Study of Plato', in R. Kraut (ed.), *The Cambridge Companion to Plato* (Cambridge: Cambridge University Press).

LAKS, A. (2000), 'The *Laws*', in C. Rowe and M. Schofield (eds.), *The Cambridge History of Greek and Roman Political Thought* (Cambridge: Cambridge University Press).

LEE, E. N. 1976, 'Reason and Rotation: Circular Movement as the Model of Mind (Nous) in the Later Plato', in W. H. Werkmeister, *Facets of Plato's Philosophy* (Assen/Amsterdam: Van Gorcum).

LESHER, J. H. (1992), *Xenophon of Colophon—Fragments: A Text and Translation with Commentary* (Toronto: University of Toronto Press).

LEWIS, T. (1870), *Plato Contra Atheos. Plato Against the Atheists; Or, The Tenth Book of the Dialogue on Laws* (New York: Harper).

LIPSIUS, J. H. (1905–15), *Das attische Recht und Rechtsverfahren*, 3 vols. (Leipzig: Reisland).

LLOYD, G. E. R. (1968), Review of I. Düring, *Aristoteles: Darstellung und Interpretation seines Denkens, Journal of Hellenic Studies*, 88: 163–6.

MARTIN, M. (1990), *Atheism: A Philosophical Justification* (Philadelphia Phil.: Temple University Press).

MAYHEW, R. (1997), *Aristotle's Criticism of Plato's Republic* (Lanham, Md.: Rowman & Littlefield).

—— (2006), 'Plato, *Laws* 10, 905E3: *ENTEΛEXΩΣ* or *ENΔEΛEXΩΣ*', *Classical Quarterly*, 56: 312–17.

—— (2007), 'Persuasion and Compulsion in Plato, *Laws* 10', *Polis: The Journal of the Society for Greek Political Thought*, 24: 91–111.

McPHERRAN, M. (2000), 'Does Piety Pay? Socrates and Plato on Prayer and Sacrifice', in N. D. Smith and P. B. Woodruff (eds.), *Reason and Religion in Socratic Philosophy* (Oxford: Oxford University Press).

MENN, S. (1995), *Plato on God as Nous* (Carbondale and Edwardsville, Ill.: Southern Illinois University Press).

MERLAN, P. (1960), *Studies in Epicurus and Aristotle* (Wiesbaden: Otto Harrassowitz).

MOHR, R. (2006), *God and Forms in Plato* (Las Vegas: Parmenides; rev. and expanded edn. of *The Platonic Cosmology* (Leiden: Brill, 1985)).

MORROW, G. R. (1960), *Plato's Cretan City: A Historical Interpretation of the Laws* (repr., with a foreword by C. Kahn, 1993) (Princeton, NJ: Princeton University Press).

NAILS, D. (2002), *The People of Plato: A Prosopography of Plato and Other Socratics* (Indianapolis, Ind.: Hackett).

NIGHTINGALE, A. (1993), 'Writing/Reading a Sacred Text: A Literary Interpretation of Plato's *Laws*', *Classical Philology*, 88: 279–300.

PANGLE, T. (1980), *The Laws of Plato* (New York: Basic).

PARKER, R. (2005), 'Law and Religion', in M. Gagarin and D. Cohen (eds.), *The Cambridge Companion to Ancient Greek Law* (Cambridge: Cambridge University Press).

PENDRICK, G. (2002), *Antiphon the Sophist: The Fragments* (Cambridge: Cambridge University Press).

POST, L. A. (1944), Review of J. B. Skemp, *The Theory of Motion in Plato's Later Dialogues American Journal of Philology*, 65: 302–3.

PRICE, S. (1999), *Religions of the Ancient Greeks* (Cambridge: Cambridge University Press).

SAUNDERS, T. J. (1970), *Plato: The Laws* (Penguin).

—— (1972), *Notes on the Laws of Plato* University of London, Institute of Classical Studies, bulletin supplement no. 28.

—— (1973), 'Penology and Eschatology in Plato's *Timaeus* and *Laws*', *Classical Quarterly*, 23: 232–44.

—— (1991), *Plato's Penal Code: Tradition, Controversy, and Reform in Greek Penology* (Oxford: Oxford University Press).

—— (1995), 'Plato on Women in the *Laws*', in A. Powell (ed.), *The Greek World* (London: Routledge & Kegan Paul).

—— and L. Brisson (2000), *Bibliography on Plato's Laws* (Sankt Augustin: Academia).

SCHOFIELD, M. (2003), 'Religion and Philosophy in the *Laws*', in S. Scolnicov and L. Brisson (eds.), *Plato's Laws: From Theory Into Practice. Proceedings of the VI Symposium Platonicum* (Sankt Augustin: Academia).

SCHÖPSDAU, K. (1994), *Platon, Werke: Nomoi (Gesetze): Buch I–III. Übersetzung und Kommentar* (Göttingen: Vandenhoeck & Ruprecht).

—— (2003), *Platon, Werke: Nomoi (Gesetze): Buch IV–VII. Übersetzung und Kommentar* (Göttingen: Vandenhoeck & Ruprecht).

SEDLEY, D. (2000), 'The Ideal of Godlikeness', in G. Fine (ed.), *Plato, 2. Ethics, Politics, Religion and the Soul* (Oxford: Oxford University Press).

—— (2004), *The Midwife of Platonism: Text and Subtext in Plato's Theaetetus* (Oxford: Oxford University Press).

SKEMP, J. B. (1942), *The Theory of Motion in Plato's Later Dialogues* (Cambridge: Cambridge University Press).

STALLEY, R. F. (1983), *An Introduction to Plato's Laws* (Oxford: Blackwell).

STRAUSS, L. (1975), *The Argument and the Action of Plato's Laws* (Chicago, Ill.: University of Chicago Press).

TATE, J. (1936*a*), 'On Plato: *Laws* X 889cd', *Classical Quarterly*, 30: 48–54.

——— (1936*b*), 'Plato, Socrates and the Myths', *Classical Quarterly*, 30: 142–5.

VLASTOS, G. (1995*a*), 'Equality and Justice in Early Greek Cosmologies', in Vlastos, *Studies in Greek Philosophy, 1. The Presocratics*, ed. D. W. Graham (Princeton, NJ: Princeton University Press).

——— (1995*b*) 'Disorderly Motion in the *Timaeus*' in Vlastos, *Studies in Greek Philosophy, 2. Socrates, Plato, and Their Tradition*, ed. D. W. Graham (Princeton, NJ: Princeton University Press).

WARDY, R. (1990), *The Chain of Change: A Study of Aristotle's Physics VII* (Cambridge: Cambridge University Press).

ZEYL, D. J. (2000), *Plato: Timaeus* (Indianapolis, Ind.: Hackett).

Index Locorum

General Index

Index Nominum